# CELLS

## An introduction to the anatomy and physiology of animal cells

by Ellen Johnston McHenry

**Ellen McHenry's Basement Workshop**
State College, Pennsylvania

ISBN 978-0-9825377-8-7

Ellen McHenry's Basement Workshop
State College, PA
www.ellenjmchenry.com
ejm.basementworkshop@gmail.com

Printed and distributed by Lightning Source.  www.lightningsource.com

**Most recent update of this text: Feb. 2013**

**For any additional updates or changes, go to www.ellenjmchenry.com and click on the UPDATES tab.**

# STUDENT
# BOOKLET

NOTE:  For your convenience, the video links that make use of YouTube have been posted as a playlist on *YouTube.com/TheBasementWorkshop.*

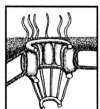
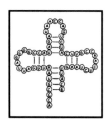

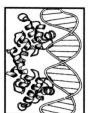

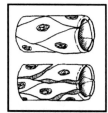

# CELLS

## An introduction to the anatomy and physiology of animal cells

Anatomy means "what the parts are"
Physiology means "how they work"

by Ellen J. McHenry

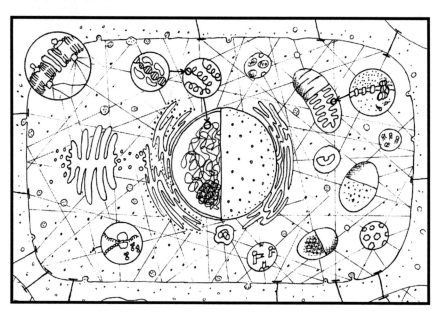

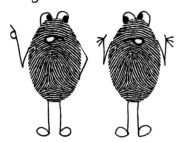

Do you know what these things are?

Nope. But I guess we'll find out soon!

# TABLE OF CONTENTS

# CHAPTER 1:  HOW DID WE FIND OUT ABOUT CELLS?

There was a time in the not-too-distant past when not a single person on earth knew that cells existed.  Galileo, who used lenses to view distant planets, knew nothing of cells. It was in the decades following Galileo (the late 1600s) that someone figured out how to use lenses to make very small things visible.  Two lenses were used, one at each end of a tube, forming a *compound microscope*.

Englishman Robert Hooke was perhaps the first to observe cells.  One day he sliced an extremely thin piece of cork and put it under his microscope.  What did he see?  Rows and rows of little box-like shapes that reminded him of the tiny rooms, or *cells*, in monasteries (where monks lived).  Today we don't use the word "cell" very much when referring to a room, except when we talk about prison cells.  But in Hooke's day the word "cell" was commonly used for a small room, so it was natural for him to use the word "cell" to describe these little compartments he saw in the cork.  He didn't really know what these cells were made of or how they functioned, but the name he gave them has been used ever since.

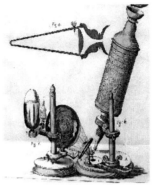 

*Hooke's compound scope*          *The famous cork cells*

*A fly's foot*

Hooke eventually wrote a book called <u>Micrographia</u> telling about his amazing microscopic discoveries.  He drew pictures of cells, parts of insects, hairs, specks of dirt and many other things that fascinated him.  He discovered that no matter how sharp he made the point of a needle, the end of it still looked dull when viewed under his microscope!  The only objects that still looked sharp when viewed under magnification were the tiny claws on the ends of insects' legs and the almost invisible "hairs" he found on the stems and leaves of plants.

Hooke was a brilliant man.  He was also a surveyor, an architect, an astronomer and a physicist.  He was working on the principles of motion and gravity at the same time that Isaac Newton was.   He didn't really want to go down in history as the man who named cells.  He would rather have been known for one of his other achievements: figuring out the laws of gravity and motion, or helping to re-design London after the fire of 1666, or proposing the the wave theory of light.  But as history would have it, most people know him as the man who gave us the word "cell."

*Hooke in a wig*      *Hooke without his wig*

*Antoni van Leeuwenhoek of Delft*

Following after Hooke came Antoni van Leeuwenhoek *(LAY-ven-hook)*, who lived his whole life in the Dutch town of Delft.  He bought a copy of Hooke's <u>Micrographia</u> while on a trip to England in 1665 (the only time in his life that he left Holland), and soon afterward began making single-lens microscopes the likes of which have never been equaled.  Leeuwenhoek perfected the art of making tiny lenses, but was careful to keep his technique a secret.  He never wrote down his method, so we can only guess what he did.  Modern glass making experts are fairly sure that Leeuwenhoek probably heated a glass rod and stretched it until it was a thin string.  Then he would take the very thin strand of glass and put it back into the flame and let the end melt until it formed a tiny round ball.  This tiny round ball would be trimmed off and used as his lens.  Other lens crafters of his day would spend hours grinding and polishing their lenses to get them into the right shape.  Leeuwenhoek

*Leeuwenhoek's microscopes were about the size of your hand.*

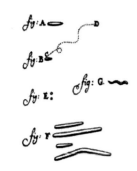

PLATE XXIV

*Leeuwenhoek observed bacteria*

just took advantage of the natural physics of hot glass. He could make these tiny glass beads fairly quickly and easily; he managed to make over 500 of these little microscopes while keeping up with a full-time job as a cloth merchant. He mounted his lenses in silver panels and attached a screw mechanism on one side. With this simple magnifier, he was able to achieve magnification of at least 300 times larger than life size!

Leeuwenhoek was an incredibly patient person. He would sit for hours watching the specimens he had mounted on his microscope. He watched long enough to be able to observe the behavior and life cycles of microorganisms. He observed the microscopic food chain and knew what each little "animalcule" would eat. He saw eggs hatch. He saw blood cells circulate inside tiny circulatory systems. He observed sperm cells swimming. Once he kept a colony of fleas in a pouch inside his sock (to keep their eggs warm) and every hour or so he would check on them to see what changes had occurred. He spent several decades reporting all his findings to the Royal Society in London. At first, his descriptions of bizarre invisible creatures were almost too much to believe. The Royal Society had to send some of their members to visit Leeuwenhoek to verify that what he was saying was true, and he wasn't just imagining his microscopic "zoo." The visitors from the Royal Society looked through the little microscopes and were amazed to see exactly what Leeuwenhoek had written about. From then on, Leeuwenhoek's reports were treated as valid science. Prominent scientists and politicians began visiting Leeuwenhoek. Peter the Great of Russia put Delft on his European travel itinerary so that he could see Leeuwenhoek's little "animalcules." Today, Leeuwenhoek is generally considered to be the father of modern microscopy.

*The man in "The Geographer" by Verneer is probably Antoni van Leeuwenhoek.*

In the early 1800s, a Scottish botanist named Robert Brown made the next advances in our understanding of cells. Brown didn't have to make his own microscopes; by this time there were technicians who specialized in making optical devices such as microscopes. Since Brown was a botanist, it was plant cells he observed. He noticed that inside every cell there was a dark blobby thing. He called this the *nucleus* but he didn't have a clue what it did. Today we know that the nucleus contains the cell's DNA.

In 1827, Brown made another important microscopic discovery. While observing pollen grains under his microscope, he noticed that tiny particles inside the pollen grains were vibrating. He wondered if these particles were alive, since they were inside a plant cell. He tried a similar experiment with dust particles and saw the dust particles moving in the same way. He knew the dust particles were not alive, so he concluded that the motion must be due to a law of physics, not biology. He was right. Molecules are in constant motion and often collide. It is these molecular collisions that cause tiny particles to look like they are moving. We call this motion *Brownian motion*, after Robert Brown.

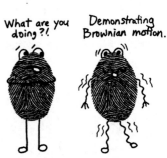

As an interesting historical side note, an ancient Greek named Lucretius was the first person to conceive of the idea of Brownian motion. In 60 B.C. he said something like this:

*Observe the dust particles in sunbeams. You will see a multitude of tiny particles moving in a multitude of ways. Their motion is an indicator of underlying movements of matter that are hidden from our sight. It originates with the atoms which move of themselves. Their collisions set in motion slightly larger particles, and so the movement mounts up from the atoms and gradually emerges to the level of our senses, so that those particles we see in sunbeams are moved by blows that remain invisible.*

In 1837, a German scientist named Theodor Schwann developed a theory that we now call "cell theory." Schwann came to realize that all living things are made up of cells that are very similar in basic structure. He also observed that cells only came from other cells. Cells could not come out of nowhere. This sounds obvious, but until Schwann's time many people still believed that living things could come from nowhere. They saw flies appear seemingly from nowhere when fruit or meat spoiled. No one knew that the flies had hatched from microscopic fly eggs.

Schwann had a friend named Matthias Schleiden who was also a botanist. Together, they figured out that the nucleus played some role in cell division. They also observed the cytoplasm (fluid) inside the cell and saw that the organelles inside the cells moved around. Schleiden is considered to be the co-founder of *cell theory*, along with Schwann. Cell theory says that cells can only come from other cells—they can't just pop into existence from nothing or from inorganic materials. (Ironically, Schleiden also accepted the theory of evolution—a theory that seemed to contradict his own cell theory.)

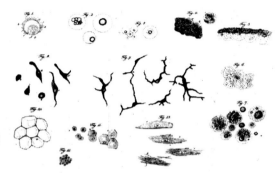

*Cells drawn by Theodor Schwann*

By the late 1800s, many different types of cells had been observed. There were fairly accurate pictures of plant cells, animal cells, and free-living single-celled organisms. The big question now was how the cells worked inside. Scientists knew that cells had some little "organelles" inside of them, but no one really knew what they did. The most obvious organelles were the nucleus (present in all cells) and chloroplasts (found only in plant cells). The chloroplasts were easy to spot because they were green. Other little spots and dots could be seen floating around inside the cell, but even the highest power on the microscopes could not enlarge them enough so that they could be studied. Another problem was that some of the little organelles were almost transparent. How can you study something you can hardly see?

A major breakthrough came when cell scientists learned how to stain cells before putting them under the microscope. The most famous "stain scientist" was Hans Christian Gram from Denmark. His technique of staining bacteria cells is still used today and bears his name: *the Gram stain*. This stain will be absorbed by some kinds of bacteria but not by others. This helps to identify what kind of bacteria you are working with. Other stain experts developed stains that would penetrate the nucleus or other organelles, making them highly visible so they could be studied more easily. Then an Austrian scientist named Camillo Golgi discovered how to use a silver compound to stain nerve cells. His stains brought to light many discoveries about nerve cells and how the nervous system works. Golgi's most famous discovery was another type of organelle found in almost all cells: the Golgi apparatus (or Golgi body).

*An electron microscope from the 1970s (now in a museum).*

Then cell science "hit a wall," so to speak. Even the very best microscopes in the world could not magnify something beyond about 1000 times. Cell scientists knew that many mysteries of the cell would not be discovered until there was a way to achieve magnifications beyond 1000. Then, in the mid 1900s, a completely new type of microscope was invented: the *electron microscope*.

Regular microscopes use light and lenses to make things look larger. Electron microscopes work on an entirely different principle; they use electrons instead of light. Electrons from a tungsten filament are "fired" at the sample being studied, and the electrons either go through it (in the case of transmission electron microscopes, or TEM) or they bounce off at various angles (in the case of scanning electron microscopes, or SEM). In both TEM and SEM, the electrons then hit a screen to form a visible image. Pictures from electron microscopes (which are known as *micrographs*) are always in black and white. Color requires light, and electron microscopes don't use light. Colored micrographs are made by adding the color afterward. (They use computer programs to adjust the graphics, just like you might use a program like Photoshop®.)

*An SEM microscope opened up to show you the vacuum chamber where the sample goes*

Modern electron microscopes can provide images that are up to 500,000 times larger than life. That's large enough to be able to see even the tiniest parts of the cell. However, electron microscopes have a big drawback. The samples being studied must be put into a vacuum chamber—no air, like outer space. Big problem for living cells. Basically, only dead specimens can be studied. Maybe really, really freshly dead specimens, but nothing alive and moving. Often you have to prepare the specimens by spraying them with an ultra-thin layer of gold or some other metal, so that means you can't sit and watch little critters moving around under an electron microscope like you can with a regular (compound) microscope. You can't watch as a cell eats or grows or divides. You only get one picture of a cell at one moment in its life. So cell scientists must collect lots and lots of still pictures, then use "detective skills" to draw conclusions based on comparing all the pictures. Sometimes scientists can think of a way to test their theories about cells by "tagging" particular molecules with radioactive or fluorescent dyes that will show up on the screen. In the next chapter, we'll read about a cell part that was discovered in this way.

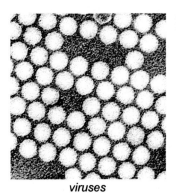
*viruses*

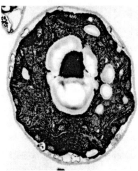
*a single-celled organism*

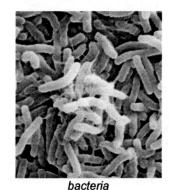
*bacteria*

*blood cells*

**TEM images look flat**          **SEM images look 3D**

Images produced by TEM electron microscopes look flat. The electrons pass through the sample in much the same way that light passes through samples on a regular (compound) microscope. This type of image can be very good for studying the insides of cells. SEM electron microscopes produce 3D images. SEMs let you see textures and shapes. It takes both types of images to give us enough information to be able to understand what a cell is really like. Scientific illustrators try to create pictures that combine information gained from both types of images. Books about cells often contain many images made by scientific illustrators.

Electron microscopes are used for more than just biology. They can be used in the fields of material science (metals, crystals and ceramics), nanotechnology, chemistry, and forensics. They have become an essential tool for many branches of science.

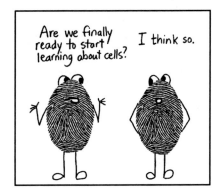

## ACTIVITY 1  Watch some informative-yet-entertaining videos about early cell scientists

Watch two short videos that feature one or more of these early cell scientists: Hooke, Leeuwenhoek, Schwann and Schleiden:  "Cell Theory" and "Microbiology Bytes" on the "Cells" playlist at YouTube.com/TheBasementWorkshop.


## ACTIVITY 2  Watch some brief explanations of how electron microscopes work

Videos available on the YouTube.com/TheBasementWorkshop channel:

1) TEM:  Transmission Electron Microscope  ("Structure and function of Electron Microscope")

2) SEM: Scanning Electron Microscope  ("Scanning Electron Microscope")


## ACTIVITY 3  (Optional)  A more in-depth video about electron microscopes

Do you really, really want to know exactly how an SEM microscope works?  Here's a video "field trip" to the University of Washington's Nanotech User Facility.  A fellow named Scott will give you almost an hour of instruction on how to operate an SEM.  He'll show you step by step how to run his SEM machine.  (If you love technical stuff, you'll think this is awesome.  For the rest of you, you might want to watch just the first five minutes or so.)

The first in this series of videos is listed near the top of the "Cells" playlist.  The others are listed at the bottom.  If you would like to find it on your own, the address is:

**http://www.youtube.com/watch?v=c7EVTnVHN-s** ("SEM part 1 of 6")


## ACTIVITY 4  Watch "Brownian motion"

Watch some Brownian motion by clicking on the videos (on the playlist) named "brownian motion," "Brownian Motion," "Brownian Motion HD," and "Brownian motion inside diatom."  The third video shows the atomic motion that creates Brownian motion.  They're not the most thrilling videos you'll ever see, but you'll be in the lucky minority of people on this planet who have been able to witness this interesting phenomenon!


## ACTIVITY 5  Look at some really neat electron microscope images

If you'd like to see some fascinating images of very small things, set your search engine to "images" (still pictures, not videos) and then use key words "TEM images" or "SEM images."

**Can you remember what you read? If you can't think of the answer, go back and read that part of the chapter again until you find the answer.**

1) The first person to ever see a cell was:
   a) Galileo    b) Hooke    c) Lucretius    d) Leeuwenhoek

2) Which one of these did Hooke NOT do?
   a) develop theories about gravity and motion        b) propose a wave theory of light
   c) help to redesign London                          d) develop cell theory

3) About how many microscopes did Leeuwenhoek make?
   a) less than 10      b) about 100      c) about 500      d) thousands

4) TRUE or FALSE?   The Royal Society immediately made Leeuwenhoek a member, as soon as they read his descriptions of "animalcules."

5) What is Brownian motion?
   a) a physical phenomenon caused by the constant motion of molecules
   b) the movement of dust particles in air
   c) a biological phenomenon found only in living things
   d) the movement of cells under the microscope

6) TRUE or FALSE?   Schwann and Schleiden proved that life could come from nonliving things.

7) TRUE or FALSE?  By the late 1800s, scientists had seen many different types of cells.

8) TRUE or FALSE?  One problem with looking at cells is that many of their parts are transparent.

9) Who is the most famous "stain" scientist?
   a) Antoni Leeuwenhoek     b) Theodor Schwann     c) Camillo Golgi     d) Hans Christian Gram

10) What is the maximum magnification you can get with most ordinary (compound) microscopes?
   a) 100x     b) 500x     c) 1000x     d) 100,000x

11) TRUE or FALSE?     TEM images look 3D.

12) What type of metal is often used as the filament in the electron "gun" in electron microscopes?
   a) platinum      b) tungsten      c) gold      d) iron

13) TRUE or FALSE?  Electron microscopes can let you watch a cell as it divides.

14) For electron microscopy, what do the specimens have to be in?
   a) a vacuum    b) suspended animation     c) a frozen state      d) high temperature environment

15) TRUE or FALSE?  There is a special kind of electron microscopy that can show you both a flat image and a 3D image at the same time.

16) What does SEM stand for? _____  _____  _____

17) TRUE or FALSE?  Electron microscopes are used exclusively for biology.

# CHAPTER 2:  THE CELL MEMBRANE and CYTOSKELETON

So now that we know a little bit about how cells were discovered, let's start learning about what cells are made of and how their insides work.  We'll start with the outer surface, the *plasma membrane*.

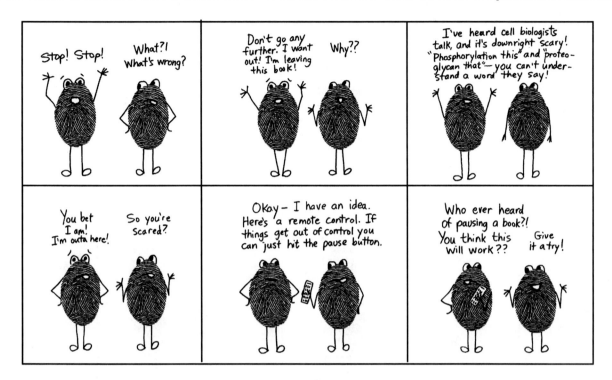

Okay, we're ready now?

Let's look at the outside of the cell first.  The outer layer of a cell, the layer that separates the inside of the cell from the outside environment, is called the *membrane*.  In plant cells there is an extra layer outside the membrane—a thick outer coating made of tough *cellulose*.  We'll discuss cellulose later when we take a closer look at plant cells. In this chapter we're only going to talk about the membrane.  The membrane is so thin that it would take 10,000 of them stacked on top of each other to be as thick as a sheet of paper.  That's pretty thin.  In fact, it's the ultimate in thin—it's only two molecules thick!  The molecules that form a cell membrane are a particular type of molecule called a *phospholipid*.
### WAIT!  DON'T PAUSE THE BOOK!

Let's look at this word and figure out what it means. The second part of the word, "lipid," basically means "fat."  You know what fats are—those white streaks in your meat, the oil you use to fry your French fries, even the cream on top of fresh milk.  Lipids are greasy and oily and don't mix with water.  Now what about "phospho"?  "Phospho" is short for "phosphate," which means some oxygen atoms attached to a phosphorus atom.  You can see that there are also some carbons, hydrogens and a nitrogen off to the side.  This second group has a separate name, but for the sake of simplicity, we are going to consider both of them together as the phosphate part of our phospholipid molecule.  This clump of atoms stays together and functions as a group.

The lipid part of the molecule is made of two long chains of carbon and hydrogen atoms (with a few oxygens thrown in).

The most important difference between the phosphate and the lipid is their reaction to water molecules. Phosphates are said to love water. Yes, scientists really do use the term "love"—but they say it in Greek, of course. They say "hydrophilic," which means "water-loving." The lipids are the opposite; they hate water. In fact, they have a phobia (fear) of water. Lipids are said to be "hydrophobic." So one wants to run away from water and the other loves it. (How could they ever vacation together?!) What holds them together?

A little clump of atoms called **glycerol** (GLISS-er-ol) holds them together. Glycerol looks very similar to the lipid, doesn't it? Just a bunch of carbons and hydrogens and oxygens. It's strange but true; everything in our bodies boils down to things that look like this. Like it or not, your body is nothing more than a really, really big clump of molecules! (But don't try that as an excuse—your parents won't buy it.)

Now, what would it look like if we connected all these molecules together and made a phospholipid?

Glycerol

| PAUSE |
| --- |

Don't worry, not even cell biologists want to draw the phospholipid molecule! So they draw a very simple picture that doesn't have any letters in it. (But they know that all the carbons and hydrogens and oxygens and phosphoruses are there.) This is the way they draw a phospholipid:

The round part at the top is the phosphate part. They call it the **HEAD**.

The **TAILS** on the bottom are the lipid chains.

They don't even bother to draw the glycerol connecting them.

 or

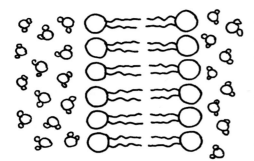

Now what happens when you throw a whole bunch of these phospholipid molecules into water? Well, the water-hating tails freak out. Then they have to find a way to cooperate so that not a single tail is in contact with the water. The molecules all line up so that the tails are facing each other (they like each other) and only the heads are in contact with the water. You can see that there are still small gaps between the phospholipid molecules, and water does sometimes sneak through. But the tails are generally pretty happy so it works out well.

The picture on the previous page shows only a dozen phospholipid molecules and has only two dimensions. But real membranes are three-dimensional. So what would thousands of phospholipids look like in three dimensions? They'd form a ball with an inside layer and an outside layer. Here is a cut-away view of the ball, so you can peek inside.

Look at the cut-away edge. Can you see all the individual phospholipid molecules lined up tail to tail? On the inside and outside of the sphere you can't see the tails at all, just heads. This is important to remember. In some pictures we will be looking at in future chapters, you won't be able to see the tails; you'll see only an endless "sea" of heads.

This phospholipid structure is the basic structure of a cell. It's not only what the outer membrane is made of, it's also the outer layer of many other cell parts.

Now we have a nice, tight, almost-leak-proof ball. Very small molecules can sneak through the cracks, but large molecules don't stand a chance of getting inside. Only one problem—the cells need to be able to bring in food molecules, get rid of waste molecules, and send molecules to other cells. The cell needs portals at various places—"gates" that let good things in and keep bad things out. The cell's gates are made out of *proteins*. This is what a simple protein looks like:

Not all proteins look just like this. But this gives you a general idea of what kind of atoms they are made of.

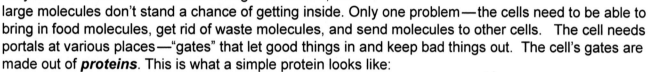

A protein doesn't look much different from a lipid or a glycerol, does it? It's made mostly of the same stuff—carbons, hydrogens and oxygens. But that letter N makes all the difference. It is a nitrogen atom. It's the nitrogen atom that makes this group of letters into a protein. But since this isn't a chemistry book, we're going to stop right here and not go any further into the chemical structure of proteins. From now on, proteins will look like little odd-shaped blobs. Let's put some protein "gates" into our phospholipid membrane:

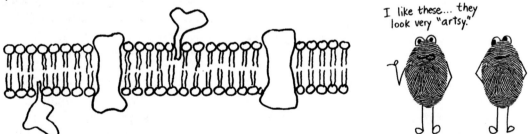

I like these.... they look very "artsy."

Those funny-shaped things are the proteins. (You recognize the phospholipids, right?) Some proteins go all the way through the membrane. These are the "gates." Other proteins are stuck on either the outside or the inside layer of the membrane. All of these proteins are called *membrane-bound proteins* because they are bound (fastened tightly) to the membrane.

The proteins that <u>go all the way through the membrane</u> are the ones that act as gates, letting certain molecules in or out. Things that the cell would want to let in would be food molecules needed for energy (like very simple sugar molecules that your body has already digested from your food), protein molecules that the cell needs as raw materials to build other proteins, or perhaps a special message molecule from another cell.

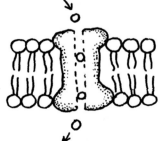

The proteins attached to the <u>outer surface</u> might do one of the following jobs:

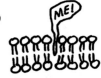

1) Act as a "flag" identifying the cell as belonging to the organism it is part of, so that it doesn't get attacked by other cells whose job it is to kill foreign invaders (such as bacteria). Cells don't have eyes, so they can't "see" each other. The way they identify each other is through the proteins on their surfaces.

2) Receive messages. Cells are usually part of a larger organism and they must all work together to keep the organism alive. Cells need to be able to communicate. They don't have ears or vocal cords so they can't talk to each other. The "messages" they send are actually molecules that travel back and forth between the cells.

3) Allow the cell to stick to other cells. The proteins can grab and hold onto the outer proteins of other cells. (You could think of them as being a bit like Velcro™ proteins.) These proteins can hold cells tightly together, or loosely together.

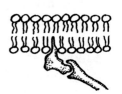

The proteins on the <u>inner side</u> of the membrane most often function as a place to attach things to, sort of like a hook or clip stuck into a wall. The most common cell part that needs to be anchored to the membrane is the cell's skeleton.

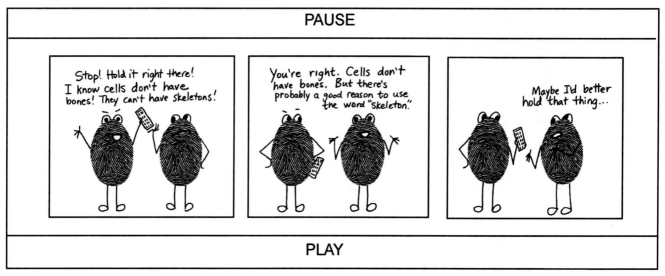

We'll come back to the skeleton in a minute. First, there's one more feature of the membrane that you need to know about: little "rafts" that can float around in the "sea" of phospholipid heads. They are called *lipid rafts* and they are made of *cholesterol*. You've probably heard a lot of talk about cholesterol and how eating too much of it can be bad for you. Cholesterol is actually something your body needs—but in moderation. (Too much of anything, even a good thing, can be bad.) Here is a picture of a lipid raft with a protein riding on it. Is this cool, or what?!

It's not only the rafts that can move around. The proteins we mentioned above can also shift their position easily. The phospholipids are not locked together. You might want to imagine a bathtub filled with ping pong balls. The individual balls can move around but there is still a continuous layer of balls covering the water.

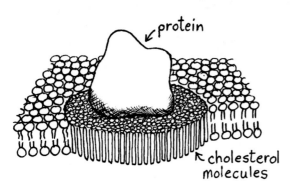

Now for the cell's skeleton...

Cells don't have bones. They are filled with a fluid called **cytoplasm**. (The word "cyto-" means "cell." So cytoplasm basically means "cell gel.") Scientists have known about the cytoplasm for well over a hundred years. What they didn't know until fairly recently (the 1970s) is that an invisible framework exists in this cytoplasm. It's invisible because it's transparent and because it's made of extremely thin filaments. It's like trying to see a fishing line underwater. Both are transparent, and the fishing line is very thin. (That's the whole idea—the fish can't see it!) Somehow scientists started to suspect there was something there that they weren't seeing, but they had to figure out a way to make it show up on their electron microscope screens. First, they found a type of molecule (an antibody) that would attach itself to these almost-invisible cell parts (but explaining exactly how they did this is way beyond the scope of this book). Next, they stained these molecules with a fluorescent dye. When injected into a cell, these fluorescent molecules covered the mysterious invisible cell parts, thus making them visible to an electron microscope. The images produced by the electron microscopes were stunning; they revolutionized cell science. The images showed an organized network of filaments, like a three-dimensional system of "roads" and "highways" traversing the cell. It was obvious that this network of fibers acted as a structural support, helping the cell to maintain its shape. Because of this structural function, this network was named the **cytoskeleton**. Just as we would be nothing but a pile of mush without our skeletons, cells would be flimsy and flat without their "skeletons."

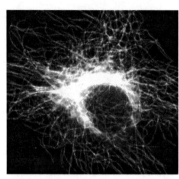

*Micrograph of part of a cytoskeleton from nl.wikimedia. (Thanks, Jeffrey81!)*

With further research, scientists discovered that the cytoskeleton also functions as a transportation system. It's like a little system of roads and highways. The roads come in three sizes: small, medium and large. The scientists who discovered them gave them these (boring) names: **microfilaments, intermediate filaments and microtubules**. If we were to make a model of a cytoskeleton we might use thread, yarn, and drinking straws to represent them.

You could create a cytoskeleton model in your room by stretching thread, yarn and straws from wall to wall!

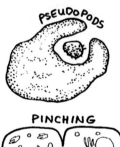

The smallest ones, the **microfilaments** (the threads in our model), are only a few molecules thick. They are very important in giving the cell its shape and helping the cell to change its shape. If a cell wants to move, it quickly builds a whole bunch of new microfilaments in that direction. The cell can build these at the rate of thousands per second. As the new little roads are built, they push the flexible membrane outward. Cytoplasm flows along with the microfilaments. Together they create what is called a **pseudopod**, or "false foot." We have white blood cells in our bodies that form pseudopods in order to surround and capture bacteria and viruses. Microfilaments are also very important when it is time for the cell to reproduce by splitting itself in half. The microfilaments cause the cell to "pinch" in the middle, in preparation for the splitting process.

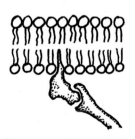

*The shapes of the anchor proteins match the ends of the filaments a bit like like jigsaw puzzle pieces that fit together.*

The medium-sized **intermediate filaments** (the yarn in our model) are especially abundant in nerve cells, skin cells, and muscle cells. They form a stretchy lattice inside the cell that help to give it strength. Remember how this lattice anchors itself to the cell membrane? The ends of the filaments hold on to certain proteins that stick out from the bottom side of the membrane. What would happen if something went wrong with those proteins? What if a cell made a mistake (and cells do make mistakes occasionally) and made those proteins the wrong shape so they could not hold on to the ends of the filaments? When this happens in muscle cells, it can cause a condition called muscular dystrophy. A person with muscular dystrophy has very weak muscles. Medical researchers are trying to find a way to help

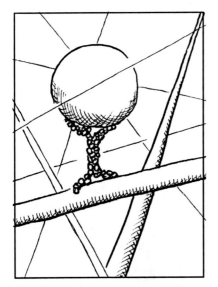

cells correct this mistake and fix these proteins.

The largest filaments, the ***microtubules*** (the drinking straws in our model), really do look like tubes. These tubes are the "highways" that the cell uses to move things about. Cells make proteins, fats and enzymes for their own use or to ship out to other cells. But these proteins, fats and enzymes don't have any way to move. They just sit there. Something must carry them to where they should go. Further research revealed how these things are transported, and scientists could harldy believe their eyes when they saw it. They saw little proteins "walking" along these roads! They looked like they were putting one foot in front of the other. What a stunning discovery! These ***motor proteins*** travel along the microtubules carrying cargo. Their cargo can be just about anything a cell makes, and sometimes even the organelles themselves. How they know where to go is still a mystery. Every time a discovery is made in cell science, it answers some questions but also creates new questions!

There is a central "hub" for the microtubules, like a railway station from which all the train tracks branch out. This central station is called the ***centrosome***. (When you see the word root "som" or "soma," it just means "body" or "thing." So "centrosome" just means "central thing." Isn't it amazing how Latin and Greek make ordinary words sound more sciency?!) The centrosome helps to organize all the microtubules when the cell starts dividing in half. The centrosome was first seen under the microscope back in the late 1800s. They could not see the microtubules but they could see that the centrosomes were somehow causing the organelles to move around. In the micrograph shown here, the big whitish blob is the nucleus and the arrow is pointing to the centrosome.

Further research on the centrosome has revealed that it is made of two parts: a pair of ***centrioles***, and a blob of protein surrounding them. The centrioles look like barrel-shaped things and they usually sit perpendicular to each other. They are made of microtubules—the same as in the cytoskeleton. Even FURTHER research has found that the "barrels" are made of nine sets of tubes, with three tubes to a set. The cell is masterfully organized right down to the molecular level!

*Two centrioles make one centrosome.*

---

STOP

OKay— my puny brain is full now. I need to stop.

CLICK

But did you learn not to be afraid of big science words? All you have to do is break them apart.

Yes! One must effectuate the dissociation of sesquipedalian vocabulary!!

?

12

## ACTIVITY 1  Watch "The Inner Life of a Cell"

This video is probably the best cell animation video in the world right now.  A team of researchers and computer animation specialists at Harvard University put together this video to show us a view of the cell that you just can't get even with the best microscope in the world.  You can't really see all these things going on in a cell.  If you saw electron microscope pictures of these things, they wouldn't look like much.  Molecules would just look like fuzzy blobs and they wouldn't be in color because electron microscopes produce only black and white images; the computer artists must add the colors.  So you couldn't ever really "see" what this video shows.   Don't let the fancy words scare you off—just enjoy the show and watch for things like phospholipid molecules, lipid rafts, microtubule highways, and lots of oddly-shaped proteins doing their jobs.

Go to www.YouTube.com/TheBasementWorkshop, click on the "Cells" playlist, then on "Inner Life of a Cell." (Note:  The upload sources for this video shift often. If this video happens to be missing in the playlist, just try searching YouTube using these keywords: "inner life of a cell harvard.")


## ACTIVITY 2  Watch a white blood cell chase a bacteria

White blood cells use their cytoskeleton to change their shape very quickly.  They can move around much like an amoeba.  They build tubules out in the direction they want to go while dissolving the tubules at the rear.  This combination of building and dissolving creates the pseudopods (which actually look more like oozy arms than they do "false feet.")  In this video clip you can see a white blood cell actually chasing some bacteria.  Go to the "Cells" playlist and click on "White Blood Cell Chases Bacteria."

If you want a slower video where you can watch the pseudopods form, watch "White Blood Cell in Action"


## ACTIVITY 3  Look at micrographs (still pictures, not videos) of the cytoskeleton

Here are some pictures that were taken with an electron microscope.

http://nanoprobenetwork.org/wp-content/uploads/2009/06/
andrebrown-stem-cell-cytoskeleton-fluo-afm.jpg


## ACTIVITY 4  Watch a few short videos about the cytoskeleton

Here is a brief video about the cytoskeleton and the various roles it plays in cells.  (You'll also see single-celled organisms that use extensions of the cytoskeleton as locomotion devices.)  Go to the "Cells" playlist and click on "Cytoskeleton Microtubules."

Intermediate filaments are what cells use to form "bridges" between cells, keeping them together.  These bridges are called "desmosomes."  (We'll officially meet them in chapter 7.)  The main point of watching this video is to gain an appreciation of the ingenious design of these little filaments.  The name "intermediate" sounds boring and we might easily take them for granted.  But they play a vital role in our bodies, especially in our skin.  They give skin its resilience and elasticity.  Go to the playlist and click on the video with the title "Intermediate Filaments."

**Can you remember what you read?  If you can't think of the answer, go back and read that part of the chapter again until you find the answer.**

1) The most natural shape for the cell membrane molecules (phospholipids) to form is a:
   a) flat surface      b) ball      c) long line    d) cytoskeleton

2) The word "lipid" basically means:
   a) protein    b) fat    c) sugar    d) membrane

3) How many layers of molecules are in the cell membrane?
   a) 2          b) 4          c) hundreds      d) thousands

4) What do you call a phosphorus atom with some oxygen atoms attached to it?
   a) a lipid        b) a protein      c) glycerol      d) a phosphate

5) What does glycerol do in the phospholipid molecule?
   a) keep the phosphate and the lipid together    b) push the phosphate toward water
   c) push the lipid away from water               d) allow the cell to stick to other cells

6) Which hates water—the phosphate head or the lipid tail? _____

7) Where would you find a membrane-bound protein?
   a) in the membrane    b) stuck to the inside of the membrane
   c) stuck to the outside of the membrane    d) all of the above

8) TRUE or FALSE?  One thing that lipid rafts can do is carry proteins around.

9) Which one of these can a membrane-bound protein on the outer surface NOT do?
   a) allow the cell to stick to other cells      b) act as an anchor for the cytoskeleton
   c) act as a "flag" identifying the cell as belonging to the organism    d) receive messages

10) What are lipid rafts made of?    a) cholesterol    b) proteins    c) microfilaments   d) wood

11) Which one of these does the cytoskeleton NOT do?
   a) form new phospholipid membranes        b) help the cell maintain its shape
   c) transport things across the cytoplasm    d) form pseudopods

12) Which one of these elements marks an organic molecule as a protein?
   a) nitrogen    b) hydrogen    c) carbon    d) oxygen

13) What is the fluid inside a cell called? _____

14) What cell part travels along the cytoskeleton "highway"? _____  _____

15) Which of these word roots means "body"?    a) cyto    b) soma    c) pseudo    d) pod

16) TRUE or FALSE?  Very small molecules can squeeze through between the phospholipid molecules and therefore don't need to go through the "gates."

17) What does the centrosome do?   a) act as a gathering point for proteins floating around the cell
b) fight invading viruses   c) act as a central point for the cytoskeleton   d) send and receive messages

18) What object do the centrioles resemble? _____

# CHAPTER 3: ATP and the MITOCHONDRIA

Cells need energy. It takes energy for those motor proteins to walk along the cytoskeleton highway. It takes energy to build microtubules. It takes energy to create pseudopods. Everything the cell does requires energy. Where does the cell get its energy? You will probably guess, and correctly so, that this energy comes from the food you eat You know that food provides energy—energy we measure in calories. You also know that the food you eat gets digested and chemically broken down so that your body can make use of that energy. But exactly how do your cells use this energy?

Surprisingly, human bodies are not that different from cars. Engines that run on gasoline use combustion to break apart the long carbon chains found in petroleum molecules. A molecule of gasoline looks something like this:

$$H-C-C-C-C-C-C-C-C-H$$

or this:

Both of these molecules have eight carbons with hydrogens attached to them. Compare these gasoline molecules with two types of molecules your body uses for energy: fat and sugar:

A LIPID MOLECULE

*This is actually the lipid tail from our phospholipid molecule.*

GLUCOSE
(a basic sugar)

The similarity is striking, is it not? All of these molecules are basically strings or clumps of carbon atoms with hydrogens attached to them. The edible molecules have a few oxygens thrown into the mix, too.

Bascially, our food is not that different from gasoline! The way an engine gets energy out of a fuel molecule is to apply a spark to it, causing it to explode. The explosion happens inside a metal cylinder that contains a movable piston. The motion of the piston is then transferred, by various shafts and gears, to the wheels. The chemical waste products created by this explosion are carbon dioxide and water (plus some miscellaneous carbon chain molecules that somehow escaped being torn apart). Both carbon dioxide and water come out the exhaust pipe. Do you want to guess what waste products your body creates as it "burns" your food? Bingo—carbon dioxide and water!

Can you see how this explains why plants we eat can also be used to make "biofuel" for cars?

Now, you'd be in big trouble if your body used sparks and rapid combustion to get the energy out of your food. You wouldn't survive past your first meal! Instead, your body uses a very gradual method, a process that involves numerous small steps, so that there is never a harmful release of too much energy all at once. Your body breaks down the large energy molecules into tiny ones that are safe for a cell to use. The tiny energy unit that a cell uses is called an *ATP*.

ATP is short for "adenosine tri-phosphate." (DON'T PANIC!) See that word "tri" in there? That tells you that there are three of something. Does the word "phosphate" look familiar? (If it doesn't, you might want to go back and read chapter 2 again.) A phosphate is a phosphorus atom with some oxygens attached to it. "Tri-phosphate" means that the ATP molecule has three of these phosphates attached to it. What about the adenosine part? What is adenosine? We'll show you what it looks like, but some of you may want to close your eyes because this looks a bit complicated...

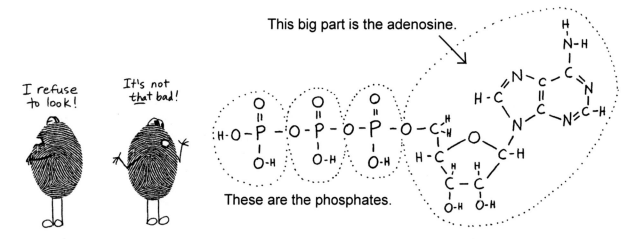

This big part is the adenosine.

These are the phosphates.

I refuse to look!

It's not that bad!

This molecule is way too complicated for scientists to draw every time they want to show ATP. So instead, they just draw it as circles—with one big circle representing the adenosine and three little circles for the phosphates. Often, they don't even put the letters in. Scientists just recognize this shape as ATP.

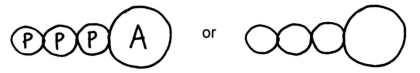

The way ATP releases energy is by popping off the phosphate on the end. There is energy stored in the bond that keeps that third phosphate on, and when it comes off, energy is released. Once the third phosphate is gone, the molecule is no longer called ATP because it no longer has three phosphates. It is now *ADP*: adenosine di-phosphate. ("Di" means "two.") ADP cannot give any more energy. The other two phosphates can't be popped off—they are stuck on too tightly. For the ATP molecule to be "recharged," the third phosphate must be put back on. Putting it back on takes energy. That's where your food energy comes in. The energy from your food is used to pop that third phosphate back onto ADP and recharge it into ATP. This is the only thing your body needs those food calories for—recharging the ATP. Once the ATPs are made, they float freely around the cell, available to any part that needs them.

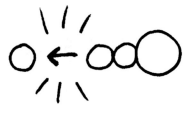

Hey- want to know something funny? Remember that biology word you were afraid of on the first page of chapter 2-- the word "PHOSPHORYLATION"? All it means is "adding on a phosphate." Pretty simple!

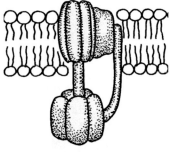

**ATP synthase**

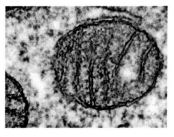

Cells have little recharging "machines" specially designed to put those third phosphates back onto ADP. These little machines make ATP. The scientific word for "make" is "synthesize." So scientists (who love Latin and Greek words!) decided to name this machine *ATP synthase*. (The "-ase" on the end of the word is the ending they always use for this type of protein. It's sort of like a last name.) This little machine looks really nifty. It's sort of a combination of an old-fashioned telephone and an old-fashioned, hand-held egg beater. You can tell from looking at this picture that it sits in the middle of a phospholipid membrane. However, it's <u>not</u> in the outer membrane of the cell. It's in organelles called *mitochondria*.

Every cell has lots of mitochondria floating around in it. This picture is a micrograph (a photograph taken with a microscope) of a real mitochondrion. You can't tell how it works just by looking at this picture. It took more than just looking at mitochondria to figure out how they work.

Scientists had to do complicated experiments on them. They also had to apply their knowledge of chemistry. The characteristics of electrons and protons play an important role in making ATP.

Here are some drawings showing the parts of a mitochondrion.

The dark area inside the wavy lines is called the **matrix**.

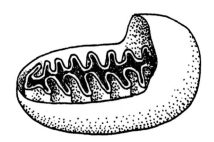

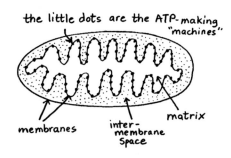

the little dots are the ATP-making "machines"

membranes

inter-membrane space

matrix

The drawing on the right is kind of flat and boring, but it shows where these little ATP synthase machines are located. They are embedded in the membrane that separates the inner matrix from the outer area (which doesn't have a nifty name like the matrix does). This membrane is made of exactly the same thing as the cell's outer membrane: a double layer of phospholipid molecules. What you can't see in this drawing is the other little embedded parts that the ATP synthase relies on. Let's zoom in and take a really up-close look at the whole assembly line.

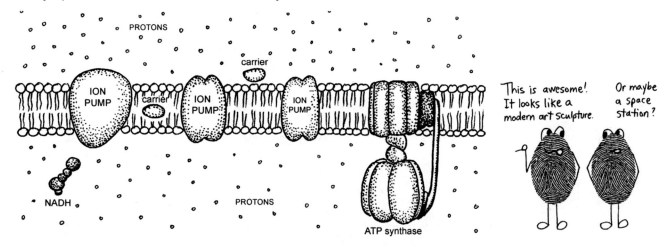

PROTONS

carrier

ION PUMP    carrier    ION PUMP    ION PUMP

NADH    PROTONS

ATP synthase

This is awesome! It looks like a modern art sculpture.    Or maybe a space station?

This is called the **electron transport chain**. The goal of this assembly line is to pump protons from underneath the membrane (meaning inside the matrix) to the top (meaning the inter-membrane space) so that there are a lot more protons above than below. The protons will then want to go back down to where it is less crowded, but the only way back down is to go through the ATP synthase machine. So down they go, and as they go down through the machine, they cause it to rotate, and this rotating motion snaps a phosphate onto an ADP.

To get things started, a pair of electrons is brought over to the assembly line by a molecule called NADH. Never mind what NADH means—all you need to know is that these electrons came from a process where sugars were digested. The chemical bonds in the sugars were broken and a pair of electrons were brought over to begin this chain of events. The path the electrons will take is shown with arrows. They are headed for an oxygen atom waiting at the bottom of the third ion pump.

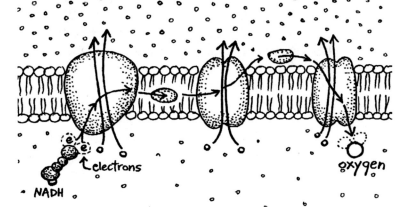

electrons

NADH

oxygen

That will be their final destination. Every time the electrons go through an ion pump, the pump pushes two protons from the bottom up to the top. Between the pumps there are two carrier molecules that ferry the electrons across the gap. As the electrons go through this chain, their energy gets used up.

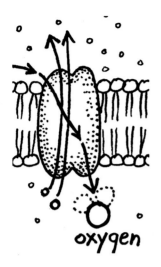

oxygen

By the time they get to the third ion pump, the electrons are worn out and don't want to do any more work. It just so happens that there are oxygen molecules hanging out around the bottom of this pump. An oxygen atom would love to turn itself into a water molecule if only it could get two hydrogen atoms. (Remember, water is $H_2O$.) Well, a hydrogen atom is nothing more than one electron and one proton coupled together. All the oxygen has to do is grab two protons that are floating by, then take the two tired electrons as they come off the assembly line, and put them together to make two hydrogen atoms. The hydrogens stick to the oxygen and presto—a molecule of $H_2O$! Your body can use this water molecule for some other process, or it can get rid of it as waste (the water vapor in your breath when you exhale).

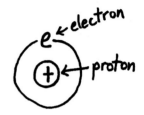

HYDROGEN

So that's what happens to the electrons. Now let's focus on the protons.

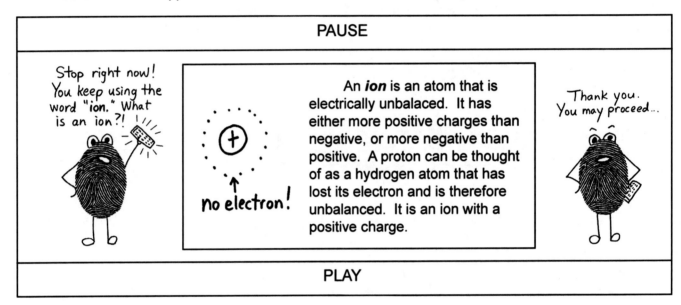

PAUSE

Stop right now! You keep using the word "ion." What is an ion?!

no electron!

An *ion* is an atom that is electrically unbalaced. It has either more positive charges than negative, or more negative than positive. A proton can be thought of as a hydrogen atom that has lost its electron and is therefore unbalanced. It is an ion with a positive charge.

Thank you. You may proceed...

PLAY

As the ion pump pushes the protons (or we could say "hydrogen ions") to the top, there are more and more protons "upstairs" and fewer and fewer "downstairs." Now imagine that you had a "sleep-over" at your house with about 50 friends, and you told them that they all had to sleep upstairs (let's assume you have an upstairs). What would happen? How long would it be until people started sneaking downstairs because of cramped conditions upstairs? Maybe some wouldn't even sneak. Maybe they would say they'd had enough, and stomp right down the stairs and out the door! Atoms and molecules don't like to be cramped, either. When they go from crowded places to less crowded places, we call it *diffusion*. The ATP synthase machine takes advantage of the diffusion of protons.

Another analogy that scientists sometimes use is a water reservoir over a water wheel. When the water spills over, it rushes down and turns the wheel (which turns machinery that grinds grain or runs a saw). In our mitochondria, the wheel is the synthase machine and the work being done is the replacement of that third phosphate onto ADP, turning it into ATP. Strangely enough, scientists are pretty sure that the synthase machine really does turn! The ADPs and individual phosphates go into that bottom part, and after the shaft twists, they pop out, joined as ATP.

## ACTIVITY 1   Watch a short video that explains diffusion

Here is a very simple and easy-to-understand video that explains what diffusion is.

**http://highered.mcgraw-hill.com/sites/0072495855/student_view0/chapter2/animation__how_diffusion_works.html**


## ACTIVITY 2   Watch animations of ATP and ATP synthase

First, a very simple video showing the "popping on and off" cycle of ADP-ATP.
Go to the YouTube "Cells" playlist and click on "ATP cycle."

Here's a video animation showing how protons go down through the ATP synthase machine, allowing the ADPs to be turned into ATPs.  You will hear the word *gradient*.  Gradient means having an area of high concentration (like the upstairs in our sleep-over example.)   Also, don't forget that when they say "hydrogen ion," this is the same as a proton.  You can access the video directly on their website, as listed below, or you can use the YouTube "Cells" playlist by clicking on "Gradients ATP Synthases."

**http://vcell.ndsu.edu/animations/atpgradient/movie-flash.htm**


## ACTIVITY 3   Watch an animation of the electron transport chain

This video will show you more about the electron transport chain.  It's very well done and very understandable after you've read this chapter.  Don't let all the scientific names of the proteins scare you!  You don't have to know them.  Just enjoy watching.  You will notice that when water is formed at the end of the process, it happens two molecules at a time.  You can access this video directly on their website, or you can use the YouTube playlist for "Cells" and click on "Cellular Respiration"

**http://vcell.ndsu.edu/animations/etc/movie-flash.htm**


## ACTIVITY 4   Compare these videos to the first two

Here are some other versions of the same information.  The artwork may look a bit different, but you will recognize all the ion pumps, the synthase, etc.  Again, don't worry about all the difficult names.

1) Inside a mitochondrion:  "Powering the Cell" on the playlist
In this video you will see a lot of blobby things floating about.  Notice that there is a progression. You start out being able to see the whole mitochondrion, then you start zooming in for close up views until you can finally see the electron transport chain.  You'll see various views, including one from the underside.  Just look for the tall blobs that are slowly rotating; these are the ATP synthase machines. Can you see the ADPs going in, and the ATPs coming out?

2) Close-up views of the synthase machine:  "ATP Synthase Top View" on the playlist
This shows you extrememly up-close views of the top and bottom of the synthase machine.  All those bumps are atoms and molecules.  That's how small this machine is!

3) Electron transport chain:
"Electron Transport Chain" and "Electron-Transport Chain" videos on playlist.

**Can you remember what you read?  If you can't think of the answer, go back and read that part of the chapter again until you find the answer.**

1)  What is the basic unit of energy used by living things? _____  (better get this one!!)

2)  Why can plants be made into fuel for vehicles?
   a)  because plants contain petroleum          b)  because plants contain protein
   c)  because plants contain strings of carbon atoms with hydrogens attached
   d)  trick question—they can't

3)  What is this thing called?

   $$O = \overset{\displaystyle O}{\underset{\displaystyle O}{P}} - O$$

   _____

4)  TRUE or FALSE?  Your body uses a slow form of combustion to burn your food.

5)  What happens when the third phosphate is popped off ATP?
   a)  a molecule of water is formed     b)  energy is released
   c)  energy is used up     d)  a proton is released

6)  The word "synthesize" means _____.

7)  Here's one for your visual memory.  How many ion pumps are in the electron transport chain? ___

8)  What happens when electrons pass through the ion pumps?
   a)  ATP is formed        b)  water is formed
   c)  two protons are pumped upward      d)  two electrons are pumped upward

9)  In what organelle would you find the electron transport chain? _____

10)  What is an ion?
    a)  a proton     b)  a pump that moves things    c)  an electrically unbalanced atom
    d)  a protein that is part of the electron transport chain

11)  What is the inside of the mitochondria called?
    a)  matrix        b)  ion       c)  membrane     d)  synthase

12)  TRUE or FALSE?  Atoms and molecules like to be packed in tightly.

13)  What is it called when a lot of something goes to a place where there is less of it? _____

14)  What is the ultimate destination of the electrons that go across the transport chain?
    a)  to be joined to an oxygen molecule    b)  to be pumped back into the matrix
    c)  to go down through the synthase machine    d)  to escape through gaps in the membrane

15)  If you join an electron and a proton, what do you get?
    a)  water    b)  a molecule    c)  a hydrogen atom    d)  an ion

# CHAPTER 4: PROTEINS, DNA and the RNA'S

So now we have a cell with an outer membrane, an organized cytoskeleton and a way to make energy. We looked at that incredible little assembly line that re-charges the ATPs. Now what would happen if one of those little machines was damaged and the cell needed to repair it? Let's say you cut your finger. Right along the cut, thousands of cells would be damaged. Your body would be left with a mangled mess of ripped-up cells that needed all kinds of repairs. The cells would have to make new ion pumps, new ATP synthase machines, new cytoskeletons, etc. How do cells know how to make and repair all their parts?

Before we can discuss the repairs, we need to learn more about the substance that biological machines are made of—***proteins***. A protein is a clump of atoms (mostly carbon, hydrogen and oxygen) that includes at least one ***nitrogen*** atom. Each type of protein has a unique shape, unlike any other type of protein. The shape and size of the protein determines what job it does in the body. The proteins fit together with other proteins like pieces in a puzzle, or like a key in a lock. (Often the way proteins work is called the "lock and key" principle.) Most proteins have weird, random shapes, but some have patterns we might recognize as lines or rings. These pictures give you a very good idea of the shape, but they don't tell you anything about the arrangement of the atoms. You can't see where the nitrogen is, or where the hydrogens attach to the carbons.

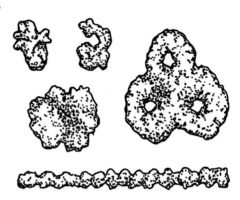

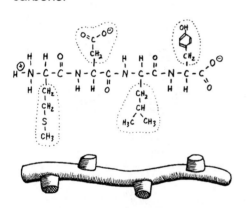

Proteins can also be drawn using letters to represent atoms: H for hydrogen, C for carbon, O for oxygen, N for nitrogen. In the past two chapters, you've seen quite a few of these letter pictures. Their main disadvantage is that they always look flat. On the left you can see two drawings of the same protein. The groups of letters that are circled in the top drawing are represented by those stump-like things in the bottom drawing. What a difference! In some situations, scientists would use the top drawing. In other situations they would use the bottom drawing. It would depend on what they were doing and what they needed the drawing to show.

Proteins are made of even smaller things called ***amino acids***. Amino acids are clumps of atoms that are arranged as shown here. Notice the nitrogen atom marking it as a protein. Also notice the question mark. The question mark represents the place where each amino acid is different. Each amino acid has its own unique combination of letters that branch off from that carbon.

Surprisingly, there aren't that many different kinds of amino acids—there are just **20** of them. That's it. Not thousands or millions, just 20. Most of them have names that end in "-ine" such as lysine, tyrosine, taurine, glutamine, alanine and proline. Amino acids link together to form long chains, like a string of beads. A typical chain has about 300 amino acids on it, but chains can have as few as 50 or as many as 2,000. Obviously, it would be way too tedious to draw a long chain of amino acids using all those letters. Usually the chains are drawn as little circles (or ovals or squares or triangles—the shape doesn't matter) with the first three letters of the name of the amino acid written on them.

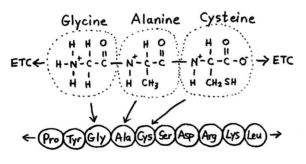

The scientists know that (Ala) is really a cluster of atoms, not a circle. But the circles sure are easier to draw! On the next few pages we will see how the cell knows which amino acids to connect together and in what order to connect them. But first, let's see what happens to these long chains after they are assembled.

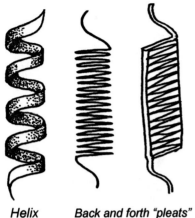

Helix          Back and forth "pleats"
               end up looking like a ribbon.

Chains that have hundreds (or thousands) of amino acids could get really tangled. If you've ever worked with yarn or string (or even an extension cord) you know how easy it is for something long and thin to get tangled. What a mess a cell would be if these chains got all tangled together! Not to worry, however. These chains are organized in a highly efficient way. The chains are *folded* into compact shapes. This process is simply called *protein folding.* (For once scientists didn't give something a hard name!) Amino acid chains often coil up, forming a shape called a *helix.* They can also fold back and forth many times, ending up looking like a *ribbon.* A third option is to form something kind of random that doesn't really have a recognizable shape that we can put a name to. Some proteins use just one or two of these options, but others use a mixture of all of them. It just depends on the protein.

---

## PAUSE

Pause!! I don't get it. Where did all those little circles go? What is that coil?

When you see the circles, it's a super-close-up view. If you "zoom out" it looks more like a coil or ribbon.

So that coil and that ribbon up there are made of little amino acid circles even though you can't see them.     Right!

## PLAY

---

Yes, don't forget that those coils and ribbons are made of long chains of amino acids. Also don't forget that amino acids don't really look like little balls, either. They are made of atoms.

After the chain makes its coils and folds, a second round of folding occurs. The entire chain bends and folds and takes on a three-dimensional shape. The final shape a protein folds into is determined by how the molecules in the chain interact with each other. Some of them are hydrophobic or hydrophilic. The water-hating molecules all try to get together (pulling their part of the strand along with them in the process) to create a special water-hating zone. Water-loving molecules try to move to the outside of the shape (pulling their part of the strand along with them in the process), giving them a better chance of being able to hang out with water molecules. In addition to these hydrophilic and hydrophobic issues, some places on the chain have an electrical attraction to each other, causing them to "stick" together (a bit like magnets stick together). The strands are pushed and pulled by all these interactions, and as a result the protein takes on a unique three-dimensional shape—a shape that will determine what job it will

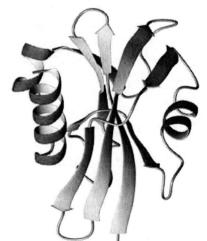

do. Some proteins end up as ion pumps in a mitochondrion. Others will go to the bloodstream and carry oxygen from the lungs. Some specialized proteins become part of long flexible "strings" that connect skin cells and give skin the ability to stretch. Many proteins end up as "messengers," sent as a signal to another cell. There are millions of jobs that need to be done in the body, and there is a specific protein for each job.

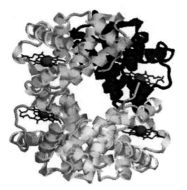

*Hemoglobin picks up four oxygen molecules as it goes through the lungs and carries them to cells.*

Now let's go back to the scenario we opened with. There's been some damage to the cell and its biological equipment must be repaired. Amino acids must be strung together and then folded. But a cell doesn't have a brain. It can't figure out what to do. There must be an automatic system that doesn't involve thinking. Umm... this is going to seem like another side track, but before we can actually start making the proteins for those ion pumps, we really need to take a few minutes to talk about DNA and the cell's nucleus. We really will get to those damaged ion pumps, but first...

In the middle of the cell there is a very large organelle called the **nucleus**. The first person in history to see a nucleus was Leeuwenhoek in 1719. All through the eighteenth and nineteenth centuries, scientists continued to see these large blobs inside almost every cell they looked at, but they had no way of figuring out what the blobs did. The function of the nucleus remained a mystery until the 1900s, when the electron microscope was invented. Using the electron microscope, scientists were able to see the structures inside the nucleus clearly enough to be able to figure out what role they played in the cell. They determined that the material in the nucleus was critical for the manufacturing of proteins and was probably controlling the process somehow. But this was as far as the electron microscopes could take them. The pictures couldn't tell them exactly how this process worked.

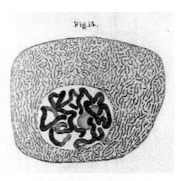

*A drawing from 1882 (Fleming)*

There was disagreement in the scientific community about the source of the cell's information. Many scientists thought it had to be on the proteins themselves. Others believed the information was stored in the nucleus, encoded onto a protein they had identified as **deoxyribonucleic acid**. *(Pronounced: dee-ox-ee-ri-bo-new-clay-ick)* This isn't an acid like hydrochloric acid or battery acid. It isn't dangerous at all. The only reason it is called an acid is that it has a certain grouping of atoms attached to it: COOH. This configuration of carbon, oxygen and hydrogen is what makes something an acid, even if it is an extremely weak one. (We're guessing maybe you've had enough pictures of molecules, so we'll skip drawing this one.) This was a very long name to write and to pronounce so they started calling it **DNA** for short.

*Most people associate Linus Pauling with his work on vitamin C.*

Using x-ray crystallography (crystallizing the molecule, then taking a picture of it using x-rays), they figured out that DNA has three basic parts: **phosphates**, **sugars**, and nitrogen-containing **bases**. They were pretty sure the phosphates and sugars were connected to each other, and a few researchers wondered if they formed some kind of helix shape, like those proteins on the previous page. Three leading researchers who were working on this problem in the 1950s were Linus Pauling, James Watson, and Francis Crick. Linus Pauling was already a famous chemist. He would eventually win four Nobel Prizes. Watson (an American) and Crick (an Englishman) were much younger and just at the start of their careers. Pauling was the first to announce his theory. He proposed a three-sided model. Watson and Crick looked carefully at his model,

Watson is on the left, Crick on the right. Their famous model is now in the science museum in London.

however, and realized that it disobeyed a fundamental law of chemistry. In his model, Pauling had put together three molecules that would actually repel each other in real life. How could such a famous chemist make such a basic mistake? It seemed almost unbelievable! But when Watson and Crick realized Pauling's mistake, they knew they now had a chance to be the first to solve the DNA mystery. Working together, they brainstormed different possibilities for how the molecules could be arranged. One day (Feb. 28, 1953), they hit upon an idea that just clicked. They knew almost immediately that they had solved the mystery. Legend has it that

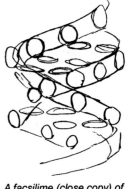

A facsimile (close copy) of Watson's first sketch of his idea about DNA.

they went into town and walked into a pub (because they were in England) and announced to the crowd, "We have discovered the secret of life!"

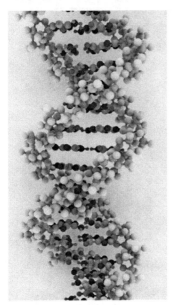

A model showing all the atoms in DNA. (For picture credits, see the list right before the bibliography.)

Watson and Crick figured out that DNA is made of two helix shapes joined at the middle by "rungs," like a twisted ladder. This shape is often called a **double helix**. The sides of the ladder are made of an alternating pattern of sugar molecules and phosphate molecules. Attached to the sugars on the rungs are things called **bases**. A sugar, a phosphate, and a base fit together to form a **nucleotide**. (More about these in a minute.)

The picture on the left shows a model of DNA that someone constructed using plastic beads to represent atoms. That's how small DNA is. It's just clusters of atoms stuck together. Most often, we see pictures that show DNA looking smooth and sleek, like the picture on the right. It's hard to draw real DNA. It's also hard for the viewer to make sense of all those bumps and lumps, so it can actually be helpful to use a more simplified picture.

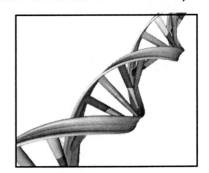

The rungs of the DNA helix are made of pairs of molecules called bases. There are four bases: **adenine, thymine, cytosine and guanine (A, T, C and G)**. Two of these bases bond together to form a **base pair**, which becomes a rung on the DNA ladder. **A** always pairs with **T**, and **C** always pairs with **G**. (This is easy to remember if you notice that the letters A and T are made of straight lines, and the letters C and G are both curved lines.) Let's look at an incredibly non-realistic picture of one section of DNA. We'll just use lines and geometric shapes to represent the molecules, so it will look deceptively simple. We'll show the base pairs as matching shapes so that it's obvious they are designed to go together. They aren't really matching shapes in real DNA. What keeps real base pairs together is an electrical attraction between the molecules.

It would be even more clear if the parts were colored... Maybe our reader can do that for us?

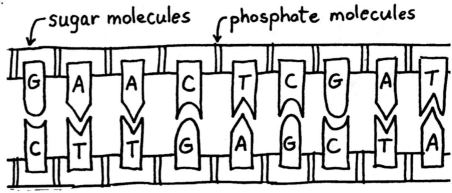

sugar molecules   phosphate molecules

The arrangement of the letters on the rungs isn't just random. One side of this ladder forms a secret code. The side with the code is called the "sense" side and the other side, which is just a mirror image, so to speak, and doesn't carry any information, is called the "nonsense" side. On the "sense" side, there are three-letter "words." A few of these letter combinations actually spell English words, like CAT, GAG and TAG. But mostly they don't look like real words. (For example: GGT, ACG, AAA or GCT) These three-letter words have a secret-sounding name: **codon**. A codon is one "word" in the DNA secret code. Can you circle the codons on the "sense" side? The first is ACG, the second is GAT, and so on.

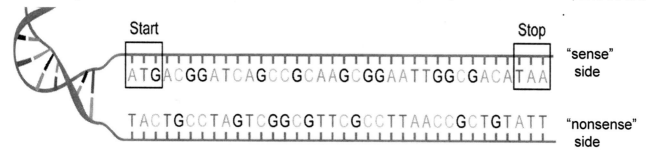

How many three-letter combinations can you make with this code? There are four letters and three possible positions for each letter (first letter, second letter, third letter). If we apply the correct math formula, we get $4^3 = 64$. There are 64 possible words.

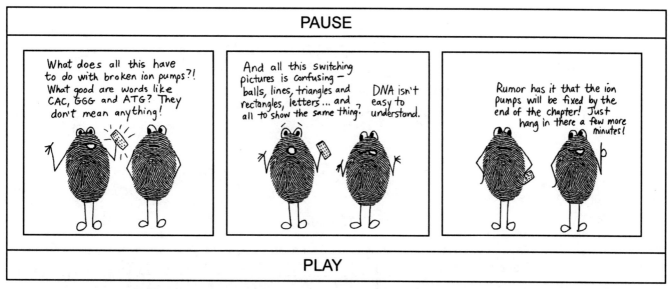

Now, we are just about ready to fix that ion pump. This is where we put what we learned about proteins and protein folding together with the information about DNA.

What is an ion pump made of? An ion pump is a very long chain of amino acids that is folded up in a certain way. The cell needs to make another chain that's identical to the first one. If it's identical, it will fold up the same way. Presto—a new ion pump!

In the nucleus, there is a part of the DNA that has the code for how to make this particular protein chain. The code is written as a series of these three-letter codons. It might look something like this (only a lot longer, with hundreds or thousands of codons):

AAT GGC GGA GAT TTT TAA GTT AAG AAG GAG CAC TTC TAT ACT GAT CCG

There's a big problem, though. These instructions can't leave the nucleus. It's not just that they aren't allowed to leave—they <u>can't</u> leave. They are too large to fit through the tiny holes in the membrane of the nucleus. They are stuck in the nucleus! (We'll take a closer look at these large pieces of DNA in a future chapter.) So a special messenger molecule called **messenger RNA** is a made. Messenger RNA is abbreviated like this: **mRNA**. (When you see "mRNA" you can say either "M-R-N-A" or "messenger RNA.")

To make mRNA, first a tiny machine (a specialized protein) unwinds and unzips the part of the DNA that will be copied. The bonds that connect the A's to the T's and the C's to the G's are fairly weak—it's not hard to pull them apart. Once the process is complete, the DNA zips right back up again.

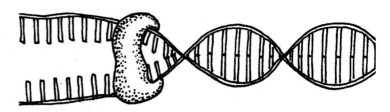

Next, another specialized protein (that looks and acts a bit like a sled) attaches itself to the nonsense side of the DNA and starts "reading" it. It knows where to start and stop reading because there are codons that mean "start" and "stop." Now this "reader" also happens to be an assembler, for as it slides down the DNA and reads each letter, it grabs the matching letter from the floating supply at hand, and sticks it on the end of the chain it has begun to form. Nucleotides go into the reader, and a string of mRNA comes out. This process is called *transcription*. "Trans" means "across," and "script" means "write." (Just in case you would like to know, the correct name for the sled is **DNA polymerase**.)

*(poll-LIM-er-ace)*

mRNA ← available nucleotides

The little "readers" in your cells can add hundreds of bases to mRNA every second!

nonsense side of DNA     "reader" →

When the mRNA is complete, it looks very similar to DNA, except that it has only one side. It's an exact copy of the sense side of the DNA, but with one small difference. For some unknown reason, mRNA doesn't have the letter T. It has A, C and G, but not T. Wherever there should be a T in mRNA, there is a **U** instead. U stands for **uracil** *(yoor-ah-sill)*. The U works the same way as T, and basically means T, except that it's a U. Sorry for having to add a little more confusion to this already long chapter, but that's just the way it is with mRNA.

When finished, mRNA looks like one half of DNA.

G A A C U C G A U U

CLOSE UP VIEW

*(Remember, there aren't any letters or geometric shapes in real mRNA. mRNA looks like clumps of atoms, like that DNA model made of beads.)*

I'd like to register a complaint about uracil. It's a stupid-sounding word, and it makes this chapter even harder!

When it has finished this process, the mRNA looks like the sense side of the DNA (except for having U's instead of T's). The mRNA has become a copy of the sense side of the DNA. Then the mRNA snakes out through one of the tiny pores in the membrane of the nucleus. The hole is big enough to let RNA pass through, but small enough that the DNA can't get out. (You could think of it as the nucleus's way of making sure its reference books stay in the library. They are too big to fit through the door!)

Once outside the nucleus, the mRNA heads for a

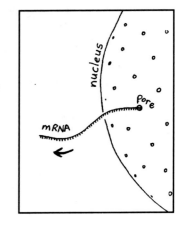

**ribosome**. A ribosome is a little manufacturing unit that assembles proteins. It has two halves, one slightly smaller than the other. When the mRNA comes along, the two halves of the ribosome close around it. (This view is sort of a "cut away" view where you can see inside. Normally, you wouldn't be able to see the whole strand of mRNA. You'd just see the ends sticking out.) Ribosomes can float freely in the cytoplasm of the cell or they can be attached to an organelle right next to the nucleus. This ribosome looks as though it is one of the free-floating ones. Notice how the mRNA has a special slot it fits into. Now it is ready for the next step: **translation**.

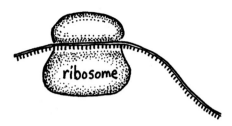

When you translate a book into another language, you replace all the words of one language with words from another language, but without changing the meaning of what is being said. In biological translation, the language of mRNA is translated from a secret code into an actual protein. mRNA contains the code, and another molecule transfers that code into actual proteins. Not surprisingly the molecule responsible for this transfer is called **transfer RNA or tRNA**. (When you see "tRNA" you can say "T-R-N-A" or "transfer RNA." Either is fine. Books always write "tRNA" because it's shorter and easier, but you can say it either way.)

Like other RNA's, tRNA is a single strand made of a "backbone" (the side of the ladder) consisting of sugars and phosphates, with nucleic acids (C, G, A and U) attached to them. Like mRNA, U replaces T. The two major differences between mRNA and tRNA are size and shape. tRNA is much shorter than mRNA. It doesn't need to be long in order to do its job, as we will see in a minute. Also, tRNA has a definite shape; it's not just a long strand like mRNA is. Artists draw tRNA a number of different ways. In real life, of course, it is a clump of atoms. In textbooks, it is drawn according to what the authors want you to understand about it. All four of these pictures represent tRNA. None of them look just like real tRNA. Each drawing has its strengths and weaknesses.

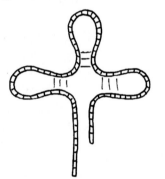
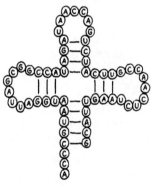

This drawing shows you the helix shape of tRNA and gives you a more accurate sense of its real 3D shape. But it's not helpful for showing how it works.

*It's a gingerbread man who got a leg nibbled off...*

This drawing is an attempt to simplify the drawing on the left. However, some places have been flattened out a bit. Like the one on the left, this drawing's main purpose is to show you its 3D shape.

The artist has flattened out the shape completely. Each loop represents a different part of that twisted helix shape. This drawing is handy for showing how tRNA works, but you don't get a good idea of what the real molecule looks like.

The purpose of this drawing is to show the nucleotide bases (A,C,G,U) that tRNA is made of. But it doesn't show the sugar-phosphate backbone (the side of the ladder). This drawing is very good for showing how tRNA does its job.

As you can see from these pictures, tRNA is really a three-dimensional twisted coil, but when the shape is flattened out by artists, it ends up looking something like a clover leaf. At the bottom, where the clover stem would be, is a special "hook" that can carry an amino acid. You can see this "hook" in all four of the drawings. It's the single strand that sticks off the molecule at the bottom.

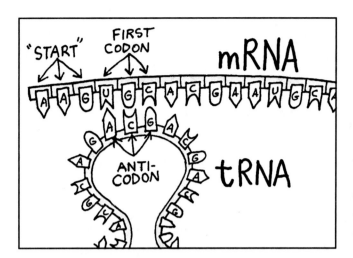

At the top of the molecule is another special part—the part that matches up to the mRNA code. The top three nucleic acids form a codon that matches up with an mRNA codon. The tRNA's codon is called an "*anti-codon*" because it has the opposite ("anti") of an mRNA codon. (Sometimes the word "anti" means something bad or negative, but in this case, it simply means that tRNA's codon has the matches for the mRNA's codon.) This drawing of tRNA is different from the four we saw on the last page. Here, we are using shapes to represent the nucleic acids. This is to emphasize that tRNA matches up with mRNA.

As you can see, the first codon, AAG, means START. Next, comes the first real codon, UGC, which is the code word for the amino acid named cysteine. Then the mRNA code keeps going, with every three letters being a code for an amino acid. Now let's see how these tRNAs do their transferring.

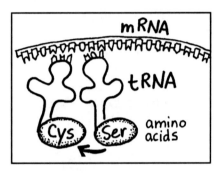

tRNA has a "hook" at the bottom that can carry an amino acid (the one that matches the mRNA code). After the first tRNA is in place, a second one comes along and matches the second mRNA codon. Then the two amino acids that they are carrying are joined together.

Now something like a relay race begins. The second tRNA must stay in place until a third comes along. After the third tRNA's amino is joined to the second's, it can leave. The third must stay until a fourth comes along. And so it goes. There must always be two tRNAs on the mRNA, until it reaches the last codon.

More and more tRNAs come to match up and to add their amino acids to the growing string. Finally, the end is reached. There is a codon that means STOP. Now the protein chain is finished and ready to be folded.

After the protein chain is complete, it just needs to be folded into the right shape and then it is ready for use—in this case for our ion pump. Some special proteins called *chaperone proteins* guide the newly formed protein as it bends and folds. There are also supervising chaperone proteins that check for mistakes. If the protein is folded wrong, it will be marked for recycling and the cell will have to start over and make a new protein chain.

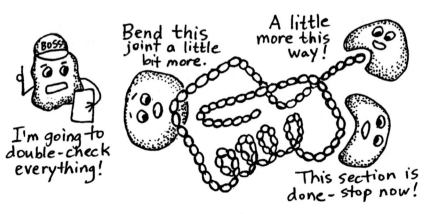

*In human society, the word "chaperone" usually means an adult who watches over children or teenagers during activities like parties or field trips.*

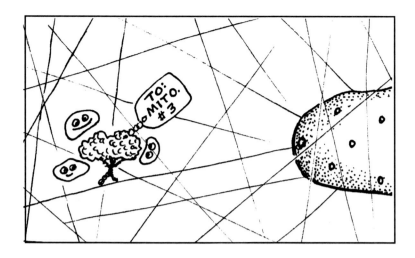

At last, our ion pump is ready for delivery. Perhaps one of those motor proteins we learned about in chapter 2 will take the new pump to the mitochondrion, traveling along one of the microtubules of the cytoskeleton. A supervising chaperone protein over at the ribosome was kind enough to put a "mailing label" on the pump during the folding process so that the motor protein will know where to go. In our silly picture here we actually drew a label. In real cells, the label would be yet another type of protein that is specially made to "dock" at one of the portals on the mitochondria. (Those dots on the mitochondrion are the portals.) More chaperone proteins guide the protein as it travels.

Once it reaches the mitochondrion, the protein will be taken inside and guided into position. A special "clipper" protein removes the delivery tag before the pump is put in place. (Well, you take the tags off your stuff before you use them, right?) If you want to know more about this process, be sure to watch the animation video in activity 4.

Now our cell has a new problem. How do you get rid of a broken ion pump?

\* \* \* \* \* \* \* \* \* \* \* \* \* \* \* \* \* \* \* \* \* \* \* \* \* \* \* \* \* \* \* \* \* \* \* \* \* \* \* \* \* \* \* \* \* \* \* \* \* \* \* \* \* \* \* \* \* \* \* \* \*

## ACTIVITY 1   Watch some animations that show transcription and translation

Watch this video first: "Transcription and Translation" (on the playlist). It is very easy to understand and the animation is awesome! You'll get to see how fast your body can make mRNA because they show it in "real time."

Now try this video. Make sure you watch it in full-screen mode, so it is as large as possible. It's like being inside a cell. Enjoy! ("DNA Transcription and Protein Assembly")

## ACTIVITY 2   Watch two short videos about Watson and Crick

1) Watch "Secret of Life" on playlist. This video is about 9 minutes long. It tells you the story of the discovery of DNA, giving more details than we gave here in this chapter.

2) Watch "DNA Story" on playlist. This video is a very brief (less than 3 minutes) interview with James Watson and Francis Crick, originally recorded in the 1970s. (They made their discovery in '53.)

Where are they now? Francis Crick has passed away, but James Watson is still alive (as of the updating of this curriculum in 2012) and is researching the use of DNA scans for diagnosing various illnesses.
NOTE: Check the playlist for additional videos of Watson, Crick, or Franklin. New ones will be posted if and when they become available.

## ACTIVITY 3   Sing the DNA Song

You can find the music for this song on the YouTube playlist—click on "DNA Song."  There are also two videos about Rosalind Franklin, who is mentioned in the song.  If you would like a digital audio file you can use with a CD player or MP3 player, you can download them at **www.ellenjmchenry.com**. Click on the tab labeled "MUSIC."

### The DNA Song

De-oxy-ribo-nucleic acid,
Watson and Crick worked together with Franklin,*
Learned its shape from x-ray diffraction,**
Double helix, DNA.

Adenine, thymine, cytosine, guanine,
Adenine, thymine, cytosine, guanine,
Adenine, thymine, cytosine, guanine,
Are the rungs of DNA.

*James Watson was only 25 years old when he moved from America to England to work with Francis Crick.  The two of them got help from Rosalind Franklin, an expert in the field of x-ray crystallography.
** Part of the x-ray crystallography process

## ACTIVITY 4   Watch an animation of a protein being delivered to a mitochondrion

Watch "Protein Transport" on the playlist.  In this video, you will watch a protein (perhaps our new ion pump?) being delivered to a mitochondrion (remember, it's one mitochondrion, two mitochondria). You'll see the delivery tag (which they call a "signal sequence") on the front, telling where it should go, and you'll watch as it enters the mitochondrion through an entry portal (which they call a "protein translocator complex").

You will also see a name for the "clipper" that takes the delivery tag off: "signal peptidase." When you see a protein word that ends in "-ase," it means that it removes something or breaks something down.  The word "peptide" means small protein chain.  So putting it all together, "signal peptidase" just means "the little protein chain whose job it is to remove the signal tag."  Don't let big science words scare you!

The video won't show you the final process of the protein being installed as an ion pump, because the video is not about one specific kind of protein, just mitochondrial proteins in general.  (But you are welcome to imagine that the protein folds up into an ion pump and is installed in the electron transport chain.)

## ACTIVITY 5   Look at lots of crazy protein shapes

This website is devoted to helping protein chemists by posting pictures of specific proteins as they are discovered.  If you click on the little pictures, they will open up for a larger view.  There are lots of really cool shapes and designs.  Notice that some proteins incorporate extra atoms and molecules into their design.  For example, there's a protein that uses two atoms of zinc.  Can you find it? It looks like it has two beads threaded onto it.  (Its PDB code is #3070.)

http://www.thesgc.org/structures/

## ACTIVITY 4   Watch and listen to James Watson as he describes how he modeled DNA

Watch "James Watson Explains" on the playlist.  In this recent video, James Watson was asked to demonstrate how he used cardboard shapes to help figure out how base pairs go together.  This video was then enhanced with some special effects so that you can see what Watson saw in his mind as he moved these cardboard shapes into place.

**Can you remember what you read?** If you can't think of the answer, go back and read that part of the chapter again until you find the answer.

1) What type of atom marks a molecule as a protein?
   a) nitrogen   b) oxygen   c) carbon   d) hydrogen

2) TRUE or FALSE? There is only one way to draw proteins.

3) Proteins are made of long chains of _____ _____.

4) How many kinds of amino acids are there? \_\_\_\_\_

5) TRUE or FALSE? Proteins do not contain any hyrdophilic or hydrophobic areas.
                     Only phospholipids can be hydrophilic or hydrophobic.

6) Who was probably the first person in history to see a cell's nucleus?
   a) James Watson     b) Francis Crick
   c) Robert Hooke     d) Antoni van Leeuwenhoek

7) Which one of these does DNA <u>not</u> have?
   a) phosphates     b) sugars     c) lipids     d) nucleic acids

8) In DNA, the sides of the ladder are made of _____ and _____ and the rungs are made of pairs of _____.

9) How many types of bases are there in DNA?
   a) 3   b) 4   c) 20   d) hundreds

10) One side of the DNA contains a secret code, the other does not. What do you call the side that contains the code? The _____ side.

11) Which side of the DNA does the "mRNA reader" read—sense or nonsense? _____

12) Which side of the DNA is the mRNA an exact copy of—sense or nonsense? _____

13) How many nucleotides form a codon?
   a) 2   b) 3   c) 4   d) 20

a string of nucleotides

14) Which letter does mRNA <u>not</u> have?
   a) A   b) T   c) C   d) G

15) What are the cell's little protein manufacturing units called?
   a) mitochondria   b) amino acids   c) ribosomes   d) codons

16) Which of these is the smallest?
   a) DNA   b) mRNA   c) tRNA

17) TRUE or FALSE? Protein chaperones prevent the proteins from folding.

18) TRUE or FALSE? AAG means "start."

19) What does "U" stand for? _____

# TIME TO REVIEW!

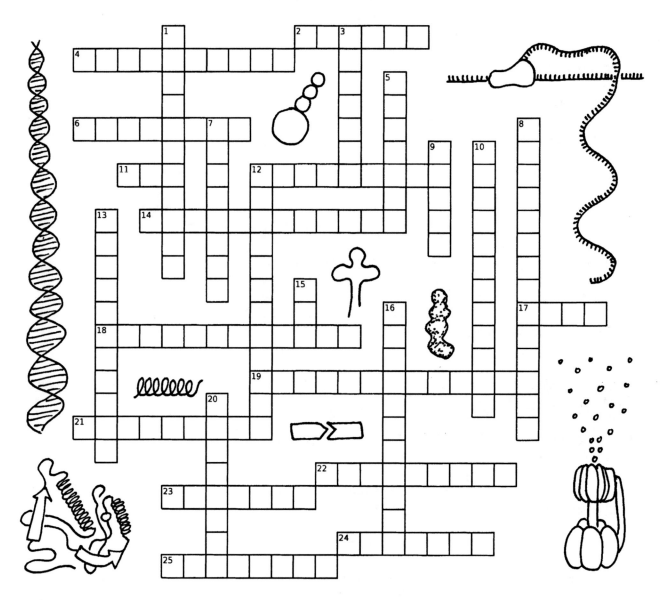

## ACROSS

2) This replaces thymine in mRNA and tRNA
4) This is the central organizing area for the cytoskeleton
6) This is the cell's protein manufacturing unit.
11) This contains the information on how to make every protein in your body.
12) This type of protein supervises protein folding.
14) These are part of the cytoskeleton and act as "highways" for motor proteins to travel on.
17) A molecule with this group of atoms (COOH) will always be an _____.
18) Membranes are made of this molecule.
19) The process of "reading" DNA to make mRNA
21) This is when a lot of something goes to an area where there is less of it.
22) This is the fluid inside a cell.
23) This is made of a very long chain of amino acids, folded up into a 3D shape.
24) DNA is found inside the _____.
25) The machine that pops the P back onto ADP is called ATP _____.

## DOWN

1) The process where tRNA turns a code into a real protein.
3) This nucleic acid is abbreviated as "A."
5) These go down through the ATP synthase machine.
7) This is what the outer layer of a cell is called.
8) These tiny fibers give the cell its shape.
9) This common folding shape looks like a coil.
10) This is the organelle that turns ADP back into ATP.
12) This is the network of fibers that gives the cell its shape as well as acting as a system of "roads."
13) This means "water-loving."
15) This is the basic energy unit that cells use.
16) This means "water-fearing."
20) This element marks an organic molecule as a protein.

# CHAPTER 5: LYSOSOMES, ER and GOLGI BODIES

So now we have some broken ion pumps sitting around. What does a cell do with garbage? Amazingly enough, cells have the equivalent of trash cans and recycling bins! The cell will put the broken pump into a recycling container called a *lysosome (lie'-so-some)*. The word lysosome comes from two Greek words, one of which you know already: "soma," meaning "body." The first part of the word comes from the word "lysis," which means to loosen or release something. You already know two words that contain "lysis." The word "analysis" means to reduce something down to its individual parts. (In this word, "ana-" means "re-.") When you analyze something, you tear it apart, even if the action is just in your mind. The word "paralysis" begins with "para" meaning "side." Often, paralysis can be described as the breaking down, loosening, or loss of function on one side of the body. Of course, paralysis can involve the whole body, too, but often it is one side, or one part, of the body. If you go on to study cell science at a deeper level, you will run into other words that have "lysis" or "lys" in them, such as hydrolysis, glycolysis, lipolysis, and autolysis.

So what does the lysosome loosen or release? It loosens chemical bonds that keep atoms and molecules together. Once loosened, the atoms and molecules go back to being individual units that can be used to build something else. It's exactly like taking apart a Lego® structure you've built. You can take apart the airplane you made and use those very same parts to make a building or a

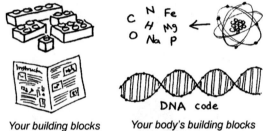

*Your building blocks and the instructions*

*Your body's building blocks (chemical elements—atoms) and the DNA instructions*

space station or a vehicle. The individual blocks are the basic units you use no matter what you are building. It's the same with chemistry. The basic building blocks are oxygen, carbon, hydrogen, nitrogen and other elements from the Periodic Table. These atoms can be used to build anything in the universe; you just need the instructions for how to put them together in the right order. As we just learned in the last chapter, the instructions for how to make biological things are written as DNA code.

Let's take a look at a lysosome and see how it works. As you might guess, it has an outer membrane made of phospholipids, just like the cell's plasma membrane. (Most organelles in the cell have phospholipid membranes.) The lysosome's membrane differs from the plasma membrane in the proteins and sugars that are embedded in the membrane. The plasma membrane has portals that let things in and out of the cell, identification tags on the outside, and anchors for the cytoskeleton on the inside. The lysosome doesn't need these types of proteins. It only needs things relevant to doing its particular job— digesting and recycling proteins, lipids (fats) and carbohydrates (sugars).

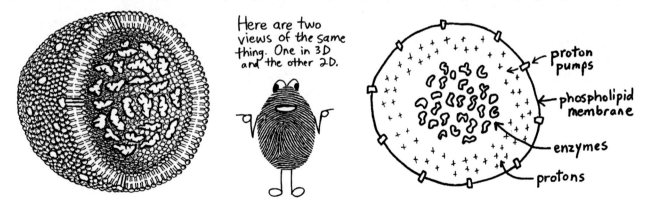

Here are two views of the same thing. One in 3D and the other 2D.

proton pumps

phospholipid membrane

enzymes

protons

One of the things the lysosome has embedded in its phospholipid membrane is a particular type of ion pump. This pump is similar to the ion pumps in the mitochondria in that it pumps protons.

The way it works, however, is much different. You'll remember that the mitochondria's ion pumps <u>produce</u> ATP. The lysosome's ion pumps <u>use</u> ATP. The lysosome's pumps use ATP energy to bring protons inside its membrane, causing the number of protons inside the lysosome to be much greater than outside. (If you want to know more about how the lysosome's proton pumps work, check out the info and the video in activity 1 at the end of this chapter.) Why does a lysosome need so many protons inside? The answer requires a very brief chemistry lesson before we go on.

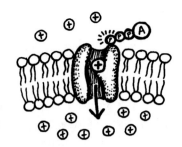

# A Very Brief Chemistry Lesson

**WHAT IS AN ACID?** The definition of an acid is a substance that accepts (or "wants") electrons. Examples of acids you are familiar with would include lemon, orange and cranberry juice, vinegar, and soda pop (drinks that are fizzy). That tart taste that lemons have (bet your salivary glands are tingling just thinking about lemons!) is because they are acidic. Their opposites, the bases (also called alkaline substances), are bitter. Baking soda and soap are alkaline. Scientists have a scale for rating how acidic or how alkaline something is. It is called the *pH scale*. The scale goes from 1 to 14. The middle number, 7, is neutral—neither acid nor base. The lower the number, the more acidic the substance is. The higher the number, the more alkaline it is. Plain water that does not contain any dissolved minerals ("distilled" water) is neutral, at 7. Orange juice and vinegar have a pH of about 3. Lemon juice is at about 2.5. The acid in your stomach ranges from 1 to 3. On the other end, baking soda is about 8 and ammonia (often used in cleaning products) is at about 12. (Surprisingly, normal rain water scores a pH of about 5.7. Acid rain is 5.2.)

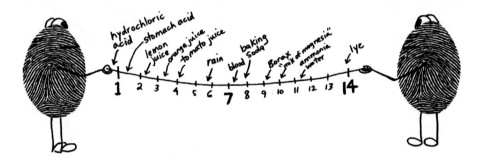

**WHAT DOES pH MEAN?** It means "*potential hydrogen*." If you put an electron and a proton together, you get a hydrogen atom. We saw this back in chapter 3 at the end of the electron transport chain. Remember when those electrons came out of the last ion pump and were captured by an oxygen atom? The two electrons were matched with two protons, creating two hydrogen atoms for the oxygen to use to make itself into a water molecule. The pH number indicates the degree to which a substance wants to get, or to get rid of, electrons or protons. If it wants to get electrons, it is an acid. The more it wants them, the more acidic it is. If a substance wants to get protons (or the reverse, to get rid of electrons) the more alkaline it is. Confusing? Yeah, a bit. But you don't have to understand it completely to appreciate what a lysosome does.
    And now back to the lysosome...

The lysosome is constantly pumping protons inside itself. What happens as a result? Those protons would gladly accept electrons. (As they say, opposites attract!) By definition, the interior has become acidic because it is now an electron acceptor. It has a pH of about 4.7. (Different books and web sites will give you different numbers for the pH of lysosomes, but they will always be between 4.5 and 5.) Now let's find out why the lysosome needs to make its interior acidic.

Inside the lysosome are proteins called enzymes. An enzyme is a protein molecule that assists either in putting together other molecules or in tearing them apart. In this case, all of the lysosome's enzymes tear things apart. There are about 40 different kinds of enzymes inside a lysosome. Some of these enzymes break apart proteins, others break apart lipids or carbohydrates or nucleic acids (DNA and RNA). Each enzyme can only break apart one type of molecule, so many enzymes are needed to break apart the many types of molecules the lysosome must digest. (You might want to think of these enzymes as little "keys" that can unlock the chemical bonds that hold, or "lock," the molecules together. Each lock needs the correct key.) The enzymes need an acidic environment in order to function properly. It's the same in your stomach. The enzymes in your stomach also need acid in order to do their job, so your stomach makes itself acidic. If you've ever burped up any stomach juice by accident, you could feel the acid burn in your esophagus. Your stomach has a protective mucus lining that keeps it from being burned.

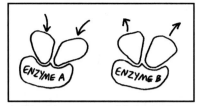

In this picture, enzyme A is joining two molecules. Enzymer B is splitting them.

The lysosome also has ways of protecting itself from its acidic environment and from the action of the enzymes, but scientists are still studying it so we can't tell you how it works. Perhaps one reason that the lysosome need an acidic environment is for the protection of the cell itself. What if a lysosome broke open and all the digestive enzymes got out? They would go around digesting the cell's organelles and the cell might die as a result. Because they need acid in order to function, if the lysosome bursts open, the enzymes suddenly find themselves in an environment that is no longer acidic, and therefore they can't digest very well. Thus, the cell is saved. (What a brilliant design!)

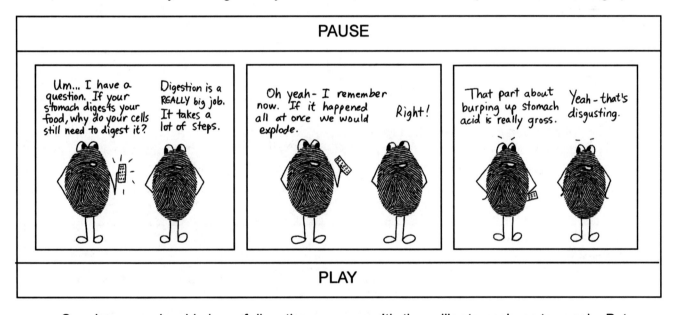

So a lysosome is a big bag of digestive enzymes. It's the cell's stomach, so to speak. But unlike a stomach, it isn't connected to a mouth. There's no hole that things go into. The membrane is continuous all the way around. The only way to get into a lysosome is to merge with it. (If you've ever experimented with oil droplets you know what happens when two oil droplets touch each other; they merge and become one slightly larger oil droplet.) If the cell can wrap its food or garbage inside a phospholipid sphere, and launch the sphere towards a lysosome, when that sphere touches the lysosome the two will merge together. After they merge, the garbage or food particles will then be on the inside of the lysosome.

A phospholipid sphere created for the purpose of transporting things (or merging things) is called a *vesicle*. Vesicles are what cells use instead of cardboard boxes. When they need to ship something or carry something, they put it into a vesicle. Vesicles can be used to hold all sorts of things, including broken ion pumps. Let's put that broken old ion pump into a vesicle, then give it a push towards a lysosome and see what happens. It drifts off towards the lysosome... it touches the lysosome, and... presto—it's gone! As soon as it touched the lysosome, it disappeared. The vesicle merged into the lysosome. What used to be the membrane of the vesicle is now part of the membrane of the lysosome. And the ion pump? It's inside with all those enzymes. In a matter of seconds, the old pump is reduced to a pile of amino acids. Then the lysosome will put those amino acids back into the cytoplasm, expelling them through portals in the membrane. The pieces can either be used by the cell to make more proteins, or they can be exported out of the cell and eventually into a blood vessel.

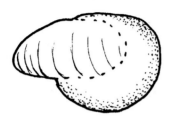

If the mitochondrion had lots of broken ion pumps, the cell might decide to scrap the whole thing and just make a new one. The old mitochondrion will be sent to the ER where it will be wrapped in a phospholipid membrane. (Even though its own outer membrane is made of phospholipids, it is still wrapped.) The wrapped mitochondrion will then be sent to merge with a lysosome. After merging, the lysosome's enzymes will dissolve all the parts of the mitochondrion and release the amino acids back into the cytoplasm.

A lysosome can also digest things that come into a cell from outside. Some cells take in food particles by creating a "dent" in the plasma membrane that will eventually be pinched off and turn into a vesicle. Even bacteria can be gotten rid of in this way.

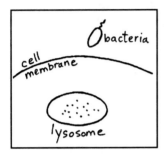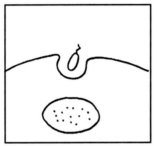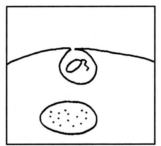

Your white blood cells have lots of lysosomes. You've already seen a video (chapter 2) of a white cell chasing down a bacterium. When it catches it, it will engulf it and create a vesicle to bring it inside the cell. Then the vesicle will merge with a lysosome and it's good-bye bacterium!

Ah, yes. Well, let's move on.

We mentioned this before, but a cell not only uses "micro machines" and organelles, it also has to manufacture them. Cells have to make ribosomes, mitochondria and lysosomes. We'll get to ribosomes and mitochondria later. Right now, let's find out how a cell makes a lysosome.

The first step in making a lysosome is to make the enzymes that will be inside it. An enzyme is a specialized protein. In the last chapter we saw how those little parts called ribosomes take mRNA (that came from the nucleus) and work together with tRNA to hook amino acids together. The ribosome we saw making a protein was working all by itself as it floated in the cytoplasm. Then the protein was transported to the mitochondrion and taken inside. This method won't work for a lysosome. You can't make a phospholipid ball, then stuff it with enzymes. The ball must be created around the enzymes. (This process is fascinating but a little complicated, so hold on and buckle your cellular seat belts for a few pages!)

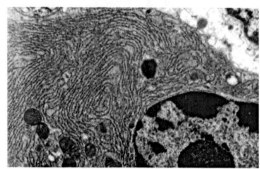

The ribosome begins to read the mRNA for how to make one of these digestive enzymes. The first 50 or so rungs on the mRNA have a special meaning. (Remember, mRNA is a copy of the DNA secret code instructions.) This first part of the code means, "Take me to the ER." In this case, the ER isn't the Emergency Room. It's something called the **endoplasmic reticulum**.

Now you've been reading this book long enough that you can guess what's coming next, right? Exactly. We are going break down those huge words and make them easy and understandable. "Endo" just means "in" or "within." "Plasmic" refers to the cell's cytoplasm (the fluid,

*A micrograph of ER outside the nucleus of a cell. The nucleus is the large circle in the lower right corner. (The black spots are mitochondira.)*

or "cell gel"). So "endoplasmic" simply means "in the cytoplasm of the cell." Not too hard. The word "reticulum" comes from the Latin word "reticulatus," meaning "net-like" or "network." So this organelle isn't round like a mitochondrion or a lysosome. In fact, it's a complicated network of long tubes that are connected at various places. Even scientists find these long words a bit of a bother and they hardly ever use them. They almost always refer to the endoplasmic reticulum by its initials, **ER**. From now on, we'll do as the cell biologists do, and we will write "ER". When you see "ER" you can say "E-R' or you can say "endoplasmic reticulum," whichever you prefer.

Now back to our story. When the ribosome begins reading this particular piece of mRNA—the instructions on how to made a digestive enzyme—the first part of the code tells the ribosome to take it to the ER. Why? Because the ER is the organelle in the cell that can put phospholipid membranes around things. The enzymes must be inside a membrane for reasons we shall see shortly. Follow along with these pictures as we watch what happens next:

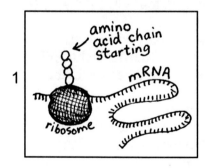

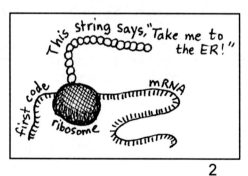

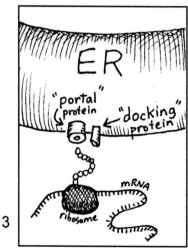

**1)** The ribosome is just starting to make the amino chain.
**2)** The first part of the code is complete. It says, "Go to the ER." The ribosome cannot make any more of the chain until it has anchored itself to the ER. The mRNA just waits.
**3)** There are little "docking ports" on the outside of the ER, where a ribosome can come and attach itself, sort of like a boat coming in to a dock. In fact, there are even little "tug boat" proteins that go out and help guide the ribosome into the dock! There are two parts to the little dock. One part is the place where the ribosome is secured so it doesn't drift off (like the "cleat" on a real dock). The other part, right next to it, is a portal (a hole). The ribosome sticks the end of the protein through the portal so that it goes inside the ER.

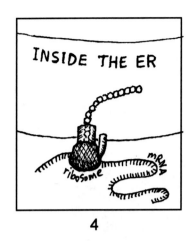

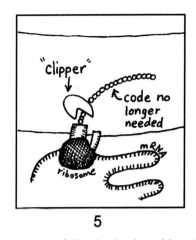

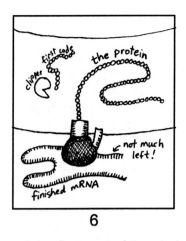

|       4       |       5       |       6       |

**4)** In this picture, the ribosome has successfully docked and has inserted the first part of the chain.

**5)** Little "clippers" come over and cut off the end of the protein because that part of the message isn't needed anymore. (The message said to go to the ER, and that has now been accomplished.)

**6)** Once that out-dated message is clipped off, the ribosome starts reading the mRNA again. (This picture doesn't show all the tRNAs that are bringing their amino acids over as the ribosome needs them.) As the protein chain grows, the ribosome feeds it through that portal and into the ER.

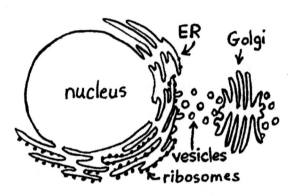

When the ribosome finishes, it detaches from the ER and goes off to find a new piece of mRNA and begins to build other proteins. This ribosome might build another one of these digestive enzymes or it might go off and build something else. As far as scientists know, ribosomes are not specific to particular jobs. They can read any piece of mRNA that comes their way.

Meanwhile, inside the ER, the newly formed protein isn't alone. Many other digestive enzymes are being formed. The ER now moves all these enzyme proteins to one of its tubes that is very close to another organelle: the **Golgi body**. (The second "g" is "soft": *Goal-jee*) The Golgi body (or **Golgi apparatus**) is named after Italian scientist Camillo Golgi, who discovered it in 1897. (He was the first to see it but he didn't know what it did.) Golgi bodies stay right close to the ER. They don't touch it, but they stay close.

The ER has a phospholipid membrane, just like mitochondria, lysosomes, and vesicles. The ER now pushes the enzymes outward so they make a bulge in the membrane. Then it pinches off those bulges, and voila... they become vesicles. The vesicles then do their job and transport those enzymes over to the Golgi body.

Now take a wild guess what the outside of the Golgi body is made of. Hmm... how about phospholipids? Yes, of course, and for a good reason. All a vesicle has to do is make contact with the Golgi body and it instantly merges with the Golgi membrane. Whatever the vesicle was carrying is then inside the Golgi body. (If you watch the animation videos in activities 2, 3 and 4, you'll see vesicles merging. In this case, watching it happen is better than reading about it.)

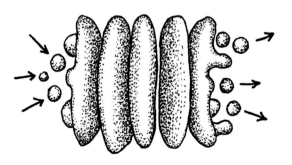

Now for the weird part—the Golgi body itself. This might be the most bizarre organelle in the cell. It looks like a stack of pancakes with bumps stuck to the first and last cakes. But that's not the weirdest part. The Golgi body is in constant flux. The overall shape stays pretty much the same, but the parts are always changing. Watching an animation is the best way to see this, but here is a quick description. The first pancake is made of vesicles that are merging together to make one large

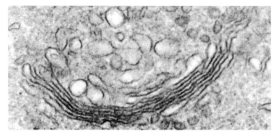
*A micrograph of a Golgi body (Notice the vesicles.)*

pancake. (Those are the bumps you see.) Then there are about three pancakes in the middle, then a final pancake. That last pancake is constantly breaking apart into vesicles. Those bumps on the last pancake are vesicles budding off. Eventually the last pancake completely disintegrates and the pancake right behind it moves in and takes its place. Then the next pancake down the line has to move up and take the place of the pancake that just moved into last position. And so on it goes, back to the first pancake. As the first pancake moves up to take the place of the second, new vesicles move in and start forming a new first pancake.

(SIDE NOTE: This theory of how a Golgi body's pancakes constantly shift (called the "maturation theory") is generally accepted by most scientists right now, but not everyone is convinced. If you browse around on the web, you might find a site that doesn't agree with this theory.)

All scientists agree that despite any shifting of Golgi pancakes, the little "micro machines" inside the Golgi body stay in place. The pancakes of the Golgi body contain proteins similar to the chaperone proteins we met in the last chapter. The Golgi's chaperone proteins act like post office workers packaging, sorting, and labeling the proteins and enzymes that come through. In the case of our lysosomal enzymes, the Golgi protein "workers" fold them into the right shape, tag them with labels that identify them as lysosomal enzymes (scientists call the lysosomal "zip code" M6P), gather all of them into one place, then package them into vesicles. The Golgi body also makes sure that the future lysosome has two special types of proteins in its membrane: those proton pumps we learned about, plus "portal" proteins that allow the digested particles to exit the lysosome and go back into the cytoplasm. The pumps and portals were manufactured in the ER in much the same way that the digestive enzymes were.

After all the enzymes, pumps, and portals have been labeled and put into vesicles, the vesicles then bud off the last pancake and drift away from the Golgi body out into the cytoplasm. These vesicles will either develop into lysosomes or merge with an existing lysosome.

So how do the Golgi's own protein "workers" stay in the apparatus when the pancakes are constantly shifting and changing and moving on? Scientists are still studying this. They don't know. There are many things about cells that we still don't know.

Golgi bodies process other things, too, not just lysosomal enzymes. Cells make all kinds of things. Sometimes they even make things that need to be delivered to other cells—even cells that are in another part of the body. The Golgi's job is to put the correct label on each protein that comes through so that it will be delivered to the right place. If the items in question must be delivered outside the cell, then the Golgi puts them into a vesicle that will drift all the way out to the plasma membrane and merge with it. The result of merging with the outer membrane is that the contents of the vesicle end up outside the cell. The Golgi is sort of like a packing and processing factory and a post office all in one. It packs proteins and gets them to where they need to be.

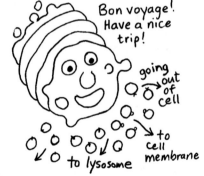

Here's a horrible thought—what if the Golgi body messes up and puts the wrong tag on something? Does it still get delivered? What happens to it? In the case of lysosomal enzymes, if they don't get labeled properly, they don't end up inside a lysosome. So you've got "lost" enzymes and empty lysosomes. What a disaster! You'd have cellular garbage piling up and no way to get rid of it. The cells would eventually be so full of garbage that they could not function anymore. When something like this happens, it is called **lysosomal disease.** There are many kinds of lysosomal diseases because there are many different kinds of lysosomal enzymes. Babies born with a lysosomal disease have very severe health problems and usually die before the age of six or eight. The most famous lysosomal disease is Tay-Sachs disease. Most adults have heard of this disease but they have no idea what causes it. (Your average adult-on-the-street has no idea what a lysosome is or what it does. Try asking around at your next family gathering. How many of your relatives know what a lysosome is?)

The root problem that causes lysosomal diseases is faulty instructions from the DNA. Because every cell has an identical copy of the DNA, every cell makes the same mistake. If just one or two Golgi bodies make a mistake, the body will hardly notice. But if every Golgi in every cell of the body makes the same mistake, that's a serious problem. Researchers are working very hard to find a way to make these faulty Golgi bodies start tagging the enzymes correctly.

Other diseases caused by incorrect protein folding include Alzheimer's, cystic fibrosis and many types of cancer. (In the case of Alzheimer's, it seems that certain proteins clump together because they are the wrong shape, then these clumps get stuck in various places in the brain.) Even though cells have chaperone proteins that are supposed to supervise the folding, things can still go wrong. The chaperones can have something go wrong with them, too.

Believe it or not, you can help researchers who are working on modeling protein folding. Even though it only takes a cell a millionth of a second to fold a protein, it can take a computer up to 30 years to calculate what the cell did! But many computers working together can shorten this time to just a few days. A research group at Stanford University (in California) has developed software that allows anyone to donate some of their computer's "spare time" to work on figuring out how a protein folds. See the link listed in activity 5 for more information.

\* \* \* \* \* \* \* \* \* \* \* \* \* \* \* \* \* \* \* \* \* \* \* \* \* \* \* \* \* \* \* \* \* \* \* \* \* \* \* \* \* \* \* \* \* \* \* \* \* \* \* \* \* \* \* \* \* \* \* \* \*

## ACTIVITY 1    A video about the lysosome's proton pumps

Here is a short animation that shows how the lysosome's proton pumps work.

**http://highered.mcgraw-hill.com/olcweb/cgi/pluginpop.cgi?it=swf::535::535::/sites/dl/free/ 0072437316/120068/bio05.swf::Proton%20Pump**

## ACTIVITY 2    A video about lysosomes

Here is a computer animation showing what lysosomes do:

**http://highered.mcgraw-hill.com/sites/0072495855/student_view0/chapter2/animation__ lysosomes.html**

## ACTIVITY 3   A video about Golgi bodies

Watch "Golgi Apparatus" on the playlist. This video has no narration, just music. You will see the processes we discussed in this chapter. You will see the work of the Golgi being represented by a conveyor belt and cardboard boxes. The boxes represent vesicles. Notice the mailing labels being applied to the boxes. In real life, Golgi mailing labels are made of things like sugars. (If you want to know the exact details of how a sugar molecule can be a mailing label, you'll have to study cell biology in college some day. That's a bit beyond the scope of this introductory book!)

## ACTIVITY 4  A video showing how a lysosome is made

Here is a video that covers a lot of what we learned in this chapter.

**http://vcell.ndsu.edu/animations/proteinmodification/movie-flash.htm**
("Protein Modification" on playlist)

Don't let the vocabulary in this video scare you off.  (Turn off the sound if it does!)  This video will show you a vesicle leaving the ER, floating over to the Golgi body and merging with it.  Then you'll see some orange chaperone proteins inside the Golgi body putting on a tag (mailing label) called the "Mannose 6-phospate" (M6P).  This the label for vesicles going to lysosomes.  The enzymes will then pass through the Golgi till they get to the last pancake.  In the last pancake, the enzymes will attach themselves to some red proteins that will act like seats on a shuttle bus.  A vesicle will form (this is the shuttle bus) and will float over to the endome (which is a baby lysosome).  The vesicle merges, and the enzynes are thus delivered.  Then the shuttle bus returns to the Golgi body for another load.

Here is a little dictionary of terms, so you don't get confused while watching:

- hydrolase = digestive enzyme (they are gray or green in this video)
- oligosaccharide = complex sugar  (sugars are shown as little colored hexagons)
- glycosylation = adding a sugar
- M6P = the "mailing label" that means "deliver this to a lysosome"
- endosome = baby lysosome
- cis cisterna = first pancake (where vesicles are merging)
- trans Golgi cisterna = last pancake (where vesicles bud off)
- M6P receptor proteins = the docking sites on the Golgi membrane that anchor only enzymes with the M6P tag on them (sort of like "seats" on the vesicle "shuttle buses")

## ACTIVITY 5    An opportunity to help protein folding researchers

We mentioned that Stanford Universtity has developed a way for ordinary folks to help researchers learn more about protein folding.  Even if you are not interested in donating computer time, check out their web site.  You can learn more about protein folding (click on SCIENCE) and even see a video that shows what it looks like when a computer tries to figure out how a protein folds (click on RESULTS).   If you want to see more videos of computer protein models folding, use a video search engine with key words, "protein folding simulation."

**http://folding.stanford.edu/English/Main**

Here's another site that has made protein folding into a lot of fun.  They've made a high-tech "video game" where you solve protein puzzles.  Pretty awesome!

**http://fold.it/portal/**

## ACTIVITY 6    Learn more about lysosomal disorders and the people who live with them

Here is the web address of a huge national association in the United States, devoted to helping those with lysosomal disorders.  They are trying to raise public awareness of these rare disorders and also raise money to help the researchers who are trying to find a cure.

**http://www.hideandseek.org**

**Can you remember what you read? If you can't think of the answer, go back and read that part of the chapter again until you find the answer.**

1) One of the jobs of the lysosome is to:
   a) make proteins out of amino acids        b) break down protein chains into amino acids
   c) make amino acids from nucleic acids      d) help proteins fold properly

2) The environment inside a lysosome is very:
   a) acidic    b) basic    c) warm    d) salty

3) Lysosomes have a special pump in their membranes that bring lots of what inside?
   a) ATP    b) proteins    c) electrons    d) protons

4) How does the lysosome get its enzymes?
   a) It makes its own enzymes.      b) They come in from the bloodstream.
   c) A vesicle brings the enzymes from the Golgi body.
   d) The enzymes are brought into the lysosome by pumps in its membrane.

5) TRUE or FALSE?  If a lysosome breaks open, the enzymes kill the cell.

6) TRUE or FALSE?   The Golgi body processes only enzymes destined for lysosomes, not for
   any other organelle.

7) Why do ribosomes bind to the docking ports on the ER?
   a) They bump into it by accident.      b) Because the ribosome would fall apart otherwise.
   c) Because the first part of an mRNA strand told them to go there.
   d) Because the ER is the only place you can find a supply of amino acids for tRNA.

8) The outsides of the ER and Golgi body are made of what?
   a) phospholipids    b) proteins    c) enzymes    d) ribosomes

9) TRUE or FALSE?  Lysosomes can digest only proteins.

10) TRUE or FALSE?  Some of your cells contain amino acids that used to be germs.

11) What part of the body is a lysosome most like?
   a) heart    b) stomach    c) liver    d) mouth

12) How do the Golgi's own "worker" proteins stay inside the Golgi body even though the Golgi
    body is constantly shifting and changing around them?
    a) They anchor themselves to the proteins in the membrane.
    b) They tag themselves so they don't get lost.
    c) They stay inside vesicles.      d) We don't know.

13) Which is the correct order for the process of making an enzyme?
    a) Golgi body, ER, vesicle, ribsome          b) vesicle, ribosome, ER, Golgi body
    c) ribosome, ER, vesicle, Golgi body         d) ER, vesicle, Golgi body, ribosome

14) TRUE or FALSE?  Some enzymes put things together, others take things apart.

15) Which one of these diseases is NOT caused by incorrect protein folding?
    a) Alzheimer's    b) pneumonia    c) Tay-Sachs    d) cystic fibrosis

16) TRUE or FALSE?  A lysosome has the same kind of ion pumps that are found in mitochondria.

# CHAPTER 6: THE NUCLEUS, AND HOW RIBOSOMES ARE MADE

Now we know how a lysosome is made. We aren't going to study the manufacturing process of each and every organelle (we've got to leave *something* for you to study in college!), but let's look at one more manufacturing process. Let's find out what ribosomes are and how they are made. For this, we need to head back to the nucleus.

We took a quick look at the nucleus in chapter 4 when we learned how DNA is copied by mRNA in order to make proteins. We learned that DNA never leaves the nucleus, making it necessary to send mRNA copies of the DNA out into the cytoplasm. We saw the single-strand mRNA leave the nucleus through a pore in its membrane. In order to understand ribosomes, we need to go back inside the nucleus and find out more about it. When we get to the center of the nucleus, we'll see ribosomes being made. We'll start from the outside and work our way in.

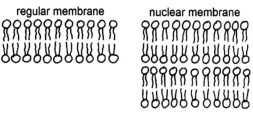

The membrane surrounding the nucleus is twice as thick as the cell's plasma membrane. There are two phospholipid bilayers instead of one. This double-thick layer is called the **nuclear envelope**. One reason for having a double layer is so that the nucleus can be connected to the ER without actually being part of it. The outer layer of the nuclear envelope is "continuous with" (is part of) the outer membrane of the ER. In this picture you can see that the outer membrane of the nucleus becomes the ER membrane. The inner layer is not connected to the ER. The inner layer forms sort of an interior sac around the contents of the nucleus. We also drew a few ribosomes sticking to the ER, inserting their proteins, as we learned in the last chapter. ER that has ribosomes stuck to it is called **rough ER**. When scientists first saw it under their microscopes, it looked like it had a rough texture, so they called it rough ER. (Finally, they used a normal, ordinary word for something!) You can also see nuclear pores in this picture—we'll get to them in just a minute.

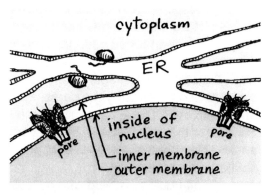

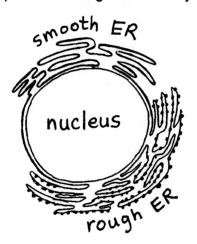

So if there is *rough* ER, might there be *smooth* ER, too? Yes. ER that doesn't have any ribosomes stuck to it is called **smooth ER**. It has the same basic structure as rough ER (except no ribosomes) but it does things that the rough ER does not do. The exact jobs the smooth ER does depends on what kind of cell it is in. If it is in a muscle cell, one of its main jobs is to store calcium ions that will be used in muscle contraction. (Where does smooth ER get calcium? Only from what you eat and drink. Drink your milk and eat your vegetables!) In all cells, the smooth ER helps to manufacture lipids (fats), especially a certain type of lipid called **steroids**. Steroids are a whole family of molecules that control body processes such as growth of muscle and bone, preventing inflammation, breaking down carbohydrates, and developing and maintaining characteristics that make us look and act male or female. (That's quite a diverse list. These things don't seem related, do they?)

I'll be the ER and you be the mitochondrion.

We can call this game "cholester-ball."

In some cells, the smooth ER and the mitochondria work together to make steroids. They pass the molecules back and forth, each one adding something or clipping something off until the steroid molecule is finished. (The mitochondria have a few other jobs besides making ATP.) After the steroid molecule is finished, proteins inside the ER will tag it so that it gets delivered to the right place.

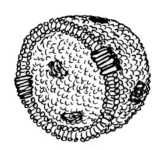
*Lipid rafts embedded in a vesicle, ready for delivery.*

The smooth ER would also be the place where cholesterol rafts are manufactured, since cholesterol is a type of lipid and the smooth ER is in charge of making lipids. How would the smooth ER get those rafts out to the membrane? Just like the rough ER sends things to the Golgi body—by way of a vesicle. A slight difference would be that since the lipid rafts are made of lipids and are embedded in lipid bilayers (lipids, lipids everywhere), the rafts wouldn't have to be inside a vesicle; they could be part of its membrane. When the vesicle touches the plasma membrane it merges with it and the lipid rafts suddenly find themselves part of the plasma membrane instead of a vesicle.

Now back to the nucleus itself. The nucleus's double-layer membrane contains 3,000-4,000 *pores* that let things in and out. The picture on the right shows pores, but not nearly enough of them. The problem with illustrations is that by the time you get the pores small enough to be accurate, you'd no longer be able to see them! So we decided to make the pores larger and a bit out of scale, but the benefit of doing this is that your visual memory will (we hope) file this picture and remember that the nuclear membrane is full of tiny holes.

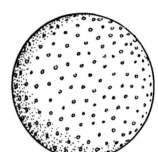

A close-up view of these pores shows them to be very strange-looking indeed—sort of a combination of a basketball hoop and a collar. In this picture, the pore has been sliced in half. Notice the phospholipid bilayer. It's been sliced, too. In reality it would be a continuous sheet all the way around the pore. The basket sticks down into the nucleus. The ring at the bottom can open and close to some degree. (There would be chaperoning proteins by the pores, too, checking on the "traffic" coming in and going out.) Those filaments on the top are probably for anchoring the nucleus to the cytoskeleton, but they could have other jobs, too. This is an on-going area of research right now, so we can't say for sure what the filaments do or don't do.

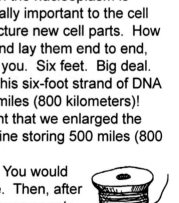

The nucleus is filled with fluid similar to the cytoplasm ("cytosol") found in the rest of the cell. However, the fluid in the nucleus has its own special mix of proteins and ions floating around in it (sort of like its own soup recipe), so cell biologists felt a need to create a special name for it. They decided to call it *nucleoplasm*. (You might have predicted this. It's just the plasm of the nucleus.) So if we say something is found in the nucleoplasm, that means it is inside the nucleus.

Now we are ready to examine the contents of the nucleus. Floating in the nucleoplasm is something we've already looked at: DNA. You'll remember that DNA is critically important to the cell because it contains all the information that the cell needs in order to manufacture new cell parts. How much DNA is there in the nucleus? If you could take all the stands of DNA and lay them end to end, they would measure about 6 feet (2 meters). That probably doesn't impress you. Six feet. Big deal. But you have to remember how incredibly thin DNA is. If you could enlarge this six-foot strand of DNA until it was as thick as a piece of thread, its length would measure over 500 miles (800 kilometers)! That's a bit more impressive. If we enlarged the nucleus by the same amount that we enlarged the DNA, the nucleus would be about the size of an average bedroom. So imagine storing 500 miles (800 km) of thread in your room. How would you do it?

The first thing you would probably do is wind the thread onto spools. You would need over 2,000 spools (and endless hours of winding!), but it could be done. Then, after all your thread was wound onto spools, you could organize the spools into boxes or onto shelves. Would all 2,000 spools fit in your room? Amazingly enough, they would all fit onto shelves on just one wall. You'd have most of the room still open. Spools are great for organizing things that are very thin and very long. So it's not too surprising that cells use spools, too. The cell's spools, called *nucleosomes*, are made of proteins called *histones*. Eight histone proteins join together to make one nucleosome spool. One nucleosome can wind a section of DNA that is about 146 rungs long. You can see from the picture that the DNA loops around the nucleosome twice.

DNA

8 histones

A ninth histone protein (called H1) acts like a piece of tape and keeps the two loops of DNA from falling off the spool. There isn't a whole lot more known about this histone, so we can't tell you much more. This is another frontier of science.

DNA researchers are pretty sure that the binding histones (the pieces of tape) are partially responsible for controlling which parts of the DNA get copied. Remember, if a cell needs to copy some of the information from the DNA, the "ladder" must be unzipped so that mRNA can be made using the nonsense side. So if the DNA is tightly wound onto

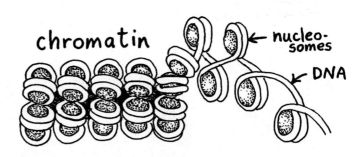

DNA

binding histones

a spool, it is harder to access. There also seem to be molecules on the nucleosomes that control the winding and unwinding of the spools by acting as "switches." There are special proteins whose job it is to turn these molecular switches on and off. When the proteins switch them off, the spools relax and let the DNA unwind so that it can be unzipped. When they are switched back on, the spools tighten again.

The next step is to deal with these long strings of nucleosomes. A cell doesn't have shelves or boxes, so it simply organizes the nucleosomes into larger clusters. The strings are curled up into a formation that we call *chromatin*. (The Greek word "chroma" means "color." When early cell scientists stained cells to look at them under their microscopes, the chromatin of DNA stained easily and showed up well on their slides.

chromatin ← nucleo-somes

← DNA

They didn't know what else to call it because they didn't know what it was or what it did.)

The strands of chromatin can be very long, but the cell has efficient ways of organizing them even further. However... we're going to have to leave you in suspense for a while because that part of the story fits in better with chapter 8.

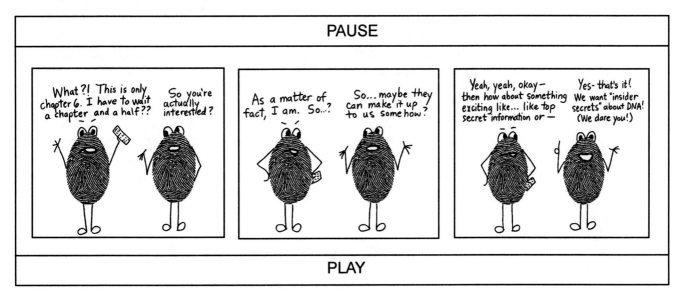

Believe it or not, we DO have some top secret information about DNA. You won't see this information in most books, especially books for kids or for high school students. This information is reserved for members of the Secret Society of Cell Biologists. (Just kidding.) Maybe the writers of most science books think this information is unimportant. Or maybe they think it's too difficult for kids? We can't even guess. But we'll let you in on their secret. The truth is that when artists draw DNA or generate virtual images of it, they leave out something very important: DNA is covered with proteins! In fact, it's so covered with proteins that you can hardly see it! The artists strip away the proteins so that you can see the DNA, but they don't tell you that they did this. Unfortunately, this leaves you, the viewer, with a wrong understanding of DNA.

Real DNA is covered with enzymes and chaperone proteins. These chaperone-type proteins control the winding and unwinding and the zipping and unzipping of the DNA with incredible accuracy. They know when to allow transcription and when to prevent it. They know which sections of DNA the cell will need and when it will need them. They "spell check" and edit. They watch over the DNA and try to keep it safe. If it gets damaged, they repair it. They are the unsung heroes of the cell!

These proteins, like all proteins, are primarily made of helices and beta sheets, but they also include some parts with cool names like "Zinc Fingers" and "Leucine *(loo-seen)* Zippers." You can see why artists leave them out when they draw DNA. They make the drawing much more complicated. If you are just studying DNA itself, the proteins kind of get in the way.

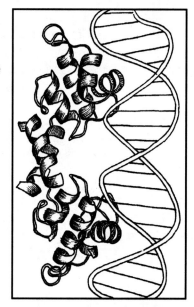

*This picture shows just one protein next to DNA. This protein has a lot of helices (that's the plural of helix) and no beta sheets.*

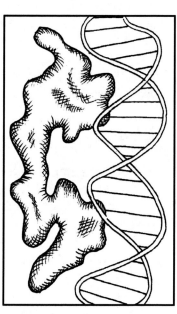

*This picture show the protein as a blob, instead of as helices. It's just a more simplified way of drawing it.*

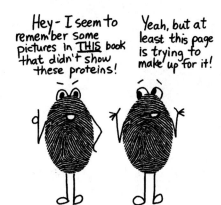

Now we're ready to move on to ribosomes. Let's zoom out a little bit and look at the whole nucleus. It looks sort of like a plate of spaghetti. The spaghetti, of course, is the DNA. At this distance, you can't see the helix shape of the DNA, nor can you see the proteins we just talked about. It just looks like a tangle of strings. See that dark patch? (No, it's not sauce.) It's a very dense part of the

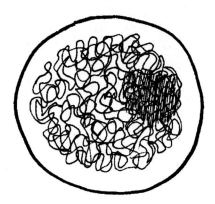

DNA and it contains the instructions for ribosomes. (DNA that has instructions for ribosomes is called "ribosomal DNA" or "rDNA.") There's not just one set of instructions—there are thousands of them. The code for ribosomes is repeated over and over again. It's like when a library has multiple copies of a popular book that everyone wants to read. In the cell, so many ribosomes have to be made (hundreds per minute) that if there was only one copy of the instructions, the cell wouldn't be able to keep up with the demand. There's a special name for this dark area: *the nucleolus*.

Now for the part that will make you shake your head for a moment while you process it. Ribosomes aren't made of phospholipids like many organelles are. Their basic structure isn't protein or sugars, either. Ribosomes are made mostly of RNA. To avoid confusion, the RNA that crumples up to form a ribosome is called rRNA. The "r" stands for "ribosomal." So now we can keep things straight: <u>mRNA</u> leaves the nucleus and <u>attaches</u> to a ribosome, and <u>rRNA</u> folds up and <u>becomes</u> a ribosome.

When new ribosomes are needed, one of those ribosomal code areas on the DNA (rDNA) opens up and that little "sled" slides along the nonsense side, just like the transcription we saw in chapter 4. (The nucleoplasm has lots of nucleic acids floating around in it, waiting to be assembled into rRNA or mRNA.) Usually that little sled produces mRNA that will be used to make proteins. In this case, the RNA produced by the sled isn't a code, it's the <u>finished product</u>! That piece of RNA is rRNA because it will fold up and become part of a ribosome. (Remember the sled's real name? *polymerase*)

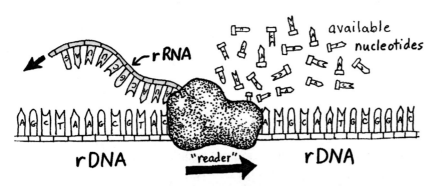

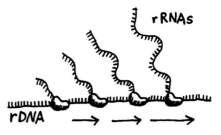

*Many sleds can be on the same rDNA. They often follow each other closely. They can even be on both sides.*

Ribosomes are made of two halves. One half is large and the other half is small. They are simply called the large sub-unit and the small sub-unit. Each half floats around in the cytoplasm by itself. Somehow or other the two halves know to come together around a piece of mRNA. When they are done making the protein, the two halves separate again.

The large sub-unit is made of three different stands of rRNA. The small sub-unit is made of only one strand. In addition to rRNA, ribosomes have some protein molecules, too. (About two-thirds of a ribosome is rRNA and about one-third is protein.) The proteins probably help the rRNA to keep its shape after it is folded.

These ribosomal proteins come from outside the nucleus. Ribosomes floating in the cytoplasm produce them. The proteins are brought into the nucleus through the pores and then are shuttled over to the nucleolus. The rRNAs are folded and then these proteins are added. The finished ribosomes are transported back out of the nucleus (through the pores, of course) and set adrift in the cytoplasm. These new ribosomes will be able to make anything. They can translate any piece of mRNA that comes their way. They might end up sticking to the ER and making proteins for lysosomes. Or perhaps they will synthesize (make) enzymes that will be secreted out of the cell and sent to another part of the body. Some of these new ribosomes will end up making more proteins for more ribosomes.

In the next chaper, we'll meet the last of the organelles and we'll see how they all work together to keep the cell alive. We'll see how cells eat and drink, and we'll also discover that they make more than one kind of toxic waste that must be dealt with. Combustion makes pollution no matter where it happens!

## ACTIVITY 1   Look at a 3D rotating virtual ribosome

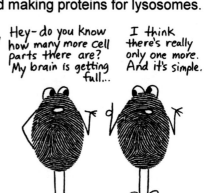

Hey- do you know how many more cell parts there are? My brain is getting full...

I think there's really only one more. And it's simple.

Look up "ribosome" on Wikipedia.com. Don't worry, you don't have to read the article. Just scroll down a bit and take a look at the animated pictures down the right side of the article. The last one, near the bottom, is an image of the larger sub-unit. The RNA is shown in orange and yellow. You can see it curled into a helix shape. The proteins are in blue. (The areas that look olive green are just areas that are in shadow.) Watch carefully as the ribosome turns around. For a split second you will be able to see a bright green dot inside. This represents the "active site" where the ribosome brings the mRNA together with the tRNAs and hooks the amino acids together.

## ACTIVITY 2    Watch a video showing DNA winding around histones

Watch "How DNA is Packaged" on the playlist. Here is an easy-to-understand video that shows what we learned about histones.

## ACTIVITY 3    Another video about histones and nucleosomes

Watch "Chromatin, Histones and Cathepsin." This video begins by talking about "epi-genetics." The word "epi" means "outside" so this is the stuff that goes on outside of the DNA, or around the DNA—the chaperones controlling the winding and unwinding of the histone spools. Watch for the little chemical "switches" that activate the winding and unwinding. If the sound track confuses you, turn it off and just watch it without sound. You don't need to know all the fancy words to be able to understand the basics of what is going on. It's just what you read about in this chapter.

## ACTIVITY 4    Dejà vu:  watch this again

Watch "DNA Transcription and Protein Assembly" again. You probably saw this animation back in chapter 4. Watch it again, but this time look specifically at the nuclear pores. They really show you those basket shapes and the filaments on the outside. Also, pay particular attention to the ribosomes. At the end of the video, what in the world is the "barrel-shaped" organelle that folds the proteins? A Golgi body? If so, we think it's a pretty poor representation of a Golgi body. Golgi bodies don't have doors that open and close. What do you think?

**Can you remember what you read?  If you can't think of the answer, go back and read that part of the chapter again until you find the answer.**

1) ER is the abbreviation for _____ _____.  (This was in chapter 5.)

2) Why is rough ER rough?
   a) It has a scratchy surface.      b) It has ribososomes stuck to it.
   c) It has ribosome inside of it.    d) It has many pores in its membrane.

3) Which of these is the ER connected to?
   a) the nucleus and the smooth ER          b) the nucleolus and the smooth ER
   c) the nucleosomes and the smooth ER      d) none of the above

4) Which of these jobs would the smooth ER never do?
   a) store calcium ions      b) make lipids    c) make ATP     d) make steroids for hormones

5) Where would lipid rafts come from?
   a) smooth ER    b) rough ER     c) the nucleus    d) Golgi bodies

6) If you unwound all the DNA in one of your cells, how long would it be?
   a) 500 miles (880 km)      b) from here to the moon     c) about a yard (a meter)     d) 6 feet (2 meters)

7) TRUE or FALSE?  The membrane of the nucleus is the same thickness as the cell's outer membrane.

8) What are nucleosomes most like?
   a) thread     b) shelves    c) switches    d) spools

9) TRUE or FALSE?  The nucleolus is where rDNA is located.

10) TRUE or FALSE?  There's only one part of your DNA that knows how to make ribosomes.

11) These get embedded into the walls of a vesicle so they can become part of a cell's outer membrane.
    a) lipid rafts    b) enzymes    c) steroids    d) chaperone proteins

12) How many histones are there in each nucleosome spool? _____

13) Ribosomes are made of how many smaller units? _____

14) TRUE or FALSE?  Mulitple "sleds" can "ride" on the rDNA at the same time.

15) Which is the correct "recipe" for ribosomes?
    a) 2/3 DNA and 1/3 protein       b) 2/3 protein and 1/3 DNA
    c) 2/3 RNA and 1/3 protein       d) 2/3 protein and 1/3 RNA

16) Chromatin is made of:
    a) nucleosomes     b) histones     c) ribosomes    d) DNA

17) TRUE or FALSE?  Some ribosomes make proteins that will be used in making more ribosomes.

18) TRUE or FALSE?  Ribosomes make DNA.

19) TRUE or FALSE?  Ribosomes make rRNA.

THESE QUESTIONS ARE REVIEW:

20) Why do ribosomes bind to the docking ports on the ER?
   a) Because they bump into it by accident.     b)  Because the ribosome would fall apart otherwise.
   c)  Because the first part of an mRNA strand told them to go there.
   d)  Because the ER is the only place you can find a supply of amino acids for tRNA.

21) The outsides of the ER and Golgi body are made of what?
   a) phospholipids    b) proteins     c) enzymes    d) ribosomes

22) In DNA, the sides of the ladder are made of _____ and _____ and the rungs are made of pairs of _____.

23) Which side of the DNA does the little sled (*polymerase*) read—sense or nonsense? _____

24) Lysosomes have a special pump in their membranes that bring lots of what inside?
   a) ATP   b) proteins   c) electrons    d) protons

25) Which of these is the smallest?
   a) DNA     b) mRNA      c) tRNA

26) What is the main reason proteins fold up?
   a) They have weak points in their amino acid chains.    b) They contain carbon atoms.
   c) They have hydrophilic areas and hydrophobic areas.    b) They contain nitrogen atoms.

27) What is the inside of a lysosome like?
   a) acidic    b) alkaline (basic)     c) warm    d) salty     e) sticky

28) Which one of these root words means "body"?
   a) cyto     b) pseudo     c) pod     d) soma

29) Which part of a phospholipid hates water—the phosphate head or the lipid tail? _____

30) How many types of bases are there in DNA?
   a) 3    b) 4    c) 20    d) hundreds

31) How many nucleic acids form a codon?
   a) 2     b) 3    c) 4    d) 20

32) Which one of these does DNA not have?
   a) sugars    b) phosphates    c) lipids    d) nucleic acids

33) What happens when a phosphate is popped off of an ATP?
   a) a water molecule is formed     b) energy is released
   c)  energy is used up      d) a proton is released

34) What is the inside of a mitochondrion called?
   a) matrix    b) ion    c) membrane     d) synthase

35) What is it called when a lot of something goes to a place where there is less of it? _____

# CHAPTER 7: CELL METABOLISM AND PEROXISOMES

The activities that go on in a cell involve either breaking things down or assembling things. We've seen how the lysosome disassembles things. In this chapter we'll learn that mitochondria do some disassembly, too, and we'll also meet a new organelle that takes things apart. The assembly jobs are divided up between the ribosomes and the ER (with the Golgi bodies helping out). This constant cycle of breaking things down, then using the parts to make other things, is called *metabolism*. (This word comes from the Greek word "metabolikos," which means "changeable.") There are special words for the two parts of the cycle. The breaking-down part is called *catabolism* ("cata" means "down") and the building-up part is called *anabolism* ("ana" means "up"). There is variation in how these words are pronounced; however you pronounce them will be fine.

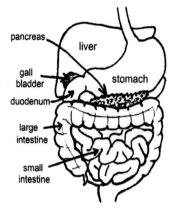

Catabolism starts when you take a bite of food and begin to chew it. Your saliva contains enzymes that begin breaking down starches right away. You can observe this happening if you put a cracker into your mouth and hold it there a while, letting it dissolve. The cracker mush will start to taste sweeter. This is the action of an enzyme called *amylase*. It breaks apart the starch molecules and turns them into simple sugars. It's not as sweet as a mouthful of white cane sugar, but the cracker will be noticeably sweeter.

When your meal gets to your stomach, more digestive enzymes go to work breaking down the various types of food you've eaten. For example, there's an enzyme called *pepsin* that begins the process of breaking down proteins. The enzymes in the stomach function at their best when in an acidic environment, so your stomach also secretes *hydrochloric acid*. (Then, to protect the stomach from its own acid, the cells lining the stomach secrete a protective mucus layer.) The stomach secretes a total of about six different enzymes. The enzymes are manufactured by ribosomes in specialized stomach cells.

When the food passes out of the stomach into the very first part of the intestines, the duodenum (*du-ODD-en-um*), it meets enzymes that have come from the pancreas. There are enzymes that start breaking down fats, and there are even more enzymes that continue to break down the starches, sugars and proteins. Also, the liver makes a contribution at this point—a dark-colored substance called *bile*. Bile works a bit like dish soap does on greasy dishes. It helps the enzymes to break down the fats.

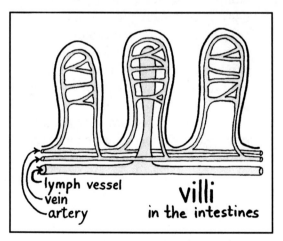

lymph vessel
vein
artery

villi
in the intestines

The walls of your intestines are lined with microscopic finger-like things called *villi*. The villi contain microscopic blood vessels and lymph vessels that come very close to the surface. As the wet, mushy food mix (which no longer resembles what you ate) is pushed along through the intestines, it comes into close contact with the villi. Sugars, amino acids, water, salts and water soluble vitamins (such as vitamins B and C) pass through the cells on the outside of the villi (a layer that is just one cell thick) and then into the *capillaries*. The tiny capillaries inside the villi are attached to slightly larger vessels, and those vessels turn into even larger vessels. Eventually, all the blood vessels end up as part of a large vein that goes to the liver.

Now the liver gets a chance to make final changes to the nutrient molecules and to strain out things that shouldn't go to the cells. If there are extra nutrients, the liver can store some of them for later use. Then the nutrients leave the liver (by way of the bloodstream, of course) and are carried throughout the body.

Fat molecules (and vitamins A and D) follow a different route (although some very small fat molecules probably do pass into the capillaries along with the sugars and amino acids). In general, the cells of the villi put the fats into little things that resemble vesicles, where they can be with other fat molecules. Remember, fat molecules are hydrophobic and hate being in water. Blood is mostly water. The fat molecules will not float along happily in the bloodstream as sugars will. So they are packaged into vesicle-like spheres called *chylomicrons* (*KY-lo-MY-krons*). Can you see the difference between chylomicrons and vesicles? Look carefully at the membrane. How many layers of phospholipids are there in a normal vesicle membrane? How many layers are in this chylomicron? Notice all the hydrophobic tails pointing to the inside of the sphere in the chylomicron. Will the fat molecules enjoy this environment inside the chylomicron? They love

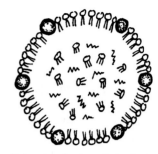

*Fat molecules in a chylomicron*

it because they are surrounded by tails that hate water, just like they do. They have their own private club in there, for water-hating molecules only. (Clubs based on hatred are not a good thing, but since fat molecules are not likely to get into politics or social networks, we'll look the other way and not bother trying to break up their club.)

The chylomicrons are then absorbed into the lymph vessels in the villi. (Look at the picture of the villi again. Notice the lymph vessel in the middle.) The chylomicrons travel up through the lymph system (through special vessels designed for carrying just lymph fluid, not blood) and are dumped into your bloodstream at a location just under your collar bone. While in the blood, the fat molecules are further broken down by an enzyme called *lipase* that is also floating in the blood. (Lipase is also present in the intestines as part of the digestive process.) The fats will eventually make several trips through the liver where they will be modified even more. Digestion sure is complicated!

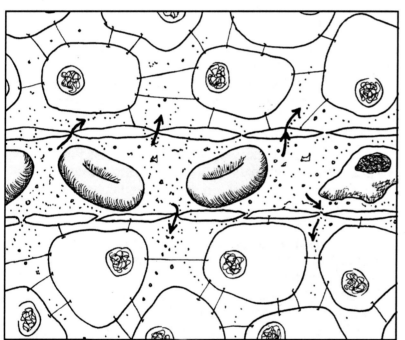

Now that we've got all these nutrients floating around in the blood, let's see how the cells are able to use them. To get nutrients, a cell must be right next to (or very close to) a blood vessel. This is why your blood vessels branch off and get smaller and smaller. They have to get so small that they can go in and among all your billions of cells. This picture shows a capillary (a microscopic blood vessel) running along next to some cells, perhaps deep in your skin. The donut-shaped things are red blood cells carrying oxygen. The fried egg thing is a white blood cell (the kind that eat bacteria). The long skinny things are the cells that form the walls of the capillary. They are very flat and curved, sort of like chunks cut out of a pipe. In the view shown here, they have been sliced so that you can't see their shape very well. We'll see their real shape when we meet them again in chapter 9.

I want to know what those lines are between the cells!

Those little lines are pieces of protein called *desmosomes*. They keep the cells linked together, but in a flexible way. There a lots of desmosomes between your skin cells. They are what makes your skin stretchy and flexible. (In other parts of the body, you might find cells more tightly packed together.) In this picture, the desmosomes look like they are attached to the cells' membrane. But would this work? Remember, the phospholipids are only loosely connected and can slide around; they would never be able to take the stress of something pulling on them. Actually, the desmosomes are anchored to the cytoskeleton. There's even a little "plate" inside to minimize stress on the membrane. A brilliant design!

NOTE: Even though we are on this page now, keep looking back at the picture on the left page.

The little dots coming out of the capillary represent sugars, amino acids, fatty acids and nucleotides. Water, oxygen and minerals are also present in the fluid (but are even smaller than these nutrients). The pressure of your blood pushing through the capillary will force many of these nutrients out through the cracks and into the space between the cells. This space between the cells is called the *interstitial* space *(in-ter-STISH-ul)*. Once the nutrients are in the interstitial space, the cells can take them in by using one of these methods:

1) DIFFUSION: Water and minerals can move in and out of cells by diffusion. If there are fewer water molecules inside a cell than outside it, water molecules will diffuse in.

2) PORTAL PROTEINS: Small or medium-sized molecules can be taken inside the cell by membrane-bound portal proteins.

3) PHAGOCYTOSIS: Large molecules are taken in by something called *phagocytosis (FA-go-cy-TOE-sis)*. "Phago" is Greek for "eat" and "cyto" (as we know already) means "cell." Phagocytosis is how a cell actually "eats." Little pseudopods (pushed out by rapidly growing microfilaments) reach out and surround a food particle. The pseudopods close in around the particle and a vesicle is formed. If the particle needs to be digested, this vesicle can be sent to merge with a lysosome.

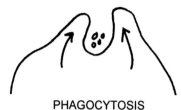

PHAGOCYTOSIS

4) PINOCYTOSIS: When a cell takes in tiny amounts of fluid from its environment, it's called *pinocytosis (PIN-o-cy-TOE-sis)*. Some biology books define pinocytosis as "drinking" and phagocytosis as "eating." But this is a little misleading, because a cell doesn't have to do pinocytosis to get water. Water can just diffuse in. Pinocytosis is basically the same as phagocytosis, just on a smaller scale. Most cells are constantly taking in little "gulps" of the fluid that is around them. The skinny cells that form the walls of the capillaries do a lot of pinocytosis. The sides of the cells that are on the inside of the capillaries gulp fluid in, then the cells "spit out" fluid on the other side—the side that faces those skin cells. Almost all cells do some pinocytosis, but some do more than others, depending on what type of cell it is. These capillaries cells do a lot because it's part of their job. Their job is to deliver nutrients to the body cells around them.

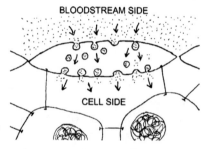

BLOODSTREAM SIDE

CELL SIDE

So that's how cells take things in. Cells can also get rid of things. When a cell wants to get rid of something, it can use basically the same methods as above, just in reverse. Carbon dioxide can diffuse out of a cell, through the interstitial space, and into a capillary. Once in the bloodstream, the carbon dioxide can then keep riding along until it reaches the lungs, where it is exhaled.

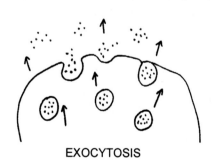

EXOCYTOSIS

When a cell does the reverse of pinocytosis, it's called *exocytosis*. (You can figure out what "exo" means because you know the word "exit.") Sometimes a vesicle that is used for exocytosis is called a *vacuole*. Vacuoles are just big, empty vesicles sitting around the cell. In plant cells, vacuoles play an important role in allowing the cell to expand or shrink while still maintaining its shape. The vacuole can getter bigger or smaller quickly and easily, according to how much extra water is in the cell. Plant vacuoles can be very large, sometimes filling half of the space inside the cell. But we digress... this book is about animal cells, not plant cells. Animal vacuoles are basically very large vesicles, and they can be used to store things or to export (dump) things outside the cell.

After the cell dumps stuff into the interstitial space, the fluid in the interstitial space (lymph fluid) drains into lymph vessels. The lymph vessels lead to lymph nodes. (You can feel some of these nodes in places such as your armpits, neck and groin.) In the nodes there are lots of white blood cells that dissolve yucky things that need to be gotten rid of. Then the fluid travels on through larger lymph vessels that go up through your chest and finally empty into your blood stream at a place under your collar bone (as we mentioned before). The blood then goes to the liver and kidneys for final clean up.

Now that we've got all your food digested and the nutrients delivered to your cells, let's see what your cells do with them. But first, let's categorize the nutrients. They can be put into four basic categories: *amino acids* (from proteins), *nucleotides* (the individual units of nucleic acids), *fatty acids* and *sugars*.

These don't look very appetizing.

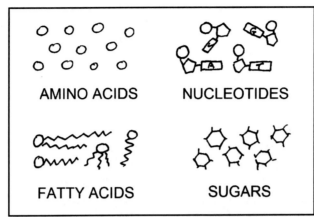

AMINO ACIDS

NUCLEOTIDES

FATTY ACIDS

SUGARS

They looked and smelled better when they were a pizza!

## AMINO ACIDS

When individual amino acids (that came from digested proteins) are taken into the cell, the cell can use them right away. The tRNAs can come and pick them up and take them over to the ribosomes, where they will be used to make proteins that the cell needs. Thus, catabolism ends and anabolism begins. We feel obligated to mention at this point, however, that many of the amino acids floating around in a cell didn't just come in from the outside. They've probaby been recycled within the cell hundreds (or even thousands) of times. A cell is constantly tearing apart proteins, even some of its own proteins, and re-using the amino acids to make new proteins.

tRNA

amino acids

Another interesting thing we need to mention is that cells have a "back-up plan" for some of the amino acids in case there aren't enough of them floating around; they can either manufacture them from scratch, or turn one kind into another. However, there are some aminos our cells can't make. These are called *essential amino acids*. You have to get these from your diet. Perhaps one of the most well-known essential amino acids is *lysine*. (Natural sources of lysine include milk and dairy products.) An interesting side note about lysine is that it is necessary for the construction of the soft, moist skin that lines your mouth, nose and throat. People who are prone to mouth ulcers and cold sores find that taking lysine supplements can help prevent these infections. Taking extra lysine gives the body a large supply of raw materials to work with. It's like giving a brick layer a huge supply of bricks to work with instead of making him scavenge the neighborhood for bricks while still trying to keep up the pace on the construction of a wall.

## NUCLEOTIDES

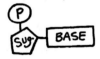

BASE

The single unit of a nucleic acid is called a *nucleotide*. We met these in chapter 4 when we first learned about DNA. A nucleotide has three parts: a sugar, a phosphate and a base. There are four bases: A (adenine), T (thymine), C (cytosine) and G (guanine). (Well, five if you count U, uracil.) Some nucleotides may come from things you ate, but many of the nucleotides floating inside your cells have been recycled. They used to be part of the DNA or RNA of other cells (even bacteria) or were taken from recycled proteins that the cell's "spell checkers" and "editors" found to be defective. If a cell finds that it doesn't have enough nucleotides, it can also manufacture them "from scratch" using phosphates, ribose sugars and other molecules that are floating around the cytoplasm. (Your cells are biochemistry geniuses!)

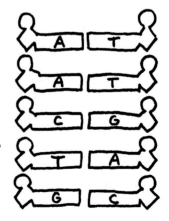

## FATTY ACIDS

The fats and oils that you eat get digested down to microscopic fatty acid molecules. They're microscopic, but many of them are still pretty long—up to several dozen

This part is the "acid."

OXYGENS

CARBONS

These little things are hydrogens.

This long part is called the "tail."

carbon atoms in the chain. Remember, the ultimate goal of of digesting fats is to break the bonds between the carbon atoms. When these bonds are broken, energy is released. But also remember that this process has to occur in lots of small steps so as not to create too much energy all at once. (No, exploding cells are not funny.)

The next step is called *oxidation* and occurs in the mitochondria. It turns out that those mitochondria can really multitask—they aren't called the "powerhouses of the cell" for nothing! The mitochondria take the fats and start chopping off pairs of carbon atoms using... well, a very complicated chemical process that we'll just call "enzyme scissors." Cells use enzymes like we use scissors and staplers. Some enzymes cut things apart, others put things together. All you need to know is that in this oxidation process, the mitochondria snip up the carbon chains into pairs of carbon atoms. Then they stick a molecule called "CoenzymeA" onto the end, using what we will call an "enzyme stapler." This produces an extremely important and useful molecule called *acetyl-CoA* (ah-SEE-till co-AY). Acetyl-CoA can be used in construction or be "burned" for energy. You might want to think of acetyl-CoA as a piece of lumber. Like acetyl-CoA, a piece of lumber used to be part of something larger (a tree). And like acetyl-CoA, a piece of lumber can be used for more than one purpose—you could use it to make a useful object such as a piece of furniture or the walls of a house, or, if you were cold and needed some heat, you could chop up the lumber and use it to make a wood fire. The cell can use acetyl-CoA as a raw material to make some cell parts, such as the "switches" on the histones that tighten and untighten the coiled DNA in the nucleus. (Interestingly, we meet the amino acid lysine again. Lysine is the amino that the histone's "switches" are made of.) Or, the cell can "decide" to use the acetyl-CoA's as fuel. To "burn" acetyl-CoA's, mitochondria have a chemical process that we are going to call the "Krebs factory."

Acetyl-CoA is "burned" using a process called the *Krebs cycle* (named after scientist Hans Krebs). Just to really confuse you and make science harder than it has to be, this cycle goes by several different names: the "citric acid cycle," or the"tricarboxylic acid cycle," or the "TCA cycle," or... you'll love this one... the "Szent-Györgyi-Krebs cycle." So many to choose from! We just decided that "Krebs" sounds pretty cool and is a word you'll be likely to remember, so we'll go with "Krebs."

The Krebs cycle is like a factory that takes in acetyl-CoA's and puts them on an assembly line where workers (enzymes, of course) process them (a 10-step process) and harvest the energy from the carbon bonds. Two things come out of the factory: some ATPs (notice the worker dumping a whole basket of them out the window) and some high-energy electrons that are taken by a "shuttle" molecule, NADH, to a nearby electron transport chain. Like many factories, the Krebs cycle produces $CO_2$ as a waste product.

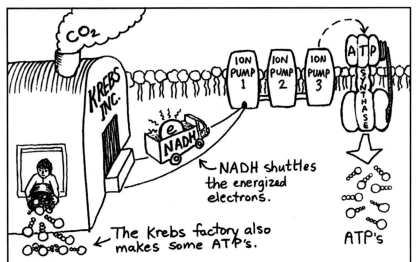

NADH shuttles the energized electrons.

The Krebs factory also makes some ATP's.

ATP's

Can you guess where those carbons in the $CO_2$ came from? That's right, those carbons used to be part of a fatty acid molecule. Now the carbons can be exhaled from your lungs as carbon dioxide and go off into the air. Perhaps a plant will then take them in and use them in photosynthesis to make glucose. And speaking of glucose, we've got one last category of nutrients to discuss...

## SUGARS

GLUCOSE

All the starches and carbohydrates you eat (rice, pasta, bread, potatoes, cookies, etc.) are digested down to simple sugars such as glucose. The cells take in these simple sugar molecules and use them for energy. Sugars can be sent to the Krebs factory where they can be burned for fuel, but first they need to be turned into acetyl-CoA's because the Krebs factory can't deal with anything other than acetyl-CoA's.

The process of preparing glucose for the Krebs cycle is called *glycolysis*. (Glucose used to be called "glycose." And you already know what "lysis" means.) Glycolysis doesn't require a special organelle. It can take place right in the cytosol (cytoplasm). There are 10 steps in glycolysis, just like there are 10 steps in the Krebs cycle. Many of these steps involve popping phosphates on and off. (It turns out that phosphates are very important in many cellular processes, not just for ATPs.) The workers who do the popping on and off of the phosphates are enzymes, of course. Our old friend lysine also plays a role in glycolysis, as do his amino buddies histidine and cysteine. The mineral magnesium is important, too; its job is to keep oxygen atoms happy while changes are being made to the molecule. (Cranky oxygen atoms can really make trouble...)

Both the Krebs cycle and glycolysis are very complicated processes. In order to really understand them, you need to know a lot of college-level chemistry. In case you are curious about what these cycles would look like in a college textbook (or perhaps an AP high school biology book), here is what glycolysis might look like:

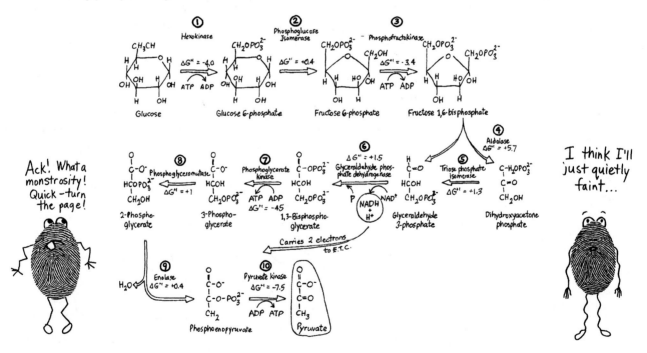

And after all of this, the necessary molecule, acetyl-CoA, still hasn't been produced! You end up with something called *pyruvate*, which is a 3-carbon molecule. The Krebs factory can only process 2-carbon molecules. But the good news is that at least some energy was produced: 2 ATPs.

Now the cell has two options of what to do with pyruvate, depending on whether oxygen is available. If there isn't any oxygen lurking in the cytosol, the cell has no choice but to use a chemical process whereby pyruvate is turned into lactic acid. Energy is released, but lactic acid has a nasty side effect. It's what makes your muscles feel sore and achy. Not the best option.

Normally, oxygen is present, so most of the time, the cell is able to convert pyruvate into acetyl-CoA by pushing it through a special portal enzyme located in the membranes of the mitochondria. You can see in this silly cartoon that the enzyme does both scissor and stapler jobs. It lops a carbon atom off the pyruvate and staples it on to an oxygen molecule, $O_2$, creating $CO_2$. Then it staples the CoA onto the remaining two carbons of pyruvate, turning it into acetyl-CoA. (Finally!) You can see why oxygen is necessary for this process. The enzyme needs somewhere to put the carbon atom it las lopped

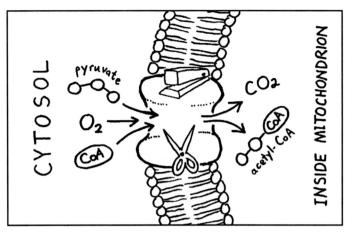

off the pyruvate. You can't just tell a single carbon atom to go off and find something to do. It might get into trouble. So the enzyme attaches the carbon atom to an oxygen molecule, and together, as $CO_2$, they float off to the lungs.

You already know what will happen to the acetyl-CoA. It will most likely be sent to the Krebs factory where the bond between the carbon atoms will be broken and the energy will be released as either ATPs or as electrons carried by NADH (or a very similar molecule called $FADH_2$). Or, as you undoubtedly remember, your cells also have the option of using acetyl-CoA to build things.

If everything goes perfectly and all parts function as they should, your body can make 36 ATPs from one glucose molecule. However, current research suggests that often little things go wrong here and there and not every glucose ends up generating the full 36 ATPs. They estimate that your cells get an average of about 30 ATPs per glucose. But if you are ever asked how many ATPs can be derived from one glucose molecule, say 36. (Occasionally you might see 38 given as the total number. The two extra ATPs are the result of using an alternative method for counting how many ATPs are made during glycolysis. It's complicated because glycolysis both *uses* ATPs and *makes* ATPs.)

Before we leave the subject of acetyl-CoA, we must mention that in a pinch, your cells can also turn amino acids into acetyl-CoA. If you ate nothing but protein, your cells would try to harvest energy out of amino acids by converting aminos to acetyl-CoA's. But it's a lot of work for your body to do this, and in the end you'd end up losing weight because your body would start tapping into your fat reserves and burning your stored fat along with the proteins. (The famous "Atkins diet" is based on this principle.)

This whole process, starting with glycolysis and ending with ATPs coming out of the ATP synthase machine, is called **cellular respiration**. The goal of cellular respiration is to provide ATPs for all the activities that go on in the cell. Your cells process billions upon billions of glucose molecules and fatty acid molecules every day. All cells, even plant cells, use cellular respiration to produce energy.

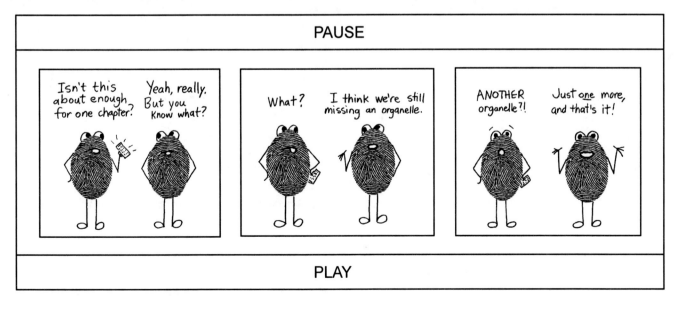

The cell has a problem we haven't mentioned yet. Some of the fatty acid chains that come into the cells are too long for the mitochondria to deal with. These extra-long fatty acid chains are sent over to an organelle called a *peroxisome*. (If you ever read an old biology book and see the term "microbodies," this is what peroxisomes used to be called.) The peroxisome looks a lot like a lysosome. It's basically a sphere made of phospholipid membrane and has lots of enzymes inside. Unlike a lysosome, however, the peroxisome has what they call a "crystalline core." Another difference is that it does not need an acidic environment, so it does not have proton pumps. It uses *oxidation* to break the carbons apart, the same way the mitochondria do. The peroxisomes just have a slightly different type of enzyme scissors. The peroxisome's enzymes are able to break apart these carbon chains into shorter lengths that can be sent over to the mitochondria for further processing.

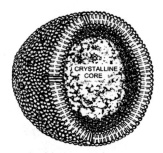

Inside a peroxisome

The peroxisome can do some other things, as well. It is able to break apart toxins such alcohol molecules. But that's not all—as an added bonus, the peroxisome can rearrange the structure of some amino acids and turn one amino acid into another. This is especially important if you have not supplied your body with an adequate amount of certain amino acids. The peroxisome can go to work and manufacture those amino acids. (But remember, it can't do this for all the aminos. There are still those "essential" aminos your cells can't make, so it really is important to eat a healthy, balanced diet.) The peroxisome can do some other jobs, too. For example, it can build lipid molecules that are critical to the proper functioning of your brain and nerves. It can also make cholesterol (necessary for rafts and for other things).

Peroxisomes are amazing little organelles! You wouldn't be able to live without them. But now for the bad news: during the process of breaking down the fatty acids, a *by-product* is produced. A by-product is an extra chemical that is produced along with the main chemical you want to produce. For example, when a plant uses photosynthesis to produce a glucose sugar molecule (the end product it wants to make), water and oxygen are produced as by-products. In photosynthesis, the by-products are not harmful at all. Water and oxygen are very beneficial to the environment. However, sometimes a by-product can be harmful or even toxic. In the case of the peroxisome, when it oxidizes fats a chemical called *hydrogen peroxide* is produced. You may be familiar with this chemical. Many people use hydrogen peroxide to sanitize cuts and wounds. It's great for killing germs. Unfortunately, it can also kill cells. The peroxisome must get rid of the hydrogen peroxide before it harms the cell. To do this, it uses an enzyme called *catalase*. (Notice the ending "-ase." Remember, almost all enzymes end with "-ase.") To understand what catalase does, we need to take a closer look at hydrogen peroxide.

The chemical formula for hydrogen peroxide is $H_2O_2$. You will notice how similar this is to the formula for water, $H_2O$. If you could remove an oxygen atom from hydrogen peroxide, you would get a harmless water molecule plus an atom of oxygen. This is what the enzyme catalase does. It

$$H_2O_2 \xrightarrow{\text{catalase}} H_2O + O_2$$

hydrogen peroxide → water oxygen

splits hydrogen peroxide molecules into water and oxygen. Water and oxygen are very useful to the cell, so this story ends "happily ever after." (Just to be chemically accurate, we need to mention that the single oxygen atoms pair up to make molecules of $O_2$. Oxygen atoms don't like to be alone. They always bond with other atoms.)

Scientists think that peroxisomes can probably be manufactured by the endoplasmic reticulum. More often, though, the cell increases its number of peroxisomes by a process called *binary fission*. ("Bi" means "two" and "fission" means "splitting," so binary fission just means "splitting in two.") The peroxisome enlarges itself a bit, then pinches together in the middle, cutting itself in half. (Mitochondria can also do this.) The process of binary fission allows a cell to rapidly scale up its ability to deal with a sudden increase of molecules that need to be oxidized. If a cell has only 400 peroxisomes, it can increase to 800 in a very short time. Each peroxisome just splits in two. If the ER had to make all those new peroxisomes, it might take too long.

BINARY FISSION

Since the liver is the main place where fatty acids and alcohols are broken down, liver cells have hundreds of peroxisomes and mitochondria. The liver is made of millions of cells. Each cell has hundreds of peroxisomes and mitochondria. The liver is able to process billions of fatty acid molecules every day. And on top of that, the liver has hundreds of other jobs, too. It's another one of the incredible multitaskers in your body.

There's one type of cell in your body that doesn't have any mitochondria or peroxisomes—red blood cells. Red blood cells are designed to carry oxygen molecules to cells. If they had mitochondria and peroxisomes inside them, those organelles would always be stealing the oxygen molecules for their oxidation processes. This would make red blood cells far less efficient for carrying oxygen. As we'll see in the last chapter, each type of cell is specialized for its role in the body.

 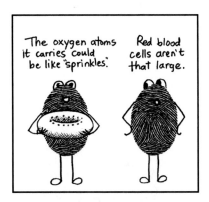 

* * * * * * * * * * * * * * * * * * * * * * * * * * * * * * * * * * * * * * * * * * * * * * * * * * * * * * * * * * * *

## ACTIVITY 1   An interactive online quiz game about the parts of a cell

Test your knowledge of organelles with this interactive online quiz game:
**http://www.cellsalive.com/cells/cell_model.htm**


## ACTIVITY 2   Video animation of the Krebs cycle (optional)

If you like chemistry and want to know a little more about the Krebs cycle, here is a simple explanation and animation you can watch.
**http://highered.mcgraw-hill.com/sites/0072507470/student_view0/chapter25/animation__ how_the_krebs_cycle_works__quiz_1_.html**

Here is a video that shows pyruvate being formed and going into the matrix of mitochondrion. Watch "Cellular Respiration Occurs in Mitochondria" on the playlist.


## ACTIVITY 3   A totally awesome free video game about the cell!

Yes, there is a totally free, totally awesome video game about cells! It was developed by a team of cell biologists, so even though it is hosted by cartoon platypuses (no kidding) it has a pretty high level of science. The first thing you'll notice is how handy it is to have a mitochondrion. You'll go from producing just 2 ATPs every time you gobble up a glucose, to producing over 30 ATPs per glucose. You'll find peroxisomes come in handy, too, especially when you are being attacked by invaders.

You can play this game "live" online, or you can download it to your computer. (Bear in mind that if you want to save your game and pick up where you left off, you'll have to download the game.)

**www.cellcraftgame.com**

**Can you remember what you read?  If you can't think of the answer, go back and read that part of the chapter again until you find the answer.**

1) Reducing nutrients down to their individual components is called:
   a) metabolism     b) catabolism     c) anabolism     d) oxidation

2) What does pepsin break down?
   a) proteins     b) nucleic acids     c) fats     d) carbohydrates

3) What enzyme is produced by the salivary glands in your mouth?
   a) catalase     b) amylase     c) dehydrogenase     d) hydrochloric acid

4) What tiny structures line your intestines?
   a) capillaries     b) lymph vessels     c) villi     d) chylomicrons

5) Where would you find hydrochloric acid?
   a) in your stomach     b) in your intestines     c) in your duodenum     d) in your liver

6) What is inside a chylomicron?
   a) glucose   b) phospholipid membranes   c) amino acids     d) fatty acids

7) What do you call the protein fibers that form connections between cells?
   a) ligaments   b) desmosomes   c) chromosomes   d) tendons

8) Which one of these is NOT a way that something could get into a cell?
   a) diffusion   b) portal proteins   c) exocytosis   d) pinocytosis   e) phagocytosis

9) A very large storage vesicle in a cell is called:
   a) peroxisome   b) chylomicron   c) vacuole   d) villi

10) What is in the space between cells?
    a) nothing     b) blood     c) lymph fluid     d) water

11) Where do fats get oxidized (with "enzyme scissors")?
    a) in the cytosol     b) in mitochondria     c) in lysosomes     d) in the ER

12) Where does glycolysis (mainly) occur?
    a) in the interstitial space     b) in the peroxisomes     c) in the nucleus     d)  in the cytosol

13) What can acetyl-CoA be used for?  (choose two)
    a) energy   b) transporting electrons   c) making cell parts   d) eliminating toxins   e) lumber

14) Which of the following is NOT a job that peroxisomes do?
    a) break down alcohols   b) break down fats   c) make amino acids   d) get ATPs from glucose

15) How many ATPs can be produced from one glucose molecule?
    a) 2     b) 10     c) 32     d) 36

16) What is the end product of glycolysis?
    a) acetyl-CoA     b) glucose     c) citric acid     d) pyruvate

17) What does the Krebs "factory" produce as a by-product (waste)?
    a) oxygen     b) carbon dioxide     c) ATPs     d)  electrons

# CHAPTER 8: MITOSIS AND MEIOSIS

Like all living things, cells need to reproduce. There's a constant need for new cells, whether for growth or repair. The normal method of cell reproduction in your body is called *mitosis*. The word mitosis comes from the Greek word "mitos," meaning "thread." This is the same "mitos" that begins the word "mitochondria." The "thread" being referred to is chromatin (DNA).

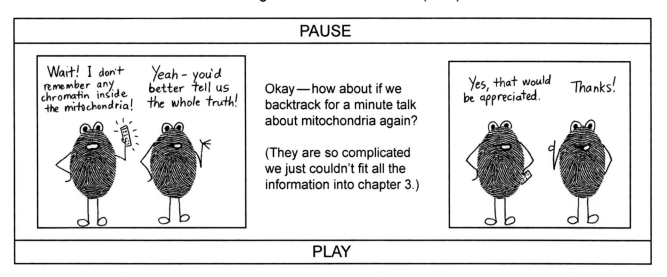

All right—we'll explain. The mitochondria do contain chromatin, but just a little bit of it—a tiny fraction of the amount of chromatin found in the nucleus. It's called *mitochondrial DNA (mtDNA)*. Two interesting facts about mitochondrial DNA are that: 1) it is arranged in a circle, and 2) you inherit your mitochondrial DNA only from your mother, not your father. When an egg is fertilized, only nuclear DNA is donated by the sperm. Most of the sperm's mitochondria are located in the tail (providing energy for rapid movement) and the tail never enters the egg. So the mitochondria present in the egg cell (donated by the mother) will be the source of all of the mitochondria for the developing organism. Because of this direct inheritance of mitochondria from only the mother, mtDNA is very useful for things like tracing the ancestry of people groups. It has also been used to positively identify the remains of famous people such as the famous outlaw Jesse James, and the last czar of Russia, Nicolas II.

What instructions do you think are encoded in the mitochondrial DNA? A mitochondrion doesn't need most of the information that exists in the nuclear DNA. It doesn't need information about things like lysosomal enzymes, or hormones, or blood cells. A mitochondrion only needs information that pertains to itself, such as directions for how to make the proteins and enzymes it uses, especially those it uses a lot, such as the ATP synthase machine, or the electron shuttle bus, NADH. This picture shows what each section of mtDNA encodes. Strangely enough, not all of the information on how to make ion pumps is stored in mtDNA. The mitocondrion still relies on nuclear DNA for the construction of some ion pump parts as well as other proteins. No one knows why this is so. It would seem more efficient to have all the instructions in the mitochondrion. But as we saw in chapter 4, some of the ion pumps parts are made by ribosomes in the cytosol, then brought inside the mitochondrion.

A mitochondrion has more than one copy of its ring of mtDNA. It can have up to ten of them. Why the duplicates? Probably just to speed things up and make the mitochondrion more efficient.

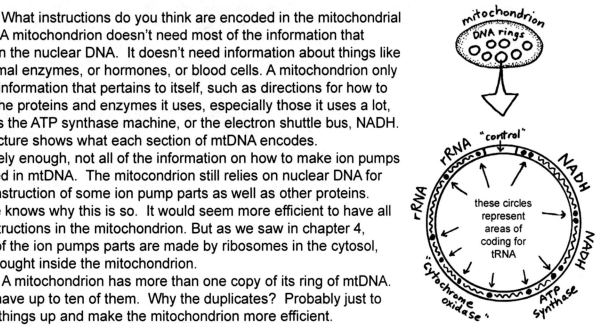

And now, back to mitosis...

Simply put, mitosis is when a cell splits in half. The original cell is called the "parent cell" and the two resulting cells are called the "daughter cells." This does not mean that the cells are feminine in any way. (Ships and hurricanes are given female names, and they aren't feminine, either.) Mitosis may sound very similar to a process we mentioned briefly in the last chapter: **binary fission**. Binary fission is the term used to describe the dividing process used by cells or organelles that do not have a nucleus. This includes mitochondria and peroxisomes, and also bacteria.

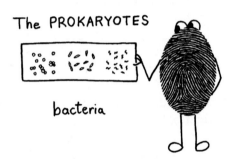
BINARY FISSION

To do mitosis, you must be a cell with a true nucleus—a nucleus with a membrane that envelopes all of the DNA and keeps it separate from the rest of the cell. (One of the steps in mitosis is to dissolve the nuclear membrane. If you don't have a nuclear membrane to dissolve, then you can't do mitosis, right?) Cells that have true nuclei are called **eukaryotic** cells (you-care-ee-ot-ic). "Eu" means "true" and "karyo" means "kernel" (referring to the nucleus). Animal and plant cells are all eukaryotic, and so are fungi and protozoa. The only type of cell that isn't eukaryotic is the bacteria. Bacteria cells <u>do</u> have DNA, but it is not contained within a nuclear envelope. Bacteria are called **prokaryotic** cells. "Pro" means first, or "before." (This refers to some scientists' belief that prokaryotes existed before eukaryotes.) The words *eukaryotic* and *prokaryotic* are used frequently in cell biology, and you will see them again at some point in your education. We really won't need to use these words in the rest of this book, but we just thought it would be a good idea to let you know they exist so that next time you meet them they won't seem so strange. (Aren't they rather odd words?)

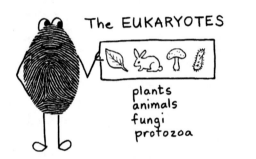

The EUKARYOTES

plants
animals
fungi
protozoa

The PROKARYOTES

bacteria

Before splitting in half, the parent cell has a lot of preparation to do. If it's going to become two cells, the original parent cell must have enough organelles for both daughter cells. The mitochondria and the peroxisomes can use binary fission to divide in half, then in half again, then in half again, until there are enough of them. Lysosomes can be generated by the ER, as we saw in chapter 5. Oodles of new ribosomes can be manufactured by the nucleosome area, although there are probably enough already floating around in the cytosol that each new cell would start out with quite a few. The ER can expand and make more of itself.

Golgi bodies seem to have several different ways of duplicating. Sometimes a Golgi will go "super-size" and will double the diameter of its "discs." Then, this super Golgi can split in half the long way, creating two normal-sized bodies. Another method scientists have observed is for the Golgi to disintegrate itself into small blobs. Then, after the cell splits, each of these little blobs can grow into a whole new Golgi body. (There's a tiny flatworm called a planaria that can do a similar trick. If you cut it up into pieces, each piece will grow into a new worm!) Lastly, a cell's ER can probably manufacture new Golgi bodies if necessary. Golgi reproduction still remains somewhat of a mystery. There is still a lot we don't know about cells.

The most difficult replication task a cell faces is the duplication of the DNA in the nucleus. This is a huge task. First, the entire DNA "library" has to be copied. We saw this process in chapter 4. The little unwinding machine (helicase) unwinds the DNA, then the little sled (polymerase) runs along the open DNA, producing duplicate strands. In chapter 4, our process stopped as soon as the needed section of DNA had been copied because we were only copying just a tiny section. In this case, the entire length of the DNA has to be copied—all 6 billion rungs! The cell has a tricky job making sure that those two copies don't get tangled together. That's where those histone spools (nucleosomes) come in. (We like to call them "histone spools" because the word "histone" is more memorable than the word "nucleosome." Words that are based on roots such as "nucleo" or "cyto" or "centro" tend to all sound the same and are therefore more difficult to remember. For example, it's hard to remember the difference between centrosome, centriole and centromere. The word "histone" sounds like a word that might stick in your mind longer than the word "nucleosome." Just remember that it takes 8 histones to form one nucleosome spool.) The cell must make a whole new set of histone spools (about 300 million histones), so that each copy of the DNA can be wound up tightly and neatly. The cell must also duplicate all the chaperone proteins that surround the DNA. That's just about as large a task as duplicating the DNA!

So when the cell finally has two sets of DNA (and two sets of all the accompanying histone spools and chaperone proteins in and around the DNA) it's ready to start doing mitosis. First, the DNA organizes itself into those sticks we call chromosomes. (However, during mitosis, scientists prefer to use the word "chromatid" instead of "chromosome." Then, after mitosis is over, they go back to using "chromosome" again. As if cell biology wasn't confusing enough, right?) Keeping with the family theme, the two identical chromatids (the original and its copy) are called **sister chromatids**. (Sorry, guys—your chromatids all have sisters, not brothers.) The sister chromatids are joined at the middle by a little dot called a **centromere** (one of those hard-to-remember words). The centromere is just sticky enough to keep the chromatid sisters together, but not so strong that the bond can't be broken, as we shall see shortly.

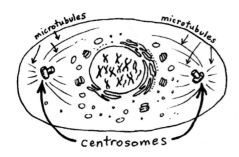

This is when the little centrosome plays its biggest role. (Remember the centrosome from chapter 2? It's made of two barrel-shaped centrioles.) The centrosome now duplicates itself. Then each centrosome starts making a long strand of microtubule, stretching it out toward one end of the cell. Then motor proteins come along and drag the centrosomes along those microtubule "roads" they just made, until the centrosomes are on opposite sides of the cell. Then the centrosomes must wait until the next step is accomplished.

The next step is to dissolve that double-thick nuclear membrane. That's right—the nuclear membrane completely disappears, leaving the chromosomes sitting there out in the open, unprotected! But this step is necessary, and the cell will just build new nuclear membranes after mitosis is complete. Fortunately, cells are very good at rebuilding their parts quickly.

Now that the nucleus is gone, the centrosomes go to work making more microtubules. These tubules stretch out forming what is called a **spindle**. Some of the spindle fibers attach directly to the chromatids. The equal pulling force on each side of the pairs of chromatids cause them to line up along the middle of the cell. Once the spindle is in place, the centrosomes start pulling even harder. They pull so hard that the pairs of chromatids snap apart right at the centromere and begin going toward opposite sides of the cell. When the centrosomes have finished pulling, each side of the cell has a complete set of chromatids. (And now we go back to calling them chromosomes.)

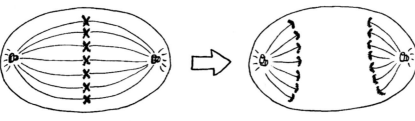

*Note: To make this illustration clear and easy to understand, we did not draw all the mitochondria, Golgi bodies, lysosomes, peroxisomes and ribosomes.*

Now for the last part of mitosis. Each side of the cell has a full set of chromosomes, plus a full set of organelles. The cell now begins to get longer. The chromosomes at each end of the cell cluster together and go back to being a blob of chromatin. Then the ER gets busy re-organizing itself and re-building the nuclear membrane around the chromatin. Soon, each end of this long cell has its own nucleus. This is technically where mitosis ends. The final splitting process is called *cytokinesis* ("cell movement"). However, most of the time when people talk about mitosis, they mean to include cytokinesis as well.

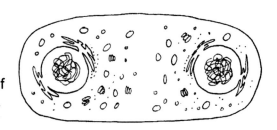

*Now the cell is ready for "cytokinesis."*

Cytokinesis is when the cell splits in half. It starts out as a pinched area on either side, then the pinch grows and grows until it's all the way down the middle. Interestingly enough (and just to show you how complicated cells are) vesicles created by the Golgi bodies seem to play a role at this point. Vesicles line up all along the middle line and help to create the new membranes. In plant cells, these vesicles are even more important than in animal cells, as they will help to create a new cell wall, not just a new membrane. (Walls are much thicker and sturdier than membranes.) Once the pinch is complete down the middle, the final separation is made, and you've got two daughter cells.

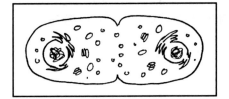 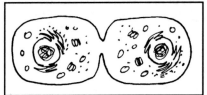 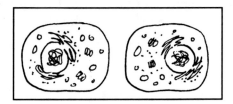

Scientists like to assign names to the steps of mitosis, to make it easier to for them to have discussions about mitosis. Then they can say things like "at the beginning of prophase" or "at the end of telophase," and all the other scientists know exactly what stage of mitosis they are talking about. So, just in case you ever need to know, here are the names they assign to the stages:

**INTERPHASE**: The "normal" state of a cell. Most of the time, a cell is in interphase. Towards the end of this phase, the organelles start to replicate more than usual, to make sure that each future daughter cell will have enough.

**PROPHASE**: The chromatin duplicates and then organizes into chromosomes. The centrosomes duplicate and go to opposite sides of the nucleus.

**METAPHASE**: The nuclear membrane dissolves, the spindle forms, and the chromosomes line up down the middle.

**ANAPHASE**: The chromatids are pulled to opposite sides of the cell. Also, all the organelles have gone to one side or the other.

**TELOPHASE**: The cell elongates (you could think of a long "<u>telo</u>scope") and new membranes are formed around the DNA, which has gone back to being chromatin.

**CYTOKINESIS**: The cell splits in half, making two daughter cells.

Eukaryotes have another other kind of cell division, in addition to mitosis. There is one situation in which you don't want a complete set of DNA in each daughter cell. In reproductive cells—eggs and sperm—you only want half of a set of DNA, not a full set. Why? Because an egg and a sperm join together to make a new set of DNA. They each donate half of the correct amount of DNA a cell needs. One half plus one half equals a whole. If an egg and a sperm each had a full set of DNA, the embryo would end up with double DNA, creating a real mess!

The special process of making an egg or sperm cell is called **meiosis** (*my-o-sis*). In meiosis, cell duplication takes place twice instead of just once. To make sure everyone knows which duplication is being discussed, scientists decided to call the first one "meiosis 1" and the second one "meiosis 2." (Sometimes you will see Roman numerals used instead of numbers: "meiosis I" and "meiosis II")

The first step of meiosis 1 is the same as in mitosis: the cell duplicates its chromosomes into pairs of sister chromatids. It does this duplicating before the chromosomes get all bunched into little sticks, so for a short time the cell has double the normal "spaghetti mess" in the nucleus.

The next step is different from mitosis. Amidst this semi-organized chaos in the nucleus, the chromosomes (or you can call them chromatids) have the unbelievable task of having to go find their "counterparts." Remember, half of a cell's DNA originally came from the father and the other half came from the mother. Humans have 46 chromosomes—23 from each parent. Each chromosome that came from the father has a similar chromosome, a "counterpart," that came from the mother. The two counterpart chromosomes carry very similar information. For example, both might carry the coding for hair color, or instructions for the production of a certain enzyme. (So how does a cell know which information to use? The answer is WAY beyond the scope of this book, so you'll have to trust us that the cell has everything under control and knows where to get the information it needs.) Each chromosome (which now is actually a pair of sister chromatids!) goes and finds its counterpart and attaches to it temporarily. Now there is a little cluster of four chromatids, two pairs of sister chromatids attached to each other. We have drawn the two pairs of sister chromatids as a set of boy twins and a set of girl twins. Even though both sets are called sisters, it can be helpful to think of one set of chromatids as brother twins instead of sister twins. The boy chromosomes represent the ones that came from the father and the girls from the mother. (You could imagine that the boy and girl chromatids are holding hands. Their hands could represent the centromere.)

*Real chromatids "crossing over" would look more like this (than like our silly cartoon of boys and girls). The dark spots are where the chromatids have traded their DNA.*

Now something bizarre happens. Those four chromatids trade some of their DNA back and forth. In our mental picture of the two sets of twins standing next to each other, it would be as if they all traded some body parts. Imagine them as plastic dolls made of individual body parts that can be snapped on and off. They could pop off their body parts, mix them up, and them pop them back on randomly. Bobby might end up with Sally's feet. Sally might end up with Betty's hair or with her left hand. Betty might end up with Jimmy's left thumb. If chromatids were people it would be a truly bizarre scene! However, chromatids look pretty boring under the microscope, and this event isn't nearly as humorous in real life as it sounds when we imagine the chromatids as people. The chromatids simply trade some DNA back and forth. Why? Remember that the purpose of meiosis is to make reproductive cells that will create offspring with brand new combinations of DNA. Children are not clones of their parents. They are their own unique selves. It's partly this step in meiosis, often called "**crossing over**," that helps to mix up the genetic information and create offspring that are different from either parent. (In large populations, such as insects, these variations can help a species to survive.)

65

Now the cell is ready to divide. Alas—those sweet couples are going to have to split up. The rules of the meiosis game say that the groups of four (the girl twins and boy twins), have to split up so that the girls go off together and the boys go off together. Just like in mitosis, the centrosomes form a spindle of microtubules. Then the chromosome pairs line up along the middle. In our imaginary scenario, the girls (or boys) wouldn't all be facing the same side. The "couples" would be arranged randomly, with some boys and some girls on each side. So when the cell finally splits, the daughter cells have a random selection of girls twins and boy twins. Theoretically, it would be possible for a daughter cell to end up with all girl twins or all boy twins, but the odds of this happening are very small. (And even if it did, it wouldn't really matter because the twins have mixed-up body parts, so the daughter cells will get some DNA from both parents no matter what happens.)

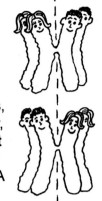

Now for the second part of meiosis. It's a good thing that chromatids don't have feelings, because now the "twins" must be separated. It's time for another cell division. This time, there is no duplication of DNA. The twins simply line up along the middle and are pulled apart by the microtubules in the spindle. It's a sad goodbye as the twins say "Adieu" and never see each other again. Once the individual chromatids are separated, the cell splits in half, forming two daughter cells that have only half the normal amount of DNA.

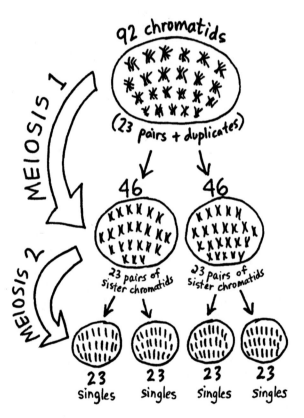

92 chromatids
(23 pairs + duplicates)
MEIOSIS 1
46
46
23 pairs of sister chromatids
23 pairs of sister chromatids
MEIOSIS 2
23 singles
23 singles
23 singles
23 singles

On the left is a diagram showing how many chromatids are in human cells during the stages of meiosis. You can see that the original cell starts out with 46 chromosomes (23 pairs). They duplicate themselves, making a grand total of 92 chromatids. After they do the "crossing over" routine to mix up the DNA, they then split apart to make daughter cells that have 23 pairs of sister chromatids (46 chromatids in all). In the second stage, the chromosomes don't duplicate, they just separate into daughter cells that have only 23 chromosomes.

So then what happens? What is the fate of those sad "ex-twins" that end up in those cells on the bottom row? These 23-chromosome cells (called **gametes**) will form into either egg cells or sperm cells, depending on whether they are in a male or female body. There are a few more twists and turns in the plot; not all female daughter cells end up as eggs. But the rest of the story is... another story. We are going to leave those reproductive cells at this stage. We can imagine them pining away for their counterparts of the opposite gender—a bittersweet ending to our cell saga.

* * * * * * * * * * * * * * * * * * * * * * * * * * * * * * * * * * * * * * * * * * * * * * * * * * * *

## <u>ACTIVITY 1</u>  Look at real cells in various stages of mitosis

If you do an Internet image search using key words "onion mitosis" you will find an endless supply of pictures showing microscopic views of cells from the tips of onion roots, a place where mitosis takes place at a very rapid rate. You'll see cells in just about every stage of mitosis.

## ACTIVITY 2   Some mitosis videos

1) Watch "Mitosis" on the playlist.  This video has nice graphics and is easy to understand.

2) Watch "Inside the Cell."  This video has no narration (but nice music), and you will see the names of the stages of mitosis printed at the bottom of the screen.

3) Watch "Cytokinesis Animal Plant."  This video shows cytokinesis in both animal and plant cells.  (NOTE:  You can click on a link on this video and it will take you to the company's official site on YouTube where the sidebars are other biology videos you might be interested in.)


## ACTIVITY 3    Some meiosis videos

1) Watch the "Meiosis" video on the playlist.  It was made by the same people who made the first mitosis video listed above.

2) In this video, "meiosis" (with a small "m" instead of a capital "M"), a school teacher explains meiosis using strings of magnetic beads.

3) Here's another nice video animation of meiosis.  "Biology: Meiosis cell division."  You'll notice that they use the words for the names of the phases (prophase, metaphase, anaphase, telophase).  This animation gives you a more detailed view of the DNA and even shows the histone spools.

4) Now for a little fun.  This video is scientifically accurate, but very silly.  It shows you meiosis as a cartoon square dance!  Watch "Meiosis Square Dance Song" on playlist.


## ACTIVITY 4   Cell number puzzle

Try to match the correct number to each clue.

**1   2   3   4   5   7   8   10   14   20   23   36   40   146   10,000   6 billion**

1) The number of ATPs that a cell can get out of one glucose molecule. ____
2) The number of histone proteins in a nucleosome spool. ____
3) The number of steps in glycolysis. ____
4) The number of electrons in a hydrogen atom. ____
5) The number of amino acids in a codon. ____
6) The number of rungs in a complete set of human DNA. _____
7) There are about this many different enzymes in a lysosome. ____
8) The number of centrioles in a centrosome. ____
9) The highest number on the pH scale. ____
10) There are this many types of amino acids. ____
11) There are this many pairs of chromosomes in a human cell. ____
12) There are this many types of nucleotide bases (including both DNA and RNA). ____
13) There are this many layers of phospholipids in the nuclear membrane. ____
14) This number is "neutral" on the pH scale. ____
15) This is the number of nuclei that could fit on the head of a pin. _____
16) There are about this many DNA rungs wound around each nucleosome spool. ____

**Can you remember what you read?  If you can't think of the answer, go back and read that part of the chapter again until you find the answer.**

1) How is mitochondrial DNA passed from parent to child?
   a) from the egg cell donated by the mother   b) from the tail of the sperm cell donated by the father
   c) from the head of the sperm donated by the father   d) from the cells of both parents

2) TRUE OR FALSE?  Mitochondrial DNA contains all the information a mitochondrion needs.

3) How is mitochondrial DNA arranged?
   a) it's disorganized, just like the chromatin in the nucleus   b) it's circular in shape
   c) it's organized into tight bundles, just like chromatids   d) it's a spherical shape

4) TRUE OR FALSE?  Only eukaryotic cells can do mitosis.

5) Prokaryotic cells mainly belong to this kingdom:
   a) animals      b) bacteria      c) fungi      d) protozoa      e) plants

6) Can you remember the correct name for the little sled that runs along the DNA?
   a) amylase     b) helicase     c) polymerase     d) trick question—it doesn't have a name

7) When a chromatid duplicates, the duplicate is called its:
   a) sister     b) daughter     c) twin     d) clone

8) Which organelle creates the spindle?  _____

9) Which of the following does the spindle NOT do?
   a) cause the chromatids to line up down the center line     b) cause the chromatids to duplicate
   c) pull the sister chromatids apart                d) extend out from the centrosomes

10) When the cell actually splits in half, it is called:
   a) mitosis     b) binary fission     c) cloning     d) cytokinesis

11)  In which process (mitosis or meiosis) will you find "crossing over"?  _____

12)  How many chromatids (chromosomes) end up in a human "gamete" cell (egg or sperm)? _____

13)  How many "gamete" cells (egg or sperm) are produced by one parent cell as the result of meiosis?
   a) 2      b) 4      c) 23     d) 46

14)  What does "crossing over" do?
   a) helps to "mix up" the DNA      b) sorts out which chromatids will go to which daughter cells
   c) causes harmful mutations      d) nothing

15)  TRUE or FALSE?  In a matched pair of chromosomes (one from the father, one from the mother) the information contained on the chromosomes is extremely similar—they both code for the same things.

16)  Which one of these is technically not part of mitosis?
   a) prophase     b) metaphase     c) anaphase     d) telophase     e) cytokinesis

17)  TRUE or FALSE?  The only place in an organism where you will find meiosis going on is in the reproductive organs.

# CHAPTER 9:  TYPES OF CELLS

Everything we have been learning about cells is true for most eukaryotic cells—animal, plant and fungal cells.  All eukaryotic cells (with just a few exceptions) have the same types of organelles and use the same basic metabolic processes.   So all of the information you've learned about cells is true for most cells.   However, cells can come in many different shapes and sizes and some have amazing adaptations that make them suitable for a particular function.  In this chapter we are going to look at a selection of cells found in human bodies (and in many other mammals, too).

## SKIN CELLS

If you asked a cell biologist what kind of cell best represents what we think of as a basic, "average" cell, he or she would probably say a skin cell.  Skin cells belong to a group of cells called *epithelial* cells.  ("Epi" means "outside" and "thelia" means "tissue.")  Epithelial cells can be found not only in the skin but also in the lungs, intestines, eye, blood vessels, and many glands.

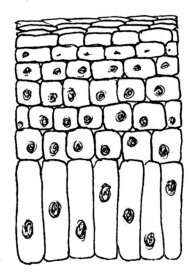

Skin cells form what we call the *epidermis* (there's that word "epi" again, plus "dermis" for skin).  The epidermis is made of layers of skin cells piled on top of each other.  Their shapes are very simple, like blocks.  The ones on top tend to be flat, the ones in the middle look like cubes, and the ones on the bottom are more rectangular.  They are packed together very tightly, connected by desmosomes.  In fact, they are so tightly packed that there aren't any capillaries running through them to nourish them.  They have to rely on diffusion from below.  The skin cells right on the surface (and therefore furthest away from the source of nourishment coming from below) don't care that they don't receive much nourishment because... they're dead!  Yes, when you look at your skin, you are seeing nothing but the outer layer of dead cells.  These dead cells no longer have any organelles, not even a nucleus. They are filled with a substance called *keratin*.  Keratin is made of long, thin strands of protein very much like the intermediate filaments of the cytoskeleton.

In the epidermal layer of skin cells, new cells are constantly being made on the bottom level.  As new cells arise, the ones above them get pushed upward.  As they go up they gradually get filled with more and more keratin.  It's sort of like the cytoskeleton takes over and kills off the organelles.  By the time they reach the top, they are totally filled with keratin.  But there's a bright side to the death of all these cells—keratin is tough and waterproof.  All that keratin (plus some oil made by oil glands under the epidermis) gives your body a fairly waterproof surface.

When cells die intentionally, as part of the overall plan to renew your body and keep it healthy, we call this "programmed cell death," or *apoptosis*.  Some people say "*a-pop-to-sis*" and others say "*a-po-to-sis*."  The reason behind the second pronunciation is the "pt" in the middle of the word.  In Greek, the "p" is silent in words that begin with "pt," such as "pterodactyl" or "Ptolemy."  You can choose which way to say it.  We think "*a-pop-to-sis*" sounds really neat (you can imagine the cells popping), but perhaps "*a-po-to-sis*" would be the way to say it if you were talking to a cell biologist.  (However, some biologists do go with "*pop*.")

*I find this section a bit disturbing...*

Most cells in your body are equipped with "suicide instructions."  Special proteins keep these instructions from being opened.  But there are triggers, either from within the cell or from outside the cell that can remove those protective proteins and let the suicide instructions begin the countdown to destruction.  The instructions are complicated and involve quite a few steps, and at various points in the sequence there is a chance for the cell to stop the process if it turns out that the cell doesn't need to die after all.  But if all the instructions are indeed carried out, the final step is often to shut down the mitochondria. Without the ATPs generated by the mitochondria, the cell will die very quickly. Occasional, the final step is to open up holes in the membrane that will allow calcium to come flooding in. Either way, as the cell starts to die, it does something called **blebbing**. The word "bleb" conjures up images of blobs, doesn't it? This is exactly what happens. The membrane starts looking like blobs oozing out everywhere. The cell breaks up into

little blobs containing bits and pieces of organelles and DNA. This mess has to be cleaned up, of course, and there is a specialized cell that does just that. It's called a **phagocyte**. "Phago" is Greek for "eating." So these "eating cells" come along and eat up all the blebbed pieces of the former cell. They digest them and the pieces can then be recycled into new cells.

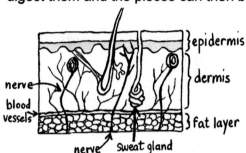

Just think what would happen if your skin cells didn't constantly die and flake off and replace themselves with new cells. That magic marker tattoo you thought was so funny to draw on your hand when you were 9 years old would still be there when you were 42! (Real tattoos obviously have to go deeper than the epidermis layer. They have to stain the much deeper layer called the **dermis**, which contains the sweat glands, oil glands, hair follicles and nerve endings.)

## CAPILLARY CELLS

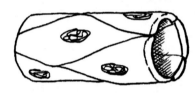

Another place where you will find epithelial cells is in your capillaries. We've already been introduced to this type of cell (back in chapter 7). The shape of this cell is very specific to its job. It looks almost like a piece of pipe. Most of the capillary cells in your body have only very small cracks between them. This fairly tight spacing keeps the red blood cells inside, while still allowing really tiny things, like water and nutrients, to leak out. (Strangely enough, white blood cells can flatten themselves out and squeeze through those very thin cracks!)

In some places in the body, such as the liver and the spleen, the red cells need to be able to enter and exit the capillaries. In these places, you will find larger cracks between the cells—cracks large enough for red cells to pass through.

Even though these cells have a very odd shape, they are still cells and have a nucleus and organelles. They are pretty lucky, though—the bloodstream rushes right past them all the time. No problem about getting enough nutrition! They are willing to share, though, and as they take in nutrition from the blood, they pass a lot of it out the other side to the cells behind them.

## VILLI

A third kind of epithelial cell is the intestinal villi, which we saw in chapter 7. These cells have holes that go right through them! They are perfect for an environment where you want more leakage than the average capillary provides, but not as much leakage as the capillaries in the liver and spleen. As we already know, the villi get the nutrients out of your intestine and into your blood.

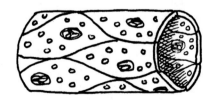

These cells are called "fenestrated" cells. The word "fenestra" is Latin for "window." (Here is yet another case where a difficult-sounding word has a very simple meaning. Fenestrated just means "full of little windows.")

## GOBLET CELLS

Gooey mucus—that's what goblet cells make. These cells are found in your respiratory tract and your intestines. Mucus helps to capture foreign particles like bacteria and dust that enter the lungs, and then washes them away. In the intestines the mucus helps to lubricate the passageways so that food flows easily. As much as we don't like too much mucus in our sinuses when we are sick, without mucus we would lose an essential form of protection from infections.

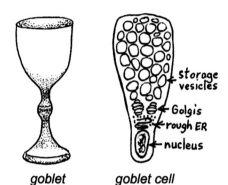

goblet          goblet cell

The goblet cells get their name from their shape: narrow on the bottom with a large "cup" on the top, like a goblet. The narrow bottom "pedestal" part of the cell contains the organelles like the nucleus, mitochondria, ER, and Golgis. The top "cup" part of the cell contains the storage vesicles. Because the top part of the cell opens out to the lining of the respiratory tract or to the intestines, it can be stimulated by something irritating, such as dust, food particles, or bacteria.

The main component of mucus is a protein called **mucin**. Like all proteins, it is made by ribosomes and then processed by the endoplasmic reticulum and Golgi bodies, which add many sugars to it, giving mucus its gooey, sticky texture. The mucins are then stored in special storage vesicles. These storage vesicles can really compress a lot of protein into a small space, thanks to calcium ions. Mucins have a lot of negatively charged areas that try to repel each other, but those areas can be "covered" over with calcium ions (which are positive and are attracted to the negative areas). When the mucin is released out of the cell through the plasma membrane, the calcium ions diffuse away and the negative ions are free to repel each other. The repulsion of the charged areas, in addition to mucin mixing with water outside the cell, causes the mucus to expand up to 600 times its previously compacted volume! (Think of a can of shaving cream... the compressed volume is very small but when you release it, it expands.)

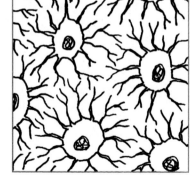

Wow! Mucus is amazing!

Yeah. Maybe we should have a "National Mucus Appreciation Day"?!

Goblet cells belong to a group of cells called "secretory" cells. (*Seh-creh-tore-ee*) Secretory cells "secrete" things like sweat, tears, saliva, milk or hormones. There are lots of different kinds of secretory cells in your body. They don't have the goblet shape, but they function in similar ways—making their products, storing them in vesicles, then releasing them at the right time.

## BONE CELLS

We all know that bones help us to stand up and keep our shape. But did you know that ounce for ounce your bones are stronger than steel? Your femur (thigh bone) is stronger than a steel bar weighing 4 to 5 times more than the bone. The average bone can hold up to five pickup trucks on top of it (but don't try that at home!). How can your bones be so strong and so light? Let's look at the cells that make our bones.

Cells called **osteoblasts** ("osteo" means "bone" and "blast" means an immature cell) make a large interwoven network using a tough but flexible protein called **collagen**. These cells have a large Golgi complex and endoplasmic reticulum to be able to process the large amounts of collagen protein they need to make. Once they have made this large spiderweb structure of protein (called a **matrix**), they begin to mineralize it using mostly calcium and phosphorus, plus magnesium and a few other minerals. These minerals bind to the flexible collagen matrix and give it lots of extra strength. The hollow spaces of the matrix keep the bone light, the protein network gives it flexibility, and the minerals give it strength. Osteoblasts can make bone in different density—denser towards the outside of the bone, and less dense towards the middle of the bone.

By now, the osteoblast is stuck inside this bone "cage" that it has made around itself, and we now change the name of the cell to *osteocyte.* An osteocyte can live inside the bone it has made for up to 20 years. Like all cells, osteocytes need nourishment from the blood. Tiny blood vessels weave their way in between the bone matrix. Osteocytes develop long-reaching arms and connect to other osteocytes. They can send signals to each other to increase or decrease the mineral content of the matrix if stimulated by pressure or force. Exercising pressurizes bones and causes the osteocytes to increase the amount of minerals in the matrix, making your bones stronger for future exercise. People who don't exercise enough or don't get enough mineral in their diet are more likely to develop something call *osteoporosis*, a condition where your bones become less dense and therefore break more easily.

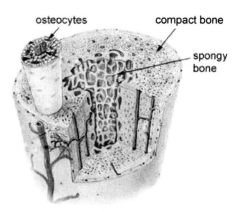

osteocytes    compact bone    spongy bone

Even though osteocytes can live a long time, not all bone lasts for 20 years. Sometimes your body needs calcium and phosphorus for other processes in the body, such as muscle contraction which requires calcium to signal the proteins to contract. When your body needs more calcium, it sends signals to a cell called an *osteoclast* so that it can begin to break down the bone matrix. You can think of the bone matrix as a warehouse for calcium and other minerals; when your body needs some minerals it calls up the osteoclasts and asks for some. Osteoclasts are derived from monocytes (see the section on blood cells for info on the monocytes) and so they are also able to phagocytize (eat) things. As osteoclasts eat away at the bone structure, they release the minerals, which go into the bloodstream to where they are needed. Osteocytes can also help with this process.

When old bone is removed, new osteoblasts come into those empty spaces to form new matrix, and mineralize it into new bone. This cycle is constantly going on in your body and helps to keep you healthy and functioning. If your body couldn't obtain calcium when it needed it, some very important functions might not be able to happen, like heart contractions or moving your diaphragm muscle to expand your lungs. Bones are not just structural supports—they are living tissues, constantly changing and replenishing themselves. (And the only way those bone cells can get the minerals they need is from what you eat and drink, so make sure you eat foods that have plenty of minerals in them!)

## MUSCLE CELLS

Like to dance? Ride your bike? Even just lift the remote to change the channel on the television? Thank your muscle cells! These amazing cells can drastically change shape, which allows them to pull on other structures like tendons and bones, causing movement.

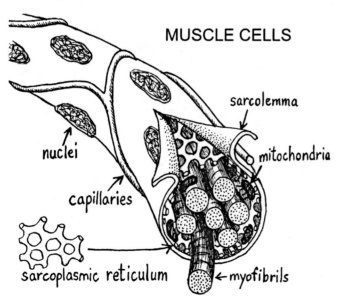

MUSCLE CELLS

nuclei

capillaries

sarcoplasmic reticulum

sarcolemma

mitochondria

← myofibrils

Each muscle cell is called a "muscle fiber." And it's not really a cell. Well, it is a cell, but it's not like any of the other cells in your body because it's more like a colony of cells all joined together into one big cell. The cells started out as single "baby" cells, then as they matured into "adult" cells, they merged together to form one long fiber. The fiber has all of the organelles from the original cells, so it ends up with a whole bunch of nuclei. A cell with more than one nucleus? How can this work?

Having multiple nuclei is an advantage to the muscle fiber (cell) because it is so long that it would be a problem if there was only one nucleus. The messenger RNAs would have to travel long distances to get to the ribosomes at the far ends of the fiber. This would slow down the process of making proteins. Your body needs to be able to renew and repair you muscles as fast as possible. So the mRNA can simply go to the nearest nucleus. All the nuclei have the same set of instructions for repairing muscles, so it doesn't matter which nucleus the mRNA chooses. Muscle cells also have all the other organelles, but they are squashed toward the outer edges to make room for the giant bundles of actin and myosin that take up most of the room in the cell.

The bundles inside the muscle cell are called **myofibrils**. They are made of two stringy proteins: **actin** and **myosin**. These are the proteins that actually move the cell. Myosin has tiny "oars" along its length that actually paddle and push off of actin when calcium is present, causing the two proteins to slide past each other. Imagine a radio antennae, and think about how the tubes slide into

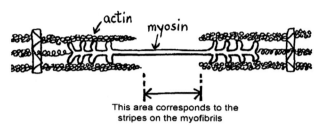

This area corresponds to the stripes on the myofibrils

each other, allow the antennae to become long (muscle relaxation) or short (muscle contraction). The sliding together and stacking of these proteins causes the whole muscle cell to shrink in length, or "contract." Then it relaxes and gets longer again.

Muscle cells have a special phospholipid membrane surrounding them called the **sarcolemma**. This membrane is special because it actually forms tunnel-like tubes that pass all the way through the diameter of the cell and out to the other side of the sarcolemma. These tunnels house nerve endings that carry electrical signals from your brain, that essentially "shock" the muscle cells. This electrical signal causes a special organ inside the cell to initiate muscle contraction. This special organ is called the **sarcoplasmic reticulum** (sounds like the endoplasmic reticulum, right?) It is similar in shape and structure to the endoplasmic reticulum. It is a phospholipid membrane network that extends through the muscle fiber and its job is to store calcium ions. When the electrical signal comes down the nerve endings through the sarcolemma tunnels, this electrical shock causes the sarcoplasmic reticulum to release its calcium ions into the cytoplasm of the muscle cell. These calcium ions bind with myosin, and cause the muscle to contract.

The muscles you can control, the "voluntary" muscles, are connected to nerves in your brain that you have conscious control over. Some muscles, like your heart muscles and the muscles in your intestines, the "involuntary" muscles, are wired to parts of your brain that automatically send signals out to them to contract and relax (otherwise you would have to remember to beat your heart!). Some muscles are connected in both ways, like the ones that expand and contract your rib cage so you can breathe. Take a couple of breaths in and out. You can control your breathing. But were you thinking about breathing before we suggested it? Good thing your subconscious brain was!


## NERVE CELLS

Nerve cells are called neurons. Their job is to send and receive electrical signals. They have a very weird shape. The three main parts of a neuron are the cell body, the axon, and the dendrites.

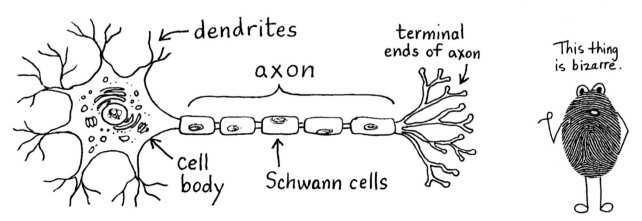

The plasma membrane of a neuron cell is different from other cells. Phospholipid membranes are great insulators—they generally won't let an electrical signal through. Kind of a problem if your job is to conduct electricity! So there are special proteins embedded in the neuron's membrane that allow electrically charged ions through. The membrane also has ion pumps.

The cell body contains the nucleus and the organelles. The dendrites stretch out from the cell body like branches from a tree. (The Greek word for tree is "dendrite.") The dendrites detect electrical signals coming from other neurons. When they pick up an incoming signal, they pass it along to the axon. The signal passes through the axon very quickly.

Those cells around the axon, called **Schwann cells** (after their discoverer, Theodore Schwann) provide insulation for the axon, like the rubber around the copper wires of a household electrical cord. The Schwann cells are separate cells from the neuron but they are never found apart from neurons. They wrap themselves around an axon and insulate, protect, and nourish it.

When the electrical signal reaches the end of the axon it goes into the terminal ends. Those terminal ends might look like dendrites, but they aren't. You'd think they could come up with a special name for those ends, but no, they are just called the terminal ends. (Terminal means "end" so they are the "end ends.") Each terminal end comes into very close contact with a dendrite from another neuron. They come incredibly close,

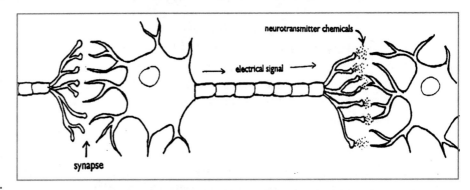

but don't touch. The tiny gap between them is called the **synapse**. Electrical signals can't jump the gap, so something must take the signal across. The electrical signal is converted into a chemicals that "float" across, like a boat going from one dock to another, except that these are little speedboats, going incredibly fast. They cross in less than 1/1000th of a second!

Some neurons are very short—microscopic, in fact. Your brain has about 100 billion tiny neurons! (There are different kinds of neurons in your brain. Some don't conduct electricity, they just take care of the ones that do.) The longest neuron in the human body is about 1 meter long (3 feet). You might be able to guess that a long neuron like this would run the length of an arm or leg.

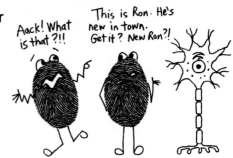

## BLOOD CELLS

There are many types of blood cells. They all float in a clear, watery fluid called **plasma**. The plasma carries all the nutrients that go to our cells: proteins, fats, sugars, vitamins, and minerals. These nutrients are incredibly small—far too small to see with a regular microscope. The blood cells are large in comparison and can easily be seen even with an average microscope, the kind you might use at home or in school.

Studying blood cells can be a bit confusing because there are many technical names for them and some cells start out being one thing and end up as another. Also, they can be classified several different ways, which makes it difficult to make the subject simple for beginning students. First, we will divide blood cells into two categories—red and white—and then we'll take a more in-depth look at 5 different kinds of white cells.

# ERYTHROCYTES (red blood cells)

The correct scientific name for red blood cells is **erythrocytes** (ee-RITH-ro-sites). This just means "red cells." (Which part of the word means "red"?) Red blood cells are very different from other cells because they have no nucleus at all. (Of course, the top layer of your skin also has cells with no nucleus but those are dead cells. Red blood cells are alive.) Red cells also live without Golgi bodies, mitochondria and most other organelles, including ribosomes. This means that they can't make proteins (so they can't repair themselves or reproduce), and they can't metabolize (so they can't "feed" themselves). So what CAN they do? Just one thing—carry oxygen.

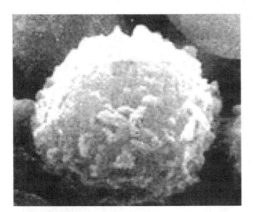

*This is an SEM (scanning electron (microscope) image of an erythrocyte.*

Red blood cells are "born" in the **marrow** (center) of your bones. A "baby" red blood cell has a nucleus, but as it "grows up" (in only one week), the nucleus disappears. As an "adult" the red blood cell looks sort of like a donut, but without the hole in the center. The cytoplasm is filled with molecules called **hemoglobin**. Hemoglobin is rich in iron, and it's the iron that gives the cells their red color. The hemoglobin molecule can grab and hold on to oxygen molecules. As the red blood cells pass through the capillaries in the lungs, the hemoglobin molecules get loaded up with oxygen molecules. Then, as the red blood cells circulate throughout the body, the oxygen molecules get distributed to cells that are in need of oxygen.

Just think—what if a red blood cell had mitochondria? Those mitochondria would be constantly stealing oxygen molecules to use for their own metabolic purposes. The red cell would then be much less efficient at delivering oxygen. But the red cells don't need mitochondria. They live in a nutrient-rich environment all the time. They get enough glucose from the plasma around them so that they don't need mitochondria like other cells do.

Red blood cells are flexible, like rubber, and can bend to fit through very, very small capillaries. The **concave** (donut-like) shape of the cell helps it to flex. When red cells have to go through capillaries that are almost too small for them to get through, they release some ATPs, which relaxes the capillary wall cells, causing the capillary to expand a bit so they can get through.

Your body has over 20 trillion red blood cells. Your body makes 2 million every second! This high production rate is necessary because red cells only live for about 3 or 4 months. When they die, they end up in the liver where a special type of white blood cell (called a macrophage) comes and digests them. The hemoglobin molecules are disassembled and the cell parts are recycled into new cells.

# LEUCOCYTES (white blood cells)

The fancy Greek name for white blood cells is **leucocytes** (LU-koh-sites) which just means "white cells." (What is the Greek word for "white"?) White blood cells contain no hemoglobin so they don't carry oxygen. They have a very different job from red cells. The white cells form a microscopic army that fights harmful invaders such as bacteria and viruses. Just like a real army is a complex society made of soldiers, officers, pilots, mechanics, sailors, cooks, doctors, nurses, truck drivers, and communications specialists, so the immune system is also very complex and has different cells that do a variety of jobs.

Strangely enough, this army of white cells looks surprisingly sparse when viewed under a microscope. For every one white cell, there are 600 to 700 red cells! If you look at a blood sample under a microscope you'll see oodles of red cells and only a few white cells (depending on what magnificaton you use). This is a bit shocking if you know how important white cells are. But remember that even though they are so outnumbered by red cells, you still have millions of white cells.

*An SEM image of a white cell. This type of image shows you the external texture. It does not tell you anything about the inside.*

There are five basic kinds of white blood cells.  Three of them have names that end in "phil" and the other two end in "cyte."  (However, just to make your academic life a little harder, some of these cells have more than one name.  Very sorry, not our fault.  Just wanted to warn you.)  Let's look at the "phil" family of cells first.

The three "phils" are ***basophils, eosinophils and neutrophils***.  We've seen the root word "phil" before,  in the word "hydrophilic."  It means "to like or love," so these cells must like something.  But not anything very interesting—just stains.  Yeah, big deal.  Basophils like blue stain, eosinophils like eosin (red) stain and neutrophils like being neutral and not taking either stain.  (Remember, everything looks pretty clear and colorless under the microscope unless you apply stains.  So stains really are important, they just aren't very exciting to talk about.)  Another thing these three types of cells have in common is that their texture is what we call ***granular***.  This means they look like they are full of tiny lumps, or granules.  The granules are tiny, lumpy proteins. These three types of cells (sometimes referred to as "granulocytes")  also have very weird-looking nuclei.

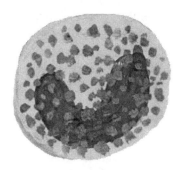

***Basophils*** (BASE-o-fills) are the least common type of white blood cell.  They account for less than one percent of your total white cell population.  (But you still have millions of them!)  The blue stain they love has a "basic" pH (as opposed to acidic), thus the name basophil.  When we tell you what they do, you may wonder why you have them at all, as they might seem to be nothing but a nuisance.  Basophils react to invaders other than bacteria or viruses—invaders such as pollen or food proteins or parasites.  Basophils freak out and burst open when they encounter these things, releasing a chemical called ***histamine,*** which causes swelling and terrible itching.  They also release chemicals that keep blood from clotting and open up the capillaries.  Basophils might sound like traitors who have gone and joined the enemy camp.  Who wants itching and swelling?  However, every cell in the immune system is there for a reason, even if it produces side effects we don't enjoy.  A certain amount of swelling around an infection can help keep it quarantined.  Also, chemicals (even unpleasant ones) can be important messengers that send signals to other cells telling them what they need to do to help out.

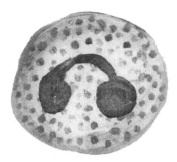

***Eosinophils*** *(EE-o-sin-o-fills)*, which like eosin stain and thus turn shades of red or pink, are able to clean up the mess that basophils leave behind after they burst.  They are slightly more abundant than basophils, and make up about 2 to 4 percent of your total white blood cell count.  Eosinophils are multi-taskers, being able to do a variety of jobs.  Besides cleaning up the messes that basophils make, they can also help to fight viral infections.  Perhaps their most notorious role in the body is to fight parasites, especially infestations of parasitic worms.  The eosinophils surround and attack these disgusting foreign invaders.

One other interesting fact about eosinophils is that the number you have in your bloodstream varies throughout the day, with the afternoon generally being the peak.

***Neutrophils*** are sometimes classified as ***phagocytes***.  You may remember that "phago" means "eat."  So these are cells that go around gobbling up bad things that you don't want in your body, such as harmful bacteria.  They only live for 1 to 2 days before they are replaced.  But this means that parasites can't live inside of them.  What?  A parasite living inside a microscopic blood cell?  Yep.  Malaria parasites love to live inside red blood cells, making them into cozy little homes for several months.  If a parasite tries to live inside a neutrophil, it will find its home disintegrating soon after it moves in (certainly before it has had time to buy furniture or stock the refrigerator) because neutrophils only live a few days.

Another important function of a neutrophil is that it can "hear" cries of pain coming from cells that are under attack from bacteria. During the attack, certain chemicals are released, which react with proteins on the capillary cells, causing a chain of events that ends with the neutrophil being pulled through the thin slits between the capillary cells and out into the interstitial space between the cells. There, the neutrophil (phagocyte) can start gobbling up the bacteria. Neutrophils are the main ingredient of the white substance we call "pus." The most obvious physical feature of the neutrophil is its very strangely shaped nucleus. The nucleus has three lobes, which are all connected to each other. The odd shape of the nucleus helps the neutrophil to get very flat and slither out of the capillary through those thin cracks between the cells.

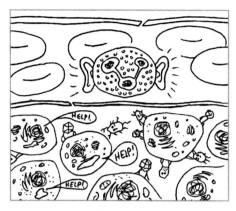

*The neutrophil is always "listening" for distress signals from cells under attack.*

An interesting fact about the neutrophil is that you can determine gender by looking at the nucleus. This can help detectives when analyzing a crime scene. They can gather blood samples, look at the neutrophils, and determine the gender of the victim. The neutrophils of women and girls have an extra bump sticking out of one of the lobes of the nucleus. This bump is the second X chromosome, which is longer than the Y chromosome that men and boys have. The cell in this illustration is from a female. Can you see the extra bump on the bottom lobe of the nucleus?

Neutrophils are the most abundant type of white blood cell. They make up about 65 percent of your white cell population.

The second category of white blood cells are the "cytes"—monocytes and lymphocytes. These cells are not granular; their texture looks smooth. They also have a large, normal-shaped nucleus, not a weird lobed one like the granular cells.

The **monocytes** float around in the blood taking it easy until they are called into action. Like the other white cells, they squeeze through the cracks in the capillaries and get out into the spaces between the cells. Once they have left the capillaries, they are called **macrophages**. This just means "big eaters." (Just to confuse you, sometimes they are also referred to as phagocytes, the same as neutrophils. We did warn you about blood cell terminology being a bit confusing!) They go around gobbling up all sorts of nasty stuff that you don't want in your body, including your own cells that have become infected with viruses.

Monocytes make up only about 5 percent of your white cell population. Half of them are stored in your spleen and are mobilized in about 8 hours if you come down with an infection. If you come down with a disease called "mononucleosis" you will have an increased number of these in your blood. Part of the diagnosis for this disease is a blood test where they count the number of monocytes.

*This lymphocyte could be a T-cell, or a B-cell, or an NK.*

The **lymphocytes** are the most complicated of all the white cells. (Buckle your intellectual seat belts!) There are three kinds of lymphocytes: **T cells, B cells and NK cells**. All lymphocytes are "born" in the bone marrow (like all blood cells) but the T-cells mature in the <u>t</u>hymus (a small organ in front of your heart and lungs) and the B-cells mature in the <u>b</u>ones. "Natural killer" cells, or NK cells, mature in the tonsils and in lymph nodes. The lymphocytes all look the same when viewed under the microscope. You can't tell the difference between a T-cell and a B-cell. You have to do chemical testing to sort out T's from B's from NK's. Lymphocytes make up about 25 percent of your total white cell population.

There are *three basic kinds of T-cells: helper cells, suppressor cells and cytotoxic cells*. Just as their name implies, the T-helper cells secrete chemicals that help the other immune cells do their job more efficiently. The T-suppressor cells keep the immune system from going overboard. Once their job is done, the killer cells need to stop killing! The cytotoxic cells are, as the name implies, toxic to cells. This type of cell can poison and kill any type of cell that it sees as "bad." This includes bacteria cells, body cells that have already been infected with viruses, and "rogue" cells such as tumor cells.

The *B-cells*' main job is to make antibodies. Antibodies are sort of like "tags" that are put on cells that need to be destroyed. A phagocyte will eat anything that has an antibody tag on it. B-cells are what allows your immune system to "remember" invaders that have come in the past. There are "memory cells" that hold onto antibodies for years. This is why you become immune to diseases you've already had (like chicken pox, for example). Your B-cells keep those antibodies tags for a very long time. If you get exposed that disease again, your B-cells are ready and they launch an immediate attack, preventing the germs from making you sick.

The *natural killer cells* are... natural killers. They are mindless robot cells that go around killing anything that has an antibody tag on it. Like the cytotoxic T-cells, they will attack bacteria, virus-infected body cells and tumor cells. (But those things have to be tagged by the B-cells first.)

We keep mentioning how abundant each type of white cell is in comparison to the other white cells. Here's a quick summary (for those of you who like statistics):

Basophils:  about 1%
Eosinophils:   about 3%
Neutrophils:  about 6%
Lymphocytes (T, B, NK):  about 25%
Monocytes (macrophages):  about 65%

The types of cells we have looked at in this chapter are not the only types of cells in the body. There are many other types of cells that secrete various fluids or chemicals, such as salivary glands (saliva), mammary glands (milk), lacrimal glands (tears), and gastric glands (digestive enzymes). There are cells in the hormonal glands such as the thyroid and pituitary. There are photoreceptors in the eyes, chemical-sensors in the nose, and taste buds on the tongue. There's liver cells, kidney cells... but we've got to end somewhere. Now that you know the basics of how cells work, you can go on and read about other types of cells and be able to understand how they are suited to their role in the body.

## ACTIVITY 1   More about blood cells

If you'd like to know more about blood cells check out this very creative video series on YouTube: "Blood Cell Bakery." Sounds gross? Actually, it's just a teacher who teaches science using cookies. Not so bad, eh? She'll teach you about blood cells using cookies and candies. (All the "Blood Cell Bakery" videos are listed at YouTube.com/TheBasementWorkshop on the "Cells" playlist.)

## ACTIVITY 2   More about bones

If you want to learn a little bit more about bones, you can find a few not-too-complicated videos by using the key words "osteoclast formation" (actual microscope footage) or "introduction to bone biology" (computer-generated animations). By using these exact key words, the intended videos should be right at the top of the list.

NOTE: Most Internet videos about types of cells are very technical or very boring (or both). They have been posted to help college students study for exams. There isn't a lot out there for younger students. It would be nice if there was a "Bone Cell Bakery" and an "Epithelial Bakery," but there isn't. (Perhaps the "Blood Cell Bakery" can inspire you to make your own edible cells!)

\* \* \* \* \* \* \* \* \* \* \* \* \* \* \* \* \* \* \* \* \* \* \* \* \* \* \* \* \* \* \* \* \* \* \* \* \* \* \* \* \* \* \* \* \* \* \* \* \* \* \* \* \* \* \* \* \* \* \* \* \* \* \* \* \* \* \* \* \* \* \* \* \* \* \* \*

**Can you remember what you read? If you can't think of the answer, go back and read that part of the chapter again until you find the answer.**

1) What does "epi" mean? _____

2) In what kind of cell would you find keratin?
   a) muscle cell   b) bone cell   c) skin cell   d) nerve cell   e) goblet cell

3) What is the scientific word for "programmed cell death"? _____

4) Which of these shapes is the closest to being like a skin cell?
   a) ball   b) box   c) cylinder   d) pyramid

5) What do goblet cells make?
   a) mucus   b) blood   c) plasma   d) keratin   e) enzymes

6) Which of these is NOT a type of epithelial cell?
   a) skin cell   b) goblet cell   c) capillary cell   d) bone cell   e) villi

7) What does "osteo" mean? _____

8) TRUE or FALSE?  Collagen is flexible.

9) What mineral do bone cells use to harden the bones?
   a) calcium   b) phosphorus   c) magnesium   d) all of these

10) TRUE or FALSE?  Once a bone is mature, the minerals are permanently "locked in."

11) TRUE or FALSE?  Bones are alive.

12) Which type of cell is most like a bone cell (in shape)?
    a) red blood cell    b) neuron    c) skin cell    d) muscle cell    e) white blood cell    f) goblet cell

13) "Sarco" and "myo" refer to:
    a) muscles    b) bones    c) blood    d) nerves    e) none of these

14) Which of these does NOT have mitochondria?
    a) muscle cell    b) goblet cell    c) white blood cell    d) red blood cell

15) What do Schwann cells do?
    a) secrete enzymes    b) protect neurons    c) mineralize bones    d) make sweat    e) filter toxins

16) Which kind of cell loses its own identity and merges with other cells to become one large cell?
    a) muscle cell    b) goblet cell    c) skin cell    d) villi    e) neuron    f) bone cell

17) What is the primary function of the sarcoplasmic reticulum?
    a) help ribosomes make proteins    b) conduct electrical signals    c) make vesicles    d) store calcium

18) Where would you find hemoglobin?
    a) in all cells    b) in nerve cells    c) in red blood cells    d) in natural killer cells    e) in muscle cells

19) What do you call the "arms" that branch off the cell body of a neuron?  _____

20) Which of these does a red blood cell not have?
    a) nucleus    b) Golgi bodies    c) ribosomes    d) ER    e) lysosomes    f) all of these

21) What kind of "phils" does your body have the most of?
    a) basophils    b) eosinophils    c) neutrophils

22) Which type of cells "spazz out" and creates a huge histamine mess?
    a) basophils    b) eosinophils    c) neutrophils

23) Which type of cells clean up after an allergic reaction?
    a) basophils    b) eosinophils    c) neutrophils

24) Where are blood cells "born"?
    a) in the blood    b) in bones    c) in lymph tisse    d) in the spleen

25) Where do B cells mature?
    a) in the blood    b) in bones    c) in lymph tissue    d) in the thymus

26) If "phil" is Greek for "to like" then what to basophils, eosinophils and neutrophils like? _____

27) Which kind of white cells give you immunity to diseases you've already had?
    a) T-cells    b) B-cells    c) NK cells    d) phagotcytes

28) How long do red blood cells live?
    a) a few days    b) a few weeks    c) a few months    d) a few years

# INDEX

This section can help you find something if you can't remember where you read it.

# TEACHER'S SECTION

# ANSWER KEY

CHAPTER 1 (page 6):
1) b, 2) d, 3) c, 4) F, 5) a, 6) F, 7) T, 8) T, 9) d, 10) c, 11) F, 12) b, 13) F, 14) a, 15) F
16) Scanning Electron Microscope, 17) F

CHAPTER 2 (page 14):
1) b, 2) b, 3) a, $0 d, 5) a, 6) lipid tail, 7) d, 8) T, 9)b, 10) a, 11) a, 12) a, 13) cytoplasm or cytosol
14) motor proteins, 15) b, 16) T, 17) c, 18) barrels

CHAPTER 3 (page 20):
1) ATP, 2) c, 3) a phosphate, 4) T, 5) b, 6) to make, 7) 3, 8) c, 9) mitochondria, 10) c, 11) a, 12) F
13) diffusion, 14) a, 15) c

CHAPTER 4 (page 31):
1) a, 2) F, 3) amino acids, 4) 20, 5) F, 6) d, 7) c, 8) sugar, phosphates, bases, 9) b, 10) sense
11) nonsense, 12) sense, 13) b, 14) b, 15) c, 16) c, 17) F, 18) T, 19) uracil

Crossword puzzle on page 32:
Across:   2) uracil, 4) centrosome, 6) ribosome, 11) DNA, 12) chaperone, 14) microtubules, 17) acid
18) phospholipid, 19) transcription, 21) diffusion, 22) cytoplasm, 23) protein, 24) nucleus, 25) synthase
Down:   1) translation, 3) adenine, 5) ptotons, 7) membrane, 8) microfilaments, 9) helix,
10) mitochondria, 12) cytoskeleton, 13) hydrophilic, 15) ATP, 16) hydrophobic, 20) nitrogen

CHAPTER 5 (page 42):
1) b, 2) a, 3) d, 4) c, 5) F, 6) F, 7) c, 8) a, 9) F, 10) T, 11) b, 12) d, 13) c, 14) T, 15) b, 16) F

CHAPTER 6 (page49):
1) endoplasmic reticulum, 2) b, 3) a, 4) c, 5) a, 6) d, 7) F, 8) d, 9) T, 10) F, 11) a, 12) 8, 13) 2,
14) T, 15) c, 16) d, 17) T, 18) F, 19) F, 20) c, 21) a, 22) sugars, phosphates, bases, 23) nonsense
24) d, 25) c, 26) c, 27) a, 28) d, 29) lipid tail, 30) b, 31) b, 32) c, 33) b, 34) a, 35) diffusion

CHAPTER 7 (page 60):
1) b, 2) a, 3) b, 4) c, 5) a, 6) d, 7) b, 8) c, 9) c, 10) c, 11) b, 12) d, 13) a, 14) d, 15) d, 16) d, 17) b

CHAPTER 8 (page 68)
1) a, 2) F, 3) b, 4) T, 5) b, 6) c, 7) a, 8) centrosome, 9) b, 10) d, 11) meiosis, 12) 23, 13) b, 14) a,
15) T
16) e, 17) T

Activity 4—Number puzzle (on page 67):
1) 36, 2) 8, 3) 10, 4) 1, 5) 3, 6) 6 billion, 7) 40, 8) 2, 9) 14, 10) 20, 11) 23, 12) 5, 13) 4, 14) 7
15) 10,000, 16) 146

CHAPTER 9 (page 79):
1) "outer" or "outside"  2) C, 3) apoptosis, 4) B, 5) A, 6) D, 7) bone, 8) T, 9) D, 10) F, 11) T, 12) B
13) A, 14) D, 15) B, 16) A, 17) D, 18) C, 19) dendrites, 20) F, 21) C, 22) A, 23) B, 24) B, 25) B,
26) stain, 27) B, 28) C

# SUPPLEMENTAL ACTIVITIES

## CHAPTER 1

Most of the recommended activities for this chapter are printed in the student booklet. If you have microscopes available and want to try viewing cork cells, that is fairly easily done. Just make sure to slice your cork in a thin wedge shape. Look for cells way out on the edge where it gets extremely thin. However, you'll find that cork cells are pretty boring and the students won't be that impressed by what they see. The cork cells are dead and look very empty.

### 1) SUPPLEMENTAL VIDEO

Here is a nice supplemental video (7 minutes long) about Leeuwenhoek that you might want to consider using. It's not listed in the student text simply because, at exactly 2 minutes and 3 seconds into it, they show a classical painting that has a female figure with one breast partially showing. Depending on your audience, this may or may not be a problem. For a high school audience, it shouldn't be a big deal. It's just a classical painting you'd see in a European art gallery. For an elementary audience, you could just put your hand over the lens at 2:02 and take it off at 2:05. Otherwise, it's a great video. Don't hesitate to use it if you are looking for more resources on Leeuwenhoek.

http://www.youtube.com/watch?v=_D5Gu_9hEus

### 2) INTERACTIVE COMPUTER ACTIVITY: HOW BIG IS A CELL?

This interactive activity lets students zoom in and out on a series of microscopic things, starting with a coffee bean and a grain of rice and ending with a carbon atom. Cells and cell parts are shown along they way, along with bacteria and viruses.

http://learn.genetics.utah.edu/content/begin/cells/scale/

## CHAPTER 2

### 1) DEMONSTRATION: A FLUID MOSAIC MODEL

This activity helps students to understand the fluid nature of the membrane. We mentioned in the text that the phospholipid molecules can move around, sort of like ping pong balls floating in a bathtub. This demonstration is a fun way to help them understand this concept.

**You will need:**
- a large, shallow metal or plastic tray of some kind (a 9x13 cake pan would be adequate)
- a pitcher of water
- a bag of "miniature" marshmallows (these will represent the heads of the phospholipid molecules)
- Chunks of apple that are slightly larger than the mini-marshmallows (You could also use chunks of Styrofoam® or anything else that is waterproof and will float.) Cut some of the chunks into thick discs you can use to represent lipid rafts. Cut some oddly shaped chunks that you can use to represent proteins.
- a few toothpicks

**What to tell the students:**
*This will be a demonstration to show what it means when scientists say that a phospholipid membrane is a "fluid mosaic." The word "mosaic" means a pattern made from small pieces. "Fluid" means "flowing." In this demonstration, we will pretend we are looking down on the outer membrane of a cell. We will only be able to see the heads of the phospholipid molecules. The marshmallows will represent these phospholipid heads. We will see how lipid rafts and membrane-bound proteins can move around in and among the phospholipids.*

**What to do:**
Pour at least an inch of water into the tray. Dump in marshmallows until they cover most of the surface of the water. Add your representations of lipid rafts and membrane-bound proteins. You might want to use a few toothpicks to create proteins that are sticking up above the surface. Fill in any remaining gaps with marshmallows.

Allow the students to gently push the rafts and the proteins around. (You could even provide very small chunks of "protein" that they could set on top of the lipid rafts.) Notice how the marsh-mallows won't allow an empty patch of water. They immediately fill any gaps you try to create. The surface of the water remains covered at all times even though the positions of the rafts and proteins are constantly changing.

**Extra tips:**
You might want to put a bath towel under your pan to absorb any slop-over accidents. You might also want to have some paper towels on hand.

## 2) DEMONSTRATION: SIMULATE THE MERGING OF MEMBRANES

This demonstration may seem almost too obvious and too simple. Because of its simplicity, we hesitated to use this demonstration with our middle school students (ages 12-14), but found that they had great enthusiasm for it and thoroughly enjoyed it.

We tried both plastic and paper plates. On our Styrofoam plates, the oil droplets tended to move to the sides. Oil is a non-polar substance and will move toward other non-polar substances, like plastic or Styrofoam, and away from polar substances, like water. (This would be an optional side discussion if you are looking for ways to emphasize chemistry.) If the paper plates are coated with wax (another non-polar substance) you may see the same thing happening. However, this problem is not a major one and if disposable plates are the obvious choice for your situation, go ahead and use them.

These instructions are for a single experiment using one plate. If you have more than two or three students, use multiple plates.

**You will need:**
- a plate (paper, plastic, or ceramic, but white or very light-colored)
- some cooking oil
- a pitcher of water
- optional: toothpicks or spoons to push oil droplets around (if you want to avoid oily fingers)
- paper towels
- optional: large containers to dispose of the used oil/water mix (if you are in a classroom)

**What to tell the students:**
*In this demonstration, we will simulate the way membranes can merge together simply by coming into contact with each other. In future chapters, we will see how important this merging of membranes is to a cell. We will be using oil to represent a phospholipid sphere. Your job to observe the behavior of oil droplets as they come into contact with each other. The behavior of the oil droplets is similar to the behavior of phospholipid membranes.*

**What to do:**

Pour some water into the plate until the bottom is covered. Then add some small circles of oil at various places on the plate. Tell the students to push the droplets around (either with fingers or the utensils—as you choose) and observe what happens when they touch. The students will observe that when two droplets touch, they instantaneously merge and become one larger droplet. Encourage the students to experiment. Is it possible to make an oil patch that looks like the letter O? How hard is it to split a large droplet into two or more smaller droplets? If left undisturbed, do the droplets initiate any movement toward each other? How close can two droplets be before they merge?

**Additional experiment:** What happens when you add a drop or two of food coloring to the water?


## 3) GROUP ACTIVITY: A "HUMAN MEMBRANE"

This activity can only be done with a fairly large group of students. You might be able to do it with a dozen students, but more is better. This activity is ideal for kinetic learners and social learners, but it's fun for everyone, too.

**You will need:**
- a fairly large space (but an average-sized classroom will do, if you move the tables and chairs)
- a few small balls (ping pong or tennis balls) and one large ball (basketball size or larger)
- a long stick to be a "flag" (cell identification marker) You might even want to tape a piece of paper to the end, that says something like, "I belong" or "I am part of the body" or even the name of one of the students.
- a camera to record this unusual event!

**What to tell the students:**

*In this activity, each of you will represent a phospholipid molecule. You will need to line up in pairs, just like real phospholipid molecules do. You can pretend that your head is the water-loving head of the phospholipid and you can stretch our your arms to be the water-hating tails. Just like in a real membrane, your water-hating tails will face each other and your water-loving heads will be on the out-side. After you have lined up and created your membrane, we will do some demonstrations that show how the membrane works.*

**What to do:**

Line up the students in two rows, facing each other, but not too close. Tell them that their heads will represent phosphate heads. Then have them put their arms out straight in front of them to represent the two lipid tails. Their hands should come close but not touch. (If you have enough students, try to form a circular membrane, as this is what phospholipids would do. One group of students would form an inner ring with their hands pointing out, and the others would form an outer ring with their hands pointing in.)

With the students lined up and modeling a piece of membrane, show the students a few small balls and tell them the balls represent very small molecules such as water or oxygen or carbon dioxide. Then gently toss or roll the balls between the students, in the spaces between legs and feet. Emphasize that this is to show that small molecules can pass right through the membrane. Then show them the large ball. Say that this represents a very large molecule, such as a food molecule or a piece of protein. Demonstrate that the molecule will not be able to slip through. (The students should be standing close enough together that the large ball can't get through the space between their legs or bodies. Then ask if anyone remembers how cells regulate the entry and exit of large molecules. *(portal proteins)* Volunteer one pair of students in the middle to be a portal protein. Have them turn to the side

and put their arms out to their sides. Designate one side to be "outside" the cell and give the ball to the portal protein who is on that side. Have the outer protein pass the ball to the inner protein. The inner protein can then just let go of the ball or give it a gentle toss into the "inside of the cell."

Volunteer a student on the outer side of the membrane to pull their hands in and a long stick to hold up. This

On the left, one student is playing the role of a portal protein. The ball is a molecule. On the right, the student with the flag is playing the role of an ID protein, letting all other cells know that it is part of the body and not an invader.

pretend to be a protein instead of a phospholipid. Then give him/her will represent an identifying "flag" that will tell all other cells that come into contact with it that it's part of the body and not a foreign invader. These tags are especially important to the cells of the immune system (white blood cells) as they go about on their search and destroy missions, looking for cells that don't belong to the body. White cells know not to attack any cell that is displaying this identifying flag.

**Extra tip:** Don't forget to take some pictures!

## 4) CRAFT:  MOTOR PROTEIN PENS

Even "craft-shy" students will probably like this craft because it is so bizarre.  The students will be making a model of a motor protein that is also a functional pen they can write with.

NOTE:  There are full-color pictures of this craft available for download at: www.ellenjmchenry.com.  Click on FREE DOWNLOADS, then on HUMAN BODY, then look for the link titled "Color pictures for "Cells" curriculum."

### You will need the following for each student:
  • a ballpoint pen (the kind with the cap that comes off)
  • a handful of assorted colored beads for each student (miscellaneous sizes, shapes and colors)
  • chenille stems (3 per student)
  • floral tape (the green tape florists use—it doesn't feel very sticky) One roll will be enough for up to 20 students.
  • some kind of ball  (You will have to determine what kind of ball will work best for your situation.  We found very inexpensive hollow plastic Christmas tree balls that worked very nicely.  You could also use a Styrofoam™ ball, or any lightweight plastic ball.  If you can't find any suitable balls, just improvise. You could use heavy card stock paper to make a cube or a dodecahedron.  (If you need a pattern, you can use the virus dodecahedron pattern at: www.ellenjmchenry.com/homeschool-freedownloads/ lifesciences-games/virusmodels.php)  Just make sure the ball is not too heavy.  A heavy ball will make writing with the pen difficult.

### What to tell the students:
*You will be making a model of a motor protein.  The ball on the top will represent a protein that is being carried.  At the bottom of the motor protein will be two things that look like legs.  In fact, they are very much like legs.  They walk along a microtubule as you would walk on a sidewalk.  The model will contain many plastic beads that will represent the structural proteins from which the motor protein is made. The nice thing about this model is that it is also useful.  It will also be a pen you can write with. You can have a lot of fun making people guess what it is, then explaining about motor proteins.*

**How to assemble the pen:**

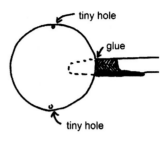
tiny hole

glue

tiny hole

1) Take the cap off the pen and put it on the other end, as if you were going to write with the pen. Press it on as firmly as you can.

2) Drill or punch a hole in the ball. The hole must be just the right size so tat it fits onto the cap at the halfway point. (see drawing at right) Adhere the ball to the pen with appropriate glue. (Recommendation: "Quick Grip" or a similar all-purpose hobby glue that is clear, has a thick texture, and dries quickly. This type of glue is often a bit smelly, but not dangerously so.)

3) Drill or punch two more holes in the ball. These should be very small holes— just large enough to accommodate the end of a chenille stem.

secure bead
at end

4) Take two of the chenille stems and secure a bead to one end of each stem. Just loop the chenille stem around, give it a twist and tuck the end back into the bead. Make sure there isn't a sharp metal end sticking out. Then thread some beads onto them until you've covered about 5 cm (2 inches) of the chenille stem. The measurement does not have to be exact.

thread on some beads

5) Lay the chenille stems alongside the pen so that the yet-to-beaded part is flush with the pen tip. (see drawing for clarification) Wrap some floral tape around at the tip, to secure them, then wind the tape up the pen about 4 cm (1.5 inches). The measurement does not have to be exact. Tear off the tape and continue wrapping until the end of the tape is sealed on. Press firmly. Floral tape won't seem very sticky so you may think it won't hold, but surprisingly, it will adhere very well and will stay in place even while the pen is being used to write with. The floral tape won't stick to fingers, just to itself. (For further clarification, look at the color pictures in the appendix.)

lay the chenilles along the sides of the pen

6) Thread some more beads along those two chenille stems until you reach about 2 cm (3/4 inch) from the end. Those two ends will fit into the small holes you drilled or punched in the ball. (Look at color picture in appendix.) You may want to glue the ends of the stems into these holes. (Ours stayed secure even without glue.)

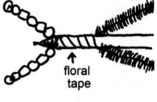
floral tape

7) You may need to make adjustments for your particular situation, depending on what you are using as a ball and how large your beads are. Use the color pictures in the appendix as guides for the general concept, then make necessary adjustments according to the materials you are working with.

8) Secure a third chenille stem to one of the side stems right at the top of the floral tape. Begin a pattern in which you alternate winding with threading a few beads on. Wind tightly. Once again, look at the color photo in the appendix to see how it will look. (Yours doesn't need to look exactly like this one.)

9) After you have wound to the top, right under the ball, secure the chenille stem to one of the beads (or the stems) right under the ball.

10) To use the pen, move the "legs" upward, out of the way of the paper. When not writing, move them back down so they look like legs again.


## 5) CRAFT: MAKE A SMALL PAPER MODEL OF A MEMBRANE

Cut and assemble a small, three-dimensional paper model of a piece of membrane. (It includes membrane-bound proteins and portal protein.) Finished dimensions: 8 cm (3 in.) wide, 18 cm (7.5 in.) long, and about 8 cm (3 in.) high. You will need paper copies of pattern pieces, scissors, clear tape or some glue sticks, and colored pencils if you want to color the model (it comes in black and white).

Go to: **http://learn.genetics.utah.edu,** click on "Teacher Resources and Lesson Plans" (top right corner), then click on "Print-and-Go Lesson Plan Index" (on right side), then scroll down and click on "Amazing Cells: Supplemental Materials" then scroll down and click on "Build-A-Membrane."

## 6) ACTIVE GAME:  MOTOR PROTEIN RELAY RACE
This activity is mainly about having fun pretending to be a motor protein.

**You will need:**
- a fairly large space (long and narrow is fine, like a hallway)
- two very large, but lightweight, objects such as beach balls (or other large inflatables) or the balance balls commonly used for exercise programs in gyms.
- a roll of toilet paper
- some duct tape or blue masking tape (painter's tape that isn't very sticky) to secure the toilet paper to the floor at each end and to make repairs to the paper if it tears.  Clear tape or regular masking tape could also be used to make repairs.  Just don't use anything on the floor that won't come off easily!  (We've found that on carpeted floors, almost any tape comes off easily.)
- two pieces of wide elastic, tied at the ends to make loops that will fit tightly but comfortably around the knees

**What to tell the students:**

In this relay race, you will play the role of a motor protein carrying a large protein molecule while walking down a microtubule road.  You will have to walk carefully so as not to tear the microtubule!  If you tear it, someone on your team will have to come and repair it before you continue.  Cells often have to repair parts of their cytoskeleton and they can do it very quickly and efficiently.  They can effect a repair in a fraction of a second.  Your repairs will take a bit longer than that!  The goal of the race is to have every member of the team take a turn as the motor protein, traveling down the microtubule and back again.

**How to set up for the race:**
You will need to roll out two long pieces of toilet paper.  Make them stretch almost the full length of your space, leaving just a bit of space at the beginning for the team members.  Secure the ends with tape.  Leave the roll of tape at the starting line so the team members can use it if they need to make repairs.

Have a loop of elastic for each team at the starting line.  (Also, have the balls ready at the starting line.)

**How to run the relay race:**
Divide the group into two teams.  (If you have an odd number of students, assign one student on the smaller team to go twice.)

The first runners stick their feet into an elastic loop and pull it up to just above their knees.  They are only allowed to move the lower part of their legs, below the elastic.  This will make them move more like a real motor protein.  (Motor proteins don't have jointed legs with ankles, knees and hips!)  It will also add a humorous "twist" to the relay race and make it more fun.  Then the runners pick up a ball and hold it over their heads.  Now they are ready to start down the microtubule road.  They must walk along the toilet paper without tearing it.  If it tears, one of the team members must take a piece of tape and go fix the tear.  The mending job doesn't have to be great.  The minimum is that the two ends of the paper must be touching.   When the runners reach the end, they turn around and come back.  Then they put down the ball and take the elastic off their legs, handing them to the next runner in the line.

The first team to get all their members down and back wins the race!

# CHAPTER 3

## 1) DEMONSTRATION: DIFFUSION

These three activities will allow the students to see diffusion happening. In the first two demonstrations, diffusion happens relatively quickly. In the third, diffusion takes place over the course of a few days.

### DEMO #1: Diffusion in the air

**You will need:**
• some aromatic items from your kitchen—perhaps a bag of coffee, or a bottle of vinegar, or a piece of citrus fruit you can slice. Just use what you have handy.

**What to tell the students:**

*In this demonstration you will not be able to see anything. You will not have to use your eyes at all. In fact, you can keep your eyes closed. You will be using your sense of smell. You will be sensing the diffusion of a certain substance into the air. It may take a while for the molecules of the substance to fill the room, but we know that they will eventually do so, because the principle of diffusion says that substances go from areas of high concentration to areas of lower concentration.*

**What to do:**

Open the jar or bag (or slice the fruit) and leave it in one corner of the room. Have the students sit in various parts of the room. As soon as a student smells the smell, have them raise their hand. The students close to the food will smell it first and those far away will smell it last. How long it takes for the smell to cross the room will depend partly on the chemistry of the food. Some substances get into the air more quickly, being more "volatile." The smell of vinegar, for example, will probably fill the room more quickly than an open bag of coffee grounds. (But you never know for sure until you try it!)

### DEMO #2: Diffusion in water

**You will need:**
• a clear glass of water
• a few drops of food coloring
• optional—watch or clock

**What to tell the students:**

*In this demonstration you will see diffusion in a liquid. You will drop some food coloring into a glass of clear water, then watch as the dye spreads out and fills the glass. Before you drop in the dye, guess how many minutes it will take for the dye to completely color the water. Then time it and see how close you were to being right. But remember—no shaking or stirring the water! Let diffusion do all the work.*

**What to do:**

Put a drop of food coloring into the glass of water and then wait to see what happens. DO NOT stir or shake the glass. Let it sit undisturbed. Observe what happens over the course of about 5 minutes. At first the food coloring will stay in a swirl, but as the minutes go by, it will gradually spread out. If you wait long enough, the dye will eventually distribute itself evenly and the original swirl shape will be gone. What do you notice about the intensity of the color in the water at the end of the demonstration compared to the intensity of the original swirl of color right when the drop entered the water? (The diffused color will be much lighter.)

**DEMO #3: Diffusion through a membrane**

**NOTE: This demonstration will take at least four days.**

**You will need:**
- an egg (or several eggs, if you want to have "back-ups")
- a glass (or small jar) of vinegar
- a glass (or small jar) of corn syrup (or you can substitute honey or pancake syrup)
- a glass of water
- a piece of string (for measuring the circumference of the egg)

**What to tell the students:**

     *This experiment involves a membrane. It will be thicker than the plasma membrane of a cell, but this membrane will function in a similar manner by allowing only small particles to pass through it. There is a special word for diffusion that happens across a cell membrane. It is called osmosis. In this demonstration you will see that water, being a very small molecule, is able to pass through the membrane. The membrane will not allow larger molecules to go through it.*

     *We will be using an egg as our cell model. The first part of this demonstration will be simply getting rid of the shell in order to expose the membrane. The second part of the demonstration will be to test diffusion through the membrane.*

**What to do:**

     Put the egg into a glass (or jar) of vinegar. (You may want to cover the glass or screw a lid on the jar in order to avoid the constant smell of vinegar.) Let it sit for a day or two until the shell of the egg has been completely dissolved and the egg has nothing but a soft membrane around it. At this point, be very careful when handling the egg. Remove the egg from the vinegar and rinse it off. Gently wrap the string around the center of the egg and make a mark on the string to indicate the size of the egg. You might even want to lay this piece of string on a ruler and get the measurement in centimeters or inches. Then put the egg into the glass of syrup. Again, let it sit for several days. Take the egg out and measure it again. Did it get bigger or smaller? Can you figure out why? Now put the egg into a glass of water and let it sit overnight. Take it out and measure it again. What happened?

**What is supposed to happen:**

     The egg should get smaller after sitting in the syrup because the water will diffuse out of the egg and into the syrup. The concentration of water is higher inside the egg than outside, so water will flow out. The syrup molecules would like to diffuse into the egg where the concentration is lower, but they cannot because they are too large to go through the membrane. After the egg is taken out of the syrup and put into water, the concentration of water is greater outside the egg, so water will diffuse back into the egg again.

**2) ACTIVE GAME: A TABLE-TOP RELAY RACE ABOUT THE ELECTRON TRANSPORT CHAIN**

     This relay race doesn't require a lot of space like a normal relay race does. It is designed to be a table-top game, but you can adapt the race to the space you are working with. We used two 8-foot tables. If you only have one table, you could put a relay each side. Or you could make just one relay set-up and have the teams take turns using it. You can use a stop watch to time each team's race, then compare their times.

     The set-up for this activity is bit lengthy. If you have enough class time, you may want to have the students work on making the parts ahead of time. If you have very limited class time for activities, you'll have to make the parts yourself and spend the class time doing the race. It takes one person about 30-45 minutes to cut and assemble all the paper parts.

**Helpful suggestion:** Before you begin preparing, watch the video demonstration of this activity. It can be accessed via the YouTube channel for this curriculum (YouTube.com/TheBasementWorkshop, "Cells" playlist, chapter 3 videos).

**You will need:**
- colored card stock (8 sheets per relay set-up)
- the patterns on the following pages
- clear tape and/or glue stick
- scissors
- some small tokens to represent electrons, protons and oxygens (I used red and white dried beans for the electrons and protons, and walnuts for the oxygens, but you can use whatever you have on hand. Just make sure they are small, like dried beans.) For each relay set-up you will need a minimum of 4 tokens for electrons, 12 for protons and 2 for oxygens.
- plastic or paper cups (two per relay set-up)
- a cardboard tube that has a diameter smaller than the bottom of the cups (one tube per set-up)
- something to represent ATPs (large and small marshmallows on a toothpick, paper circles taped to a toothpick or whatever works well in your situation—even Legos®) You will need 4 ATPs per set-up.
- black marker

**How to prepare:**

1) Print or copy the pattern pages onto the colored card stock. (If you did not purchase the CD version of this curriculum and you would like a digital (PDF) version of the patterns so you can print right from your computer, there is a free download of these patterns available online. Go to ellenjmchenry.com and click on "Curricula" then on "Cells." The downloads are at the bottom of this page.) Feed the colored card stock into either your computer printer tray or the manual tray of the copier you are using. For each relay set-up, print three copies of the first two pages (the one with the holes and the one with the two trays) and one copy of the other two pages.

2) Cut out the holes on the pages with holes, and then roll the paper into a tube. Secure with tape.

3) Cut apart the rectangles (each one being exactly one fourth of a sheet of 8.5x11 paper) and roll each lengthwise so form a small tube. You don't need to tape these smaller tubes—you can just insert them into the large cylinders and then let the small tubes expand to fill the hole, thus holding them in place (see illustration below).

4) Cut and assemble the large, shallow trays, cutting on the solid lines and folding on the dotted lines. Tape the corners so you have a square tray. Then tape a tray to the top of each large cylinder.

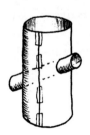 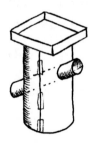

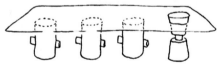

NOTE: An arrangement like this would be a more realistic representation because it would show that the pumps and the synthase machine are all connected to the same membrane, but this configuration would be more difficult to make as well as more difficult to play. Make sure the students understand that the pumps don't really have individual trays on top.

5) Cut and assemble the deeper rectangular trays, cutting on the solid lines and folding on the dotted lines. Bend the ends in to make a square corner and secure with tape. Mark one "NADH." The other two will be the shuttles between the ion pumps. The first shuttle can hold two electrons, the second only one. You may want   to label the bottom of the tray to this effect so the students won't have to remember this. They'll just look at the bottom of the tray, read the number, and know how many electrons can be shuttled. If you want to put the names of the shuttles on the trays, the first shuttle (between pumps 1 and 2) is called "Ubiquinone" *(you-BICK-wih-noan)* and the second (between pumps 2 and 3) is "Cytochrome C."

**6)** Cut out the squares with the $H_2O$ molecules on them. For each $H_2O$, cut out two short strips and one long strip and roll them so the ends overlap until the strips are the same circumference as the printed circles. Secure with tape. Then secure the circles to the "platform" by taping the tabs down. (Refer to the assembly picture on the pattern page.) Assemble the $O_2$ molecule the same way, using two long strips. If you are going to play the shorter format of the race (see "How to play" instructions) you won't need the $O_2$ molecule, and you'll only need one $H_2O$.

**7)** Now you need to make the ATP synthase "machine." Cut holes in the bottoms of the cups, the same size as the diameter of your tube. If you are making a tube out of card stock you can just cut the holes whatever size you want, roll the card stock, stick it into the holes, then let it expand (just like you did for the small tubes in the sides of the cylinders). If your synthase machine is wobbly, add some tape to make it more sturdy. You may want to label the machine, either on the cup or by adding a paper label sticking up out of the top cup. You might also want to add: 3 protons → 1 ATP so they don't forget how many proton tokens to put into the machine to get an ATP.

**8)** Prepare your ADPs and phosphates. Use whatever materials you think will work well in your situation. You may have some craft parts or food items on hand that work well. They don't even have to be round—you could use Lego® bricks. Just make sure you have three small items and one large one for each ATP. Assemble ADPs (one large and two smalls) and leave the third phosphates unattached. The phosphates will be hidden in the bottom of the synthase machine.

**9)** If you want to do more labeling, the names of the ion pumps (in order) are: "NADH Dehydrogenase," "Cytochrome b-c$_1$" and "Cytochrome Oxidase."

### How to set up the relay:

You can have any amount of space between the objects. Even though the race was designed to be a table-top race, you don't necessarily have to use a small space. If you have a large playing area and want to make the players run, you could set these quite a distance apart.

You can put out a whole bunch of tokens, enough so that every player can take their turn without having to worry about resetting the relay at the end of each turn, or you can have the last step of each turn be to reset the relay for the next player. (The shuttles, the $O_2$ and the $H_2O$ molecules will have to be re-set anyway.) If you are doing timed individual runs, you'll have plenty of time to reset. If you have multiple players going through, one after another, you'll have to make them do a quick reset.

### How to play:
(Reminder: Don't forget about the video clip that demonstrates the relay.)

**1)** The first player comes to the NADH "shuttle bus" and puts two electrons into it. He then slides the NADH box across the table until it reaches the first ion pump.

**2)** The player then puts the electrons into the top of the small tube in the first pump. The electrons will slide through and come out the other side. (The player can position the next shuttle so that it catches the electrons as they come out of the tube.) After they come out the other side and drop into the waiting shuttle, the player moves two protons from the table up to the tray on top of that pump.

**3)** The player then moves the shuttle box to the second pump. This time he must put the electrons through one at a time because the shuttle waiting on the other side can only carry one electron. He

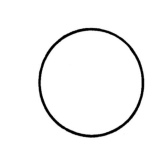

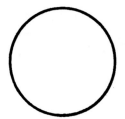

Use these three rectangles for the
smaller tubes that insert into the larger
tubes.  (Roll them lenghthwise.)

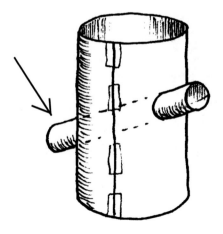

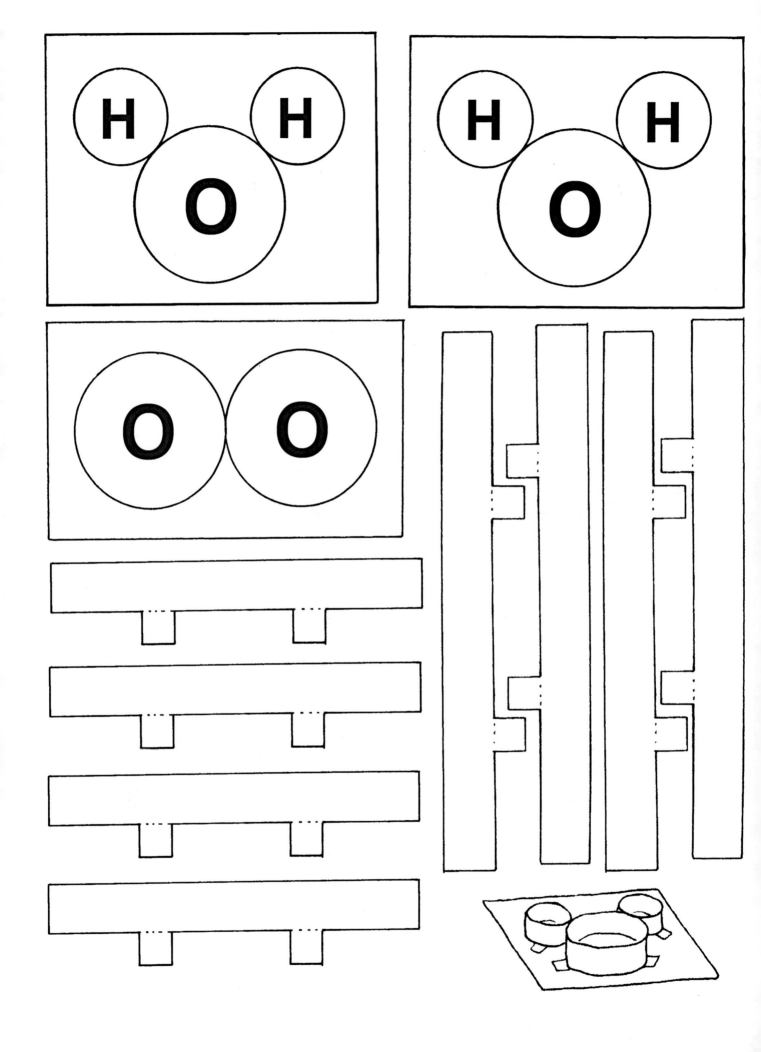

puts one electron through and moves one proton up. Then he must empty the second shuttle. So he pushes it over to the third pump, puts the electron through, and puts it into one of the "H" circles on a water molecule. Then he can go back and repeat this for the second electron. (Put it through the second pump, shuttle it over to the third pump, put it through the third pump then drop it into an "H" circle.)

4) Now the cycle starts again. The player goes back to the beginning and puts another two electrons into the NADH shuttle. The whole process in repeated until you end up with four "expended" electrons, one in each of the "H" circles.

5) Now the player must complete the water molecules by picking up four protons from the table and putting a proton with each electron. Then the oxygen molecule is "split" and one oxygen token is put into each "O" circle on the waters. Now the waters are complete and the trays can be pushed out and away, perhaps to the edge of the table.

6) The last step is to put protons down through the ATP synthase machine. There should be a total of 12 potons available, four on top of each ion pump. Drop three protons into the top cup of the synthase machine (down through the tube, if your tube is hollow), then tilt the machine and remove a phosphate from underneath it. Put this phosphate onto an ADP to make an ATP. Repeat this process until you have made 4 ATPs.

7) Now the turn is over. If you have limited tokens, the player will have to put all the protons back onto the table, the electrons back at the start, and the shuttles back at their starting points. If you have limited ATPs, perhaps the adult helping with the race can dissemble them while the players is replacing all the electrons and protons.

## SHORTER VERSION:
To play a shorter version of the relay, you can make just one water molecule instead of two. Making two water molecules is more accurate because when you split an $O_2$ molecule, the O's have to go somewhere. But for the sake of time and attention span, it may work better in your situation to run through the cycle just once and make just one water molecule and 2 ATPs.

NOTE: Save the parts from this relay! You will use them again in chapter 7.

## 3) CRAFT: ATP "POP GUN"
Instructions for this craft can be found at www.ellenjmchenry.com. Click on FREE DOWNLOADS, then CHEMISTRY.

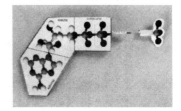

# CHAPTER 4

## 1) CRAFT: PROTEIN "PENCIL TOPPER"
The students will make a "pencil topper" decoration that resembles a computer-generated virtual protein model. This project is a guaranteed success even with students who aren't especially "crafty."

NOTE: This is an art activity. The students do not need to try to replicate an actual protein. There are so many different kinds of proteins in the world that whatever they make is likely to have some resemblance to some protein somewhere. The main point of this activity is to become familiar with what virtual protein models look like, be able to recognize the alpha helix and beta sheet structures, and to understand the importance of protein folding in determining what the protein will do in a cell or in a body. (You may also want to reinforce the concept that a protein folds into a particular shape because of the interactions of the amino acids it is made of.)

### What to tell the students:
*You will be making a model of a protein using flexible craft materials that you can bend and fold into helix or beta sheet formations. Your finished model will go on top of a pencil so it will have a dual purpose as both a scientific model and also something you can write with. (You have a motor protein pen, so now you need a protein pencil to go with it!)*

**You will need:**
- a pencil (new and unsharpened is best)
- a pencil-top eraser (see inset at right)
- about a dozen "chenille stems" of various colors
  (Chenille stems are "pipe cleaners" that are used for craft projects.)
- optional: medium-size craft beads (with a diameter that will allow them to slide onto a chenille stem)
- access to some pictures of computer-generated virtual protein models (You can use the color picture provided in the color pages supplement at www.ellenjmchenry.com, FREE DOWNLOADS, HUMAN BODY, "Color pictures for "Cells" curriculum," but you can also find your own pictures via the Internet. A good source of these virtual models is the web site listed in chapter four: **http://www.thesgc.org/structures/** )

pencil-top eraser

**How to assemble it:**

**1)** The students may make any number of alpha helices or beta sheets (also known as ribbons). To make a helix, simply wind the chenille stem around the pencil. To make a beta sheet (a ribbon) fold the chenille stem back and forth in a zigzag, pushing the zigzag together tightly so that there are no gaps. Students may also wish to have some chenille stems be curled into a random shape (see actual virtual models for ideas).

NOTE: Some proteins have, as part of their design, individual atoms, or groups of atoms, stuck on at various places. Notice the protein shown on the sample page that has two zinc atoms. (For other actual examples, consult the web address listed above.) To represent an atom, slide a bead onto the chenille stem. This is optional—it's completely up to the student whether to use beads or not. Add any beads before connecting the stems.

**2)** Next, you need to fasten all the stems together in a long line, making a continuous amino acid chain. Twist the individual stems together at the ends, overlapping them by about an inch. Make sure to twist tightly so they are secure.

**3)** Finally, bend and fold the chain into a more compact shape, like a real protein bends and folds. Choose where you want to connect your chain to the pencil and add more stem to this end. Curl this end stem around the end of the pencil tightly. (We found that no tape was required. The stem held it adequately.) Slide this curled part down just a bit and put the eraser cap on the end of the pencil, so the curled stem doesn't slide off the end of the pencil. Voila—a protein pencil topper!

**Extra tip:** Let those who finish quickly make an extra for a friend or younger sibling.

## 2) EDIBLE CRAFT: tRNA COOKIES

This craft can be adapted for special nutritional needs. You can use alternative doughs, or even an inedible version that can be just for decoration. (These would make great conversation piece cookies during the winter holiday season!)

**You will need:**
- a cookie recipe and the ingredients it calls for (rolled gingerbread is best because the finished cookies won't break easily, but a rolled sugar cookie will do)
- some very small cake decorations (we used round, flat ones)
- white icing
- some small plastic bags to make disposable "piping" bags for the icing (we found that quart size baggies were stronger and less likely to split open under pressure)
- small bits of yarn or string
- some individually wrapped candies (or you may substitute with something that fits your situation)
- a table knife if you are cutting the cookies "freehand" or an adapted gingerbread man cutter

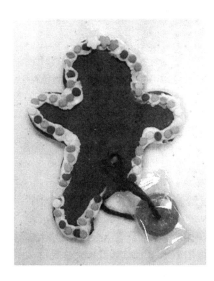

**How to prepare:**

Mix up enough dough so that each student will be able to make several cookies. If you want to use a cookie cutter, you may be able to adapt a gingerbread man cutter by crunching in a leg, folding it tightly, perhaps with a pair of pliers. We just bent ours around so that the extra slack from the missing leg was transferred to the other leg, making it a little larger (but not noticeably so, as you can see from the picture). You could also provide table knives and just cut them out freehand. Since each student will only be making a few cookies, it won't take too long.

Also prepare the icing and put it into some plastic bags, pushing the icing into one corner. Seal the bag shut, and cut a very small hole in the corner of the bag that contains the icing. By squeezing that corner, you can make the icing come out in a thin stream, making it very easy to apply to the edges of the cookies.

(A simple icing recipe is to use a spoon of shortening, a cup of powdered sugar (confectioner's sugar), half a teaspoon of vanilla and just a dribble of water. Chop the shortening into the sugar, then add the vanilla and just a tiny amount of water and stir briskly. Keep adding a few drops of water at a time until the mixture becomes the right consistency for spreading—not too thin, not too thick. (You can always add more sugar or water if you find that the icing is coming out of the bags too fast or too slow.)

**How to make the cookies:**

1) Cut out (with or without cutter) the tRNA shapes.
2) Poke a small hole in the cookie right over where the missing leg should be. (This will be where the yarn goes through.)
3) Bake.
4) Let cool.
5) Using your icing baggies, squeeze a bead of icing around the outside of the cookie. Immediately stick on the little colored decorations. (Remember, these are bases: A, G, C, and U)
6) Cut a piece of yarn and feed it through the hole in the cookie. Poke a hole in the individually wrapped candies and put the yarn through. Tie the yarn. (Lifesavers™ candy work really well.) The candy represents an amino acid.

NOTE: There is a color picture of this craft in the free downloadable file mentioned in activity 1.)

## 3) HANDS-ON ACTIVITY: TRANSCRIPTION AND TRANSLATION

This activity will reinforce what the students learned about DNA transcription and translation. There's nothing like <u>doing</u> for reinforcing concepts! The nice thing is that the activity is edible (for students without dietary restrictions) so it isn't something that will take up storage space at home. Of course, you can keep it for a while, too. No need to eat it right away!

**You will need:**

• a package of Twizzlers® (soft "licorice" sticks) If your students have food sensitivities (or you just want to encourage healthy snacking), you may also substitute a very long strip of carrot about 1/2 inch (1 cm) across and as long as possible.
• a package of colored small marshmallows (or five types of dried fruit such as raisins, cranberries, apricots, etc.)
• a box of toothpicks (thin ones are better than thick ones)
• a pair of sturdy scissors
• a piece of paper (optional—can use colored paper for different amino acids)
• a pencil or pen
• clear tape

**How to prepare:**
   If you are using carrots and dried fruit, pre-slice the carrot strips and cut any large pieces of fruit, such as apricots, so they are all about the same size (the raisins and cranberries will be your standard).

**What to tell the students:**
   *In this activity, you will be assembling a model of a short piece of DNA. You will then unzip it, like helicase does, and make a strip of mRNA by matching the bases on the nonsense side of the DNA.*

**What to do:**
   **1)** Take one strip of licorice or carrot and insert toothpick "rungs" up one side, about 1 cm (1/1 inch) apart.
   **2)** Choose five different colored marshmallows (or dried fruits) to represent A, G, T, C and U. Write a little chart for yourself telling which color (or which fruit) represents which letter. (You will need this information in step 12.)

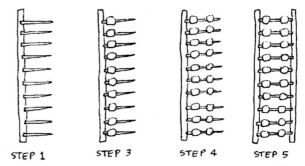

STEP 1          STEP 3          STEP 4          STEP 5

   **3)** Put a random assortment of marshmallows (or fruits) onto the toothpicks. You have now assembled one half of the DNA.
   **4)** To make the other side of the DNA you need to match each base with its complementary base. Remember, A and T are matches and G and C are matches. Slide the complementary base onto the end of the toothpick. Leave a space between them. Don't put them right next to each other. (See illustration.)
   **5)** Now you need to put on the other DNA "backbone." This might be a little tricky. When you are finished you should have something that looks like a ladder, with two bases on each rung.
   **6)** Decide which side is the sense side and which side is the nonsense side. Put a toothpick into the end of the sense side. This side is the one that has the actual code.
   **7)** Now you will make mRNA. First, you need to do the job that the enzyme helicase does—splitting the DNA down the middle. Take the scissors and cut all the toothpicks in half so that you have two long "half ladders."
   **8)** Prepare the backbone for your mRNA by taking another strip of licorice (or carrot) and putting half-toothpicks (cut or break some in half) down one side. Make sure it has the same number of toothpicks as your DNA.
   **9)** Now which side will the mRNA copy—the sense side or the nonsense side? Remember that the mRNA matches up to the nonsense side. Put your mRNA backbone next to your nonsense DNA and begin matching the bases, putting the complementary base onto the mRNA toothpicks. Remember to substitute U for T. (When you come to an A on the DNA, put a U on the mRNA.)
   **10)** After you complete your mRNA, compare it to the sense side of your DNA. Are they exactly the same? If not, try to see where you made your mistake. (First, make sure you have not "flip-flopped" one of them end for end.)
   **11)** Now you will make a short piece of protein using amino acids determined by the DNA. Your amino acids will be paper ovals. (They could also be rectangles if that is easier. It's just that most books seem to show amino acids as either circles or ovals, so we decided to use that shape, too.) Cut out some paper ovals that are as long as the space between three toothpicks on your mRNA model.
   **12)** You will need two charts for the next part. The first is the little chart you made for yourself telling

which color (or which fruit) represents which letter. The other chart is shown below. Lay your mRNA out horizontally with the toothpicks facing down. Then start at the left end, and begin "reading" the letters in groups of three. You'll remember that a group of three letters is called a *codon*. Then use the chart below to find out which amino acid corresponds to that codon. Write the name of the amino acid on the oval and put it under its codon.

**13)** Now do the next set of three letters. Write the name on an oval, set it in place under its codon and then tape it to the first one. Keep going like this until you reach the end of your strip. But why stop there? Just for fun, why not use the other strips, too? Put them all together to make one long strip and keep attaching amino acids under every three letters. You might end up with a chain of aminos that is over 12 or 15 long! (Which is still incredibly short for a protein. A small protein would still have hundreds of amino acids in it.)

**14)** You are now officially finished making a protein. (In real life, the next step would be folding it.)

**Extra tip:** Make copies of this chart for each student, or for pairs of students.

_____

| FIRST LETTER | SECOND LETTER | THIRD LETTER | AMINO ACID |
|---|---|---|---|
| A | A | A or G | Lysine |
| | | C or U | Asparagine |
| | G | A or G | Arginine |
| | | C or U | Serine |
| | C | A, G, C, or U | Threonine |
| | U | A | Isoleucine |
| | | G | Methionine |
| | | C or U | Isoleucine |
| G | A | A or G | Glutamic acid |
| | | C or U | Aspartic acid |
| | G | A, G, C or U | Glycine |
| | C | A, G, C or U | Alanine |
| | U | A, G, C or U | Valine |
| C | A | A or G | Glutamine |
| | | C or U | Histadine |
| | G | A, G, C or U | Arginine |
| | C | A, G, C or U | Proline |
| | U | A, G, C or U | Leucine |
| U | A | A or G | STOP |
| | | C or U | Tyrosine |
| | G | A | STOP |
| | | G | Tryptophan |
| | | C or U | Cysteine |
| | C | A, G, C or U | Serine |
| | U | A or G | Leucine |
| | | C or U | Phenylalanine |

## 4) TABLE GAME: "ROLLER COASTER REVIEW"

This is a board game with a twist—literally! The board is a long strip that gets twisted into a crazy roller coaster shape. The students will not mind doing more review when it's this much fun to play!

**You will need:**
- a piece of poster board (or other lightweight cardboard, or very thick paper)
- scissors
- clear tape
- colored markers (permanent markers work best)
- one paper clip for each team (a large clip, if possible)
- copies of the following 4 pages of quiz cards, printed onto heavy paper

**What to tell the students:**

*This game is called "Roller Coaster Review." The board for this game will be a long strip of paper that will represent a protein. It will end up looking more like a race track or a roller coaster than a board for a table game. Since proteins are folded into all kinds of weird shapes, your protein race track will also be twisted or folded into any shape you want, even one that looks like a corkscrew roller coaster! Since the playing surface will be going upside down at some points you will have to keep your tokens from falling off the track by using a paperclip. To advance along the track, you will answer questions about cells and proteins. If you give the right answer on your first guess, you advance three spaces on the track. If it takes you two guesses, you advance two spaces. If if takes you three guesses, you advance one space. And since there are only three answer options, this means that you will always advance at least one space. And the best part is that if you don't know the right answer, you'll learn it by the end of your turn! The first team to reach the end of their proteins wins the game.*

**How to prepare:**

**1)** Cut some long strips of poster board. You can make the track as long or as short as you want. If you are pressed for time, make a shorter one.

**2)** Divide the students into teams of two, three or four players. (The more players there are on the team, the less frequently each one will get a turn to answer questions.)

**3)** Distribute several strips to each team (one per player is ideal) and hand out markers, as well.

**4)** Have the students mark off squares on the strips. Each square will represent an amino acid. Remember, this is a strip of protein! Have them use the chart from activity 3 so they can write the names of amino acids on the squares. It doesn't matter which ones they choose. (This will help them become familiar with the names of the aminos.)

NOTE: Make sure that each team has the same total number of squares on their strip. It wouldn't be a fair race if one team had less squares to travel! You might want to pre-cut the strips ahead of time and mark in pencil how long each amino square will be. Then the students can just trace over the pencil lines with marker and add the names.

**5)** Tape the strips together, end to end, to make one long strip. Tape one end down to the table, then let the students bend or twist the strip into any shape. Then secure the other end to the table.

**6)** Give each team a paper clip to keep track of which square they are on. Start the paper clip on the first square of one end.

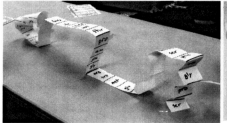 

Use a paper clip to keep track which square you are on.

**7)** You will need a set of cards for each group of teams that are playing against each other. For example, in our class we had four teams with three on each team. We had two teams play each other, so we needed two sets of cards. (If you are playing with only a few students, they can each make their own track and just use one set of cards.)

**9)** If you happen to run out of cards, just start them over again.  This time they should really know the answers if they were paying attention the first time around!

**How to play the game:**

You have some options here.  You can have an adult read the questions out loud, or you can have the students take turns drawing cards and reading the questions.  Either way, rotate turns between each team.  Read the question on the card and the three possible answers.

NOTE: Another option here would be to add a rule that says if you can answer the question without the clues being read, you can go ahead 4 spaces instead of 3.

If you have more than one person on a team, you can either have the team come up with a group answer, or you can have them take turns being the person who answers.  You can also choose whether to allow other team members to give advice if the player who is answering isn't sure of the answer.

If the correct answer is given on the first try, move the paper clip ahead 3 squares.  If an incorrect answer is given, read the question again.  This time the player knows one of the incorrect answers, so it is down to just two possible answers.  If they get the right one, move the clip head 2 spaces.  If they answer incorrectly, they get a third turn, on which they will definitely give the right answer!  Then move ahead one space.

NOTE: This game is a compromise—it's competitive without putting players on the spot and making them feel bad if they don't get the right answer.  They will always get to move at least one space.  The point of the game is to *learn*, not really to win, although one team does win in the end unless you have a tie.  (I always end game sessions with, "You're always a winner if you learned something.")

FINAL NOTE:  Some of the cards have information about particular proteins that were not mentioned in the text.  The point is to introduce a little bit of new information in a way that makes the students think about word clues and context.  In most cases, if the student stops to think about the name of the protein and listens carefully to the possible answers, they can figure it out.  In any case, they'll learn something!

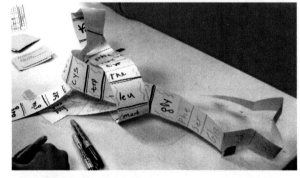

Here are some tracks that our class came up with.  Yours don't have to like these, of course.

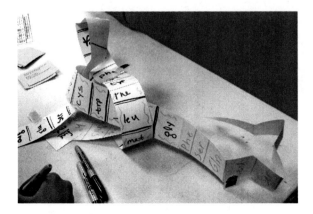

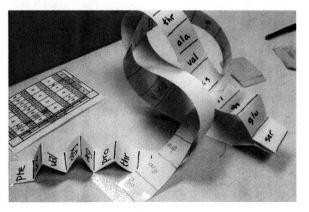

If amyloplasts are organelles in plant cells that store starch, what do you think the protein enzyme "amylase" might do in your body?

a) store extra starch in fat cells
*b) break down starches as part of digestion
c) use light from the sun to make sugar

---

What do you think the protein called "scramblase" does in your cells?

a) acts as a gateway or portal
b) runs the ion pumps
*c) flips the phospholipid molecules from one side of the layer to the other

---

What do you think the proteins called "immunoglobulins" help your body do?

*a) fight infections
b) digest your food
c) carry oxygen in the blood

---

What is an ion?

a) it's the same as a proton
b) a pump that moves things
*c) an atom that is electrically unbalanced

---

What is the inside of the mitochondria called?

a) membrane
*b) matrix
c) cytoplasm

---

What happens when the third phosphate is popped off ATP?

*a) energy is released
b) a molecule of water is formed
c) a proton is released

---

If you join an electron and a proton, what do you get?

a) a water molecule
*b) a hydrogen atom
c) an ion

---

What happens when electrons pass through the ion pumps?

a) ATP is formed
b) water is formed
*c) two protons are pumped upward

---

How many layers are in a cell's plasma membrane?

*a) 2
b) 4
c) hundreds

If the Greek word for glue is "kolla," where do you think the protein "collagen" might be found?

a) in the bones
*b) in connective tissues such as tendons and ligaments
c) in cardiac muscles

---

What does the protein "transferrin" do?

a) help the body fight viruses
*b) carry iron in the bloodstream
c) nothing

---

Where do you think you would find the protein called "pepsin"?

*a) in the stomach, digesting food
b) in the brain, transmitting signals
c) in the eye, gathering light

---

What does the protein "insulin" do?

a) regulates your heart beat
b) regulates your body temperature
*c) regulates the amount of sugar in your blood

---

What does the protein called "hemo-globin" do?

a) allows muscle cells to take up oxygen from the blood
*b) carries oxygen through the blood
c) makes new red blood cells

---

What do you think the protein called "elastin" does?

*a) gives skin its flexibility
b) help blood to clot
c) help the liver to produce bile for digestion

---

Can you guess what cells make with a protein called "tubulin"?

*a) microtubules
b) cell membranes
c) ion pumps

---

Take a guess as to what the protein "fibrin" does:

a) makes the muscles contract
*b) helps the blood to clot
c) acts as a messenger to other cells

---

What do you think the protein called "porin" does?

a) digests lipids and sugars in the intestines
b) starts the process of transcription
*c) acts as a potral or gateway in the outer membrane of cells

107

What are lipid rafts made of?

a) proteins
*b) cholesterol
c) microfilaments

---

What is the fluid inside a cell called?

a) water
b) matrix gel
*c) cytoplasm

---

What do you call a phophorus atom with some oxygen atoms attached to it?

a) phospholipid
*b) phospate
c) glycerol

---

What energy source is used to take "pictures" of DNA?

a) electrons
*b) x-rays
c) light

---

What is the most natural shape for a bunch of phospholipid molecules to form?

a) a flat surface
*b) a ball
c) a long chain

---

What kind of atom (meaning what element on the Periodic Table) marks an organic molecule as a protein?

*a) nitrogen
b) oxygen
c) carbon

---

What does the centrisome do?

a) acts as a gathering point for proteins that are floating around the cell
b) sends and receives messages
*c) acts as a central point of organization for the cytoskeleton

---

What do you call a group of three amino acids?

*a) a codon
b) a secret code
c) a nucleic acid

---

Proline, serine, lysine, arganine and tyrosine are examples of _____.

a) nucleic acids
b) hydorchloric acids
*c) amino acids

**What is the most basic unit of energy used by living things?**

a) an ion
*b) ATP
c) sugar

---

**What does glycerol do in the phospholipid molecule?**

*a) Keep the phosphate and lipid together
b) keep the phosphoate and lipid apart
c) push the phosphate toward water

---

**What is it called when a lot of something goes to a place where there is less of it?**

a) transcription
b) combustion
*c) diffusion

---

**What part of the cell helps it to keep its shape and also provides a network for transportation?**

a) cytoplasm
*b) cytoskeleton
c) plasma membrane

---

**What did Watson and Crick discover?**

a) ATP synthase
*b) the shape of DNA
c) protein folding

---

**How many ion pumps are in the electron transport chain?**

a) 1
b) 2
*c) 3

---

**What does the Greek word "soma" mean?**

*a) body
b) cell
c) center

---

**What is the name of the shape that DNA forms?**

a) coil
b) sheet
*c) helix

---

**How many amino acids are there?**

a) 4
*b) 20
c) hundreds

# CHAPTER 5

## 1) ACTIVE GAME: TRANSLATION RELAY RACE (also includes Golgi packaging)

The goal of this activity is to review the process of translation (how tRNA brings the amino acids and joins them together to form a protein chain) and the role of the Golgi bodies (folding and packing the proteins). Each team will make a protein, then fold it, package it, and ship it.

This game idea is very flexible. It can be adapted to suit the number of students who will be participating. (It was originally designed for a class of about 24 students.) You can also adapt the game to fit your space restrictions. We used the full length of a gym and made the kids run half the length of the gym to deliver their amino acids, but you don't have to do this. You can scale down the size of the parts and make it into a table top activity if necessary. You can also make the amino acid cards smaller than an index card if you need to do it as a table top activity. Adapt this activity to suit your situation. This activity could even be done by a single student, just as a learning activity, not as a race. It will be an effective learning activity no matter how it is done.

**NOTE: It may be helpful to watch the video about this relay, posted on YouTube.com/The-BasementWorkshop, on the "Cells" playlist: "Translation Relay Race Video Clips"**

**You will need:**
- index cards (one per player, plus a few extra for "mailing labels" in the Golgi body)
- envelopes (one per player)
- colored paper (half as many colors as there are players, plus black (or white) paper to represent sugars)
- a long strip of white paper (cash register tape is ideal)
- 4 rolls of clear tape (one for each ribosome station and two for the Golgi body area)
- two cardboard boxes
- black marker of some kind
- pencils

**Prep time:**
45-60 minutes for the paper items, plus additional time right before class (moving tables, etc.)

**Time needed "in class" to do this activity:**
30-60 minutes, depending now how many players you have and how many times you repeat the relay. I recommend doing the relay at least twice—the first time for practice and the second as a race.

**Preparation:**
1) Decide how many players will be on each team. This is the number of amino acids you will need to prepare. You will need a sheet of colored paper and an envelope for each amino acid. (Each player will be assigned to one particular amino acid.)

2) Cut each piece of colored paper into rectangles that are 3 1/2 inches long (10 cm) and about 1 1/2 inches wide (4 cm). You can make the rectangles narrower if you want each paper to yield more rectangles, but keep them 3 1/2 inches long. Now divide each pile of colored papers in half, so you have two piles of each color. Put each pile into an envelope so that you end up with a complete set of envelopes for each team. The picture at the top of the next page shows these envelopes. For my class, I put 8 colored slips into each envelope and we had enough to do this whole activity twice. If you are doing this activity with just one player (or as a cooperative project with several players, but not as a relay) you will need just one set of colors.

3) Assign the name of an amino acid to each color and write the name of the amino acid on the front of the envelope. For example, red might be serine, blue might be proline, orange might be valine. Each team will have an identical set of envelopes. Consult the chart at the end of activity 3 in the chapter 4 activities for a list of amino acids. It doesn't matter which amino acids you choose, or which colors you assign to them. It's up to you.

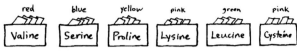

a set of envelopes for team A

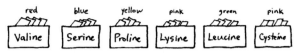

a set of envelopes for team B

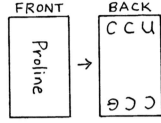

4) Each envelope will also contain an index card with the name of the amino acid written on one side, and two of its codons written on the other side. (If the amino acid only has one codon, just write it once and leave the other end blank.) For amino acids that have more than two codons associated with them, just choose any two—it doesn't matter which ones you choose.

5) Decide how long you want to make your protein chain. I recommend making a chain that is 20-30 links long. Each link in the chain will be 3 inches (7.5 cm) long, so that will give you a strip that is about 7 feet (2 m) long. Each paper link will take 15-30 seconds assembly time. You will need to estimate how many links you can reasonably put on the chain during your class time. Make sure each player gets to contribute a link at least two times. If you are working with just a small number of players, they might contribute a link five or six times.

6) Roll out a long strip of paper that is just a bit longer than the length you want to make your protein chain. (If you don't have cash register tape, you can make a long strip by cutting 2-inch wide strips of paper and taping them end to end.) **This long strip of paper represents mRNA.** The mRNA has come from the nucleus and is now ready for translation.

Write "START" on one end of the strip, then begin marking off sections that are exactly the width of an index card. (If you are adapting this game to a smaller scale, adjust accordingly.) Count off the number of links you want in your chain then write "END" after the last link. Then go back and write a codon in each of the sections. You will need to use the index cards while you do this, making sure to use each codon at least once. You might want to lay out the index cards right underneath the strip, one per section, then write in the codons on the strip. After each is written once, pick up the cards and re-position them (don't forget to turn them end-for-end so the other codon will be used) so that they are front of the remaining blank sections, then write in the remaining codons. (Hint: If the phone rings while you are working on this, let the answering machine get it! I found it a bit tedious to keep everything straight. But the preparation time was VERY worthwhile in the end, as the activity was a huge success.)

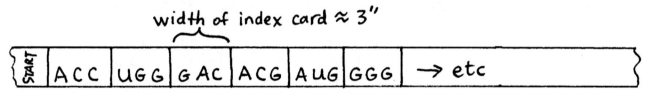

7) Make another identical strip for the other team. Mark the backs: Team A—strip 1/Team B—strip 1.

8) Repeat this process again, making a second pair of mRNA strips. The first set will be for your "practice round," and the second set will be for your race. I recommend not making this set identical to the first set, so that the players will not be able to anticipate when their codon is called. (Or, if you are short on time, you could make only one set and just switch the tapes for round two.)

**Set up needed right before class:**

1) I recommend two long tables (8 ft if possible), one for each team. (If you are playing in a smaller space or with just a few players, you'll have to adapt the game to your situation). Each table will represent a ribosome. You may want to have an adult at each table helping with the taping and making sure the assembly is proceeding correctly. In this case, perhaps the adult is the ribosome, not the

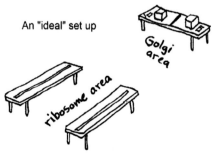

An "ideal" set up

table itself.  Roll out the first set of mRNA strips and tape one to each table.  Also make sure there is a roll of tape at each table.

**2)** You will also need an area designated as the Golgi body.  A third table would be handy for this.  You can divide the table in half, and use one half for each team.  (Once again, if your situation doesn't allow for a third table, just adapt to whatever works for you, as long as there is a definite area marked out to be the Golgi body area.)  At this site, provide these items for each team:  a box, a couple of index cards, a pencil, a roll of tape, some strips of black paper (or white paper) to represent sugars that will be added after folding and before packaging.  (You can make little paper chains out of the black (or white) paper strips if you want to get fancy.)

**3)** You will need a place that is designated as the place to which the protein will be shipped.  In our game, we just labeled the box "Outside the Cell" and had the players end the race by taking the box out through a door.  You might want to choose to have the protein shipped to a mitochondrion or somewhere else.  It could be any type of protein, shipping to just about anywhere.  Choose what is best for you.

**How to play:**
        In the first stage of this relay, the players will pretend to be transfer RNA (tRNA) and will assemble the protein at the ribosome station.  In the second stage, the players will all go over to the Golgi body area and each player will do something to prepare the protein for packing and shipping.  The game ends when the packaged protein is delivered to its destination.

**1)** Divide players into two teams.  Give one set of envelopes to each team, and have each player take an envelope.  Have the players look inside their envelopes and explain that the colored slips of paper are amino acids and the index card is their "secret code" chart that tells which codons their amino acid is associated with.  Tell them that they will be playing the part of transfer RNA.  When their codon is called, they must bring their index card and one of their slips of colored paper to the ribosome area.

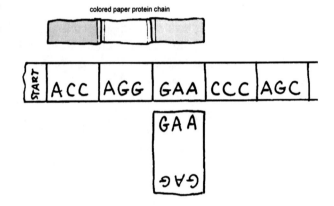

colored paper protein chain

        Explain that this first round of play will be the practice round where everyone will learn what to do.  (During this first round, the supervising adult(s) can review and reinforce information about translation and protein folding.  This can actually be high-quality teaching time—the kids will be anxious to know what to do and where to go.  You can take advantage of their desire to learn during this time!)

        Have the players come over to a ribosome table and demonstrate how they will lay their index card down to match the codon on the mRNA, then add their slip of paper to the growing paper chain above it.

**2)** Next, explain that there is a second stage to the relay,  After the protein chain is finished, they will no longer be transfer RNA.  They will then play the role of chaperone proteins and will carry the protein chain to the Golgi body area.  They will then switch from being chaperone proteins to being Golgi proteins that will fold, package, and label the protein.

**3)** Assign a Golgi body job to each player.  Each team will need someone to do these jobs:

• **Folding:** This person will fold the protein once by doing an overhand knot (the first part of tying your shoe).

• **Pinning:** This person will tape the end of the chain together after the last fold is complete (the last knot). The pinner can use tape to secure the ends together.  Then the pinner can take the end of what will now look like a paper chain, and pin them together.  The result will be a clumpy-looking paper chain.

• **Adding a sugar:** This person will tape a "sugar" (strip of black paper, or small black paper chain—whichever you have provided) to someplace on the paper protein.  (Or you could use white

paper instead of black.)
   • **Labeling:** This person will put the chain into the box, then put an "address" on an index card (you decide the address—we used "Outside of the Cell") and tape it to the box.

   If you have many players on each team, you can have multiple Folders and Sugar Adders. You will only need one Pinner and one Labeler no matter how many players there are. Once again, you can adapt this format to your particular situation and assign jobs accordingly.
   Demonstrate each job, especially how to "fold" the protein by putting an overhand knot in the chain. Tell them not to tie it too tightly. Make sure the labeler knows what to write. You might want to discuss the various options for where a Golgi body might send a protein (just about anywhere!). Ask the players what they think the Golgi body might use for making its "boxes." (Obviously, it doesn't use cardboard!) The answer is phospholipids, the same stuff the membrane is made of (as well as the outer surface of all the organelles). The Golgi body's boxes are called "vesicles" instead of "boxes."

3)   There are two ways to end the game. You might want to choose one player to be a motor protein and carry the box to the designated ending area, or you could have the labeler hold the box and all the other players surround him and pretend to be phospholipid molecules creating a vesicle. The second way strains the analogy a bit, since the cardboard box technically represents the vesicle, but if you have a large group of players and a large playing area, ending the game by having all the players escort the protein out is a fun finale. Just make sure everyone knows what to do.

4)   Ask if anyone has any questions about their role(s). If not, proceed with the practice round. Help along the way and troubleshoot if necessary.

5)   Play a second time—this time as a race between the two teams.


## 2)  GAME: LYSOSOME SIMULATION GAME

   The goal of this game is simply to reinforce the fact that the lysosome's job is to disassemble molecules. You will be using a block of Legos™ to simulate a large molecule. The players will pretend to be enzymes. Each enzyme can only do one thing. So each player will be assigned to blocks of one particular color.

**What to tell the students:**

   *In this game you will pretend to be an enzyme in a lysosome. Each team will represent a lysosome. It's a race to see which lysosome can disassemble a molecule in the least amount of time. Since an enzyme can only do one job, your team of enzymes must work together to disassemble your molecule.*

**You will need:**
 • enough Lego® bricks to make two blocks about 3 or 4 inches (8 to 10 cm) on a side  (They don't have to be Lego® brand; any type of building block will do.)

**How to prepare:**
   Make two blocks, using as many different colors as possible, and the same number of each color, if possible. Try to mix the colors as you assemble. As you can see from the picture, the block does not need to be perfectly square. In fact, have it being a little odd-shaped makes it look more like an organic molecule.

**How to play the game:**

Divide the players into two teams. Assign a color (one of the block colors) to each member of each team. Each team should have a person doing red, a person doing blue, a person doing white, etc. If you have only a few players on each team, some or all of the players will be in charge of more than one color. This means that they will be playing the part of more than one enzyme. Remind the students that an enzyme is very specific and can only disassemble (or assemble) one particular thing.

The object of the game is to disassemble the molecule down to a pile of individual blocks. (In a real cell, these "building blocks" would then be used to make other things.) Players can remove only outer blocks. In other words, if you are the red remover, you can't pull off a white block to get to a red one. Therefore, the block must be passed around to various players according to which blocks are on the outside and available for removal. The first team to completely disassemble their molecule wins.

If you want to play a second round, the blocks will have to be reassembled. To make the reassembly fun, have the teams switch sets of blocks so that they are reassembling the other team's molecule. See if they can figure out how to arrange the blocks so that it will take as long as possible for the other team to disassemble it.

**Extra tip:** To reinforce the concept that a lysosome is being simulated, have each team sit on the floor inside a large oval of string or rope (representing the outside of the lysosome).

## 3) EDIBLE CRAFT: GOLGI BODY COOKIES

Yes, yet another edible craft. But in my experience teens and pre-teens never get tired edible activities, so I use them regularly. This activity is very straightforward: make a cookie that is a model of a Golgi body.

**You will need:**
- a cookie dough recipe (and baking sheets and an oven)
- icing (something fairly stiff and not too gooey, so it doesn't drip out from between the cookies
- table knives (not sharp) for spreading icing
- optional: aluminum foil and a permanent marker

**Tip:** If you are working with a large class, have the students put their unbaked cookies on a piece of aluminum foil and then write their name on the foil. Put the foil sheets onto the baking sheets. When the cookies come out of the oven there won't be any arguing over which cookies belong to whom.

**What to do:**

Tell the students look again at the illustration of the Golgi body on page 38 of their student booklet. Then distribute dough and tell them to make each "pancake" separately, as the Golgi body will be assembled after baking, using icing. They will need to make two of the "pancakes" be the ones on the ends, which will have vesicles budding off. The exact number of interior "pancakes" is not crucial. They can make 2, 3 or 4.

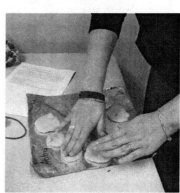

After baking the cookies and letting them cool a bit, use the icing to "glue" the Golgi "pancakes" together. Make sure the ones with the vesicles are on the ends.

# CHAPTER 6

## 1) LAB DEMONSTRATION: EXTRACTING DNA

Did you know you can easily extract the DNA from any living thing? All you have to do is break down the barriers (the phospholipid membranes) that hold it inside the cell, remove the chaperone proteins and histones that surround the DNA, then clump the DNA together so that it forms a blob big enough for you to see.

If you want a very nice online version of this experiment, go to:

**http://learn.genetics.utah.edu/content/labs/extraction/howto/**

### You will need:

• a plant or animal product you can put in the blender (liver, peas, or strawberries are often recommended, but you can use anything that contains DNA)
  • a blender
  • a small strainer
  • a bowl, a spoon, and a few small, clear glasses (or beakers or test tubes)
  • salt
  • cold water
  • liquid dish detergent
  • meat tenderizer (if you can't get this, try pineapple juice or contact lens cleaning solution)
  • isopropyl ("rubbing") alcohol (90% is better, but 70% will probably work)
  • optional: some cotton swabs for pulling DNA out of final goop

### What to tell the students:

*If you wanted to extract DNA out of a cell, what would be the first thing you would have to do? The DNA is surrounded by a nuclear envelope—a double-thick layer of phospholipids—then outside of that is the cell's plasma membrane. You will have to use a substance that can break apart phospholipid membranes. Fortunately, this type of substance is readily available. We call it "soap." You use soap to clean greasy plates that have had fatty foods sitting on them. Soap can break apart lipid substances, even the lipid membranes of cells. Your skin doesn't just dissolve away when you wash yourself with soap because your cells are tightly bound together and the soap can't penetrate very far down.*

*After you split open all the phospholipid membranes, the organelles and the DNA can spill out of the cells. The organelles that are surrounded by a phospholipid membrane, such as the Golgi bodies, ER, and lysosomes, will also get broken down by the soap, leaving whatever proteins and enzymes were inside of them just floating around.*

*Now what would be the next thing you would need to get rid of in order to get pure DNA? Remember all those proteins that surround the DNA, and the histone spools that wind it up? You'd need to get rid of those. For this, you would need something that breaks down proteins. In this demonstration you will be using meat tenderizer to do this. Meat tenderizer contains enzymes called proteases that break down proteins. (Interestingly enough, the protease enzymes in meat tenderizer were extracted from pineapples or papayas.)*

*After the proteins have been stripped away from the DNA, you then need to gather it all together in one place. One single strand of DNA is ultra-microscopic. Even thousands of strands of DNA probably can't be seen without a microscope. You will be gathering together millions and millions of strands of DNA by using a chemical reaction between DNA, salt and isopropyl alcohol. The clump of DNA will look like a bunch of stringy white goo. So what can you do with your clump of DNA? Not much. You will probably dispose of it. But if you wanted to keep it, it could be preserved for months or maybe years by keeping it in a jar of alcohol.*

**What to do:**

1)  Put your living stuff (half a cup (125 ml) of it is enough) into the blender and add about a cup (250 ml) of cold water.  Make sure to use cold water, not lukewarm water, as the temperature of the water can affect results.  Add 1/8 teaspoon (1/2 ml) of salt.  The salt will help the DNA clump together when you add the alcohol in step 7.

2)  Blend on high for half a minute or so.  The chopping action of the blender separates the cells from each other so the detergent will be able to penetrate every cell.  In the case of plant cells, it will also chop up the tough cell walls, exposing the plasma membranes.

3)  Put your strainer on top of the bowl and pour your soup into the strainer.  This step is just to get rid of larger particles, such as fiber that did not get chopped fine enough.  Then remove the strainer.

4)  Add 2 tablespoons (15 ml) of dish detergent.  Mix well, then let this mixture sit for about 5 to 10 minutes.  (However, we got the experiment to work without letting it sit.)

5)  Add a pinch of meat tenderizer to the soup and stir very gently.  If you stir too hard you might break up the DNA too much and it will be harder to see.  If you are using pineapple juice or contact lens cleaning solution, just add a few drops.  (The enzymes in the meat tenderizer were extracted from either pineapple or papaya, which is why you can substitute these.  Pineapple enzyme is called brome-lain.  Papaya enzyme is called papain.)

6)  At this point you may want to transfer your soup into some smaller containers.  You can use small, clear glasses, or you can use fancy lab equipment like beakers and test tubes, if you have them.   The main goal is use something clear so that you can see the DNA precipitate out.  However, if you want to leave all your soup in the bowl, the next step will still work.

7)  Now add alcohol to the soup.  Add enough alcohol so that you have the same amount of alcohol as soup.  You will notice that the alcohol will float to the top.

8)  Now you should see some white gooey stuff forming between the soup on the bottom and the clear alcohol on the top.  If not, swirl it very gently and then wait.  The DNA does not like to mix with alcohol.  The salt you added in step 1 will also help the DNA to clump together (or more correctly, "precipitate out" of the solution).  You can take a swab (or stick, or the end of a spoon) and pull out the stringy white blobs of DNA.  Of course, there is RNA in the goop, as well as DNA.  The cells also had a considerable amount of RNA in their cytoplasm.  What you really have is a clump of nucleic acids.

STEP 1

STEP 3

STEP 4

STEP 7

STEP 8

If you want a little bit more information and some FAQs about this demon-stration, go to the website listed in the opening paragraph.  They also have simple graphics that can help visualize what is going on.  (These extras are not on the main page.  You have to click on the blue phrases.)

For a virtual lab about extracting human DNA, go to:
**http://learn.genetics.utah.edu/content/labs/extraction/**

There is a color picture of step 8 in the supplemental down-loads on the website.

## 2) ART PROJECT: FIRST SESSION OF THE CELL "MINI-MURAL"

This project is divided into two sections because it is probably too much for one sitting, although students working at home with ample time and a long attention span could probably complete it in one long session. If you want to do it in one session, wait to begin until after the next chapter.

This drawing should be done mostly from memory (or as much as possible) so that it will be a record of just how much information the students have learned. By drawing "from scratch" and not copying it from any other source, the students' brains will be doing important processing of the information, creating procedural memories—something that reading and answering quiz questions just can't do. I found it helpful to my students if I demonstrated quickly on a white board approximately what they are supposed to sketch in each step. It was just enough visual information to stimulate their memories and to make sure that the organelles were placed appropriately on the page.

There is a color picture of this project in the downloadable file mentioned in activity 4 on pg. 88.

### You will need:
- two sheets of white card stock for each student (or substitute regular paper if necessary)
- tape
- pencils and erasers
- a compass or circle guide  (a circle guide is a flat piece of plastic with circles cut into it)
- a ruler
- recommended:  good quality drawing pens
- optional:  colored pencils or markers

### What to tell the students:
*You will be making a detailed drawing of a cell using only what you've learned, not copying from any other pictures. You will be surprised at how much you know about cells! Your cell does not need to look like an illustration from a book. It doesn't need to be perfect. The goal is just to show the amazing amount of information you have learned about cells. Also, while you are drawing, your brain will be processing the information you are recalling from your memory, and sort of reorganizing in a new way so that you will be able to remember it even better.*

### How to do the drawing:
1) Tape the two sheets of paper together to make one large drawing surface. (Match edges carefully.) Put tape on only one side. Draw on the side without the tape.

2) Begin with lightly sketching where the plasma membrane will be. Fill the page as much as possible, but leave a little bit of space around the edge, perhaps an inch or so (2 or 3 cm).

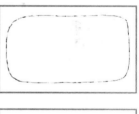

**VERY IMPORTANT:** Remember to make your first lines *very light* and sketchy. This will allow you to erase them and make changes easily.

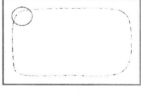

3) Now you will put in your first "inset." An inset is how illustrators show a close-up view of something inside a larger drawing. In this case, you need to show a close-up view of the plasma membrane. In the scale of your drawing, the phospholipids would be very small—too small to be able to draw them. The inset will allow you to draw the details of just a small portion of the membrane large enough to be able to see details. Use a compass or a circle guide to draw a circle in one of the corners, overlapping the membrane, as shown in the sample drawing. You can go ahead and make this circle dark, as you won't be putting anything over it. Then erase the pencil line inside it. (If you made your original sketchy line too dark, you'll now see why we recommended making them really light.) If you don't have a compass or circle guide, just make the best circle you can. (Insets don't have to be round; you could choose to make a square.)

4) Inside this inset, draw a close-up of the phospholipid membrane. Show all the heads and tails lined up correctly (heads on outside, tails to the inside), and put in some portal proteins and some other membrane-bound proteins on

both the inside and outside. You could also put in a lipid raft carrying a protein, or you could add some cytoskeleton attached to the proteins on the inside layer.  Sketch in the parts lightly with pencil first, showing where you intend to put the layers of phospholipids and where the various proteins will go. Once you have it sketched out, then you can use darker pencil lines or pen lines to draw your final version.

5)  Next, sketch out where the nucleus will go.  Put it in the center so the crack between the pages goes right down the middle. Make the nucleus about the size of your fist. Don't use a compass or circle guide for the nucleus.  You want precise circles for the insets, but not for the natural cell shapes.  Nuclei are not perfectly round in nature, just sort of round.  Draw a line down one side of the crack to divide the nucleus in half.

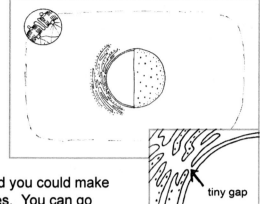

6)  On the right side, draw tiny circles to represent the pores in the nuclear membrane.  If you want to add a 3D effect, you could shade it using pencil (making it look round like a ball) and you could make the tiny circles get smaller and closer together toward the edges.  You can go ahead and finish the right side with darker lines. The left side will be your "cut away view" showing what is inside the nucleus.  We'll draw the inside in step 8.

7)  The nucleus has a double membrane so you will need to draw two lines going around the outside of the left semi-circle.  The inner line will be solid, with no gaps. The outer line will have one or more tiny gaps where the endoplasmic reticulum will join to it.  Remember, the ER is "continuous" with the nuclear membrane.  This means that you'll basically have one very long and very squiggly line going from the semi-circle out and around all the edges of the ER and then back to the semi-circle again.  You might want to sketch out very lightly where your ER squiggles will go before drawing them in with darker lines.  We will be putting a Golgi body in the space to the left, so you also might want to make some vesicles budding off the ER on that side, getting ready to drift off to the Golgi body.  After you finish the ER, put in little dots all around it to represent the ribosomes.  This side of the nucleus will have the rough ER.  We will show the smooth ER on the other side.

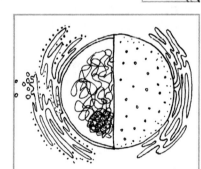

8)  Draw the smooth ER on the other side of the nucleus.  You could draw some vesicles budding off, but don't draw any ribosomes.

9)  Draw DNA in the left semi-circle.  You can just make scribbles because at this scale you would not be able to see any detail—just a bunch of DNA "spaghetti."  Make one section of the DNA a bit more dense, to represent the nucleolus.

10)  You will now add two more insets.  These will be slightly different from the first one, as they will have arrows that point to smaller circles.  Draw a very small circle around one section of your DNA spaghetti.   Then make a large circle outside the nucleus.  This larger circle should be at least an inch (2.5 cm) in diameter.  Make an arrow pointing from the larger circle to the smaller one.  The arrow indicates that the larger circle shows an up-close view of what is in the smaller circle. In this larger circle, draw the DNA as a line coiled around histone spools.

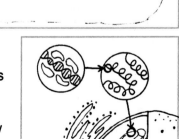

11)  Now put a small circle around one tiny section of this coiled DNA. Again, draw a larger circle near by and then draw an arrow from the larger circle to the smaller one.  In this second large circle, draw the DNA as a double helix.  Don't forget to draw a few chaperone proteins surrounding it, too.  These proteins can just be drawn beside the DNA, not covering it. You want the helix to be clearly visible. (The nucleus and rough ER are now finished.  The lines can be made final, with pen or with darker pencil lines.)

**12)** Draw a Golgi body to the left of the rough ER. It can fill most of the space between the rough ER and the left side of the cell, as we won't be putting any other organelles in this space—just the Golgi. Lightly sketch in where the "pancakes" will be. Then as you trace around the shape making your final line, add some vesicles merging with the side facing the nucleus and some vesicles budding off the side facing the plasma membrane. You could also add some vesicles floating away from the Golgi, perhaps on their way to merge with the plasma membrane. It's up to you how 3D to make your Golgi. You can try to shade the pancakes, or you can leave it as a line drawing.

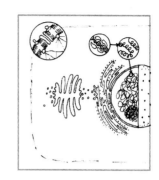

**13)** In the upper right corner of the cell, sketch an oval and a circle. The oval will become a mitochondrion and the circle will be used for an inset showing the electron transport chain. (The oval certainly does not have to be perfect. Some mitochondria are very long, some are almost round, and some are look lumpy like potatoes.) Draw a line across the middle of the oval. The top half of the oval will show the outside of the mitochondrion and the bottom half will show the inside. If you want to make your mitochondrion look 3D, you can shade the edges of the top half. Draw some lines at various places going partway across the top half. Micrographs of mitochondria usually show these lines, making the mitochondria distinguishable from other organelles. These lines are places where the inner patterns show through. On the bottom half, draw the squiggly outline of the matrix. Draw a small circle around one tiny part of the matrix line, then draw an arrow from the large circle to the small one, just like we did with the close-ups of DNA. In the circle, draw a very simple schematic of the electron transport chain. You only need to indicate the membrane, three ion pumps, the "egg-beater" synthase machine, and little dots for protons above and below the membrane. You might want to make a lot more dots above the pumps than below, to indicate that the pumps are working to increase the number of protons above the synthase machine. You also might want to put a few (very tiny!) ATPs below the synthase machine.

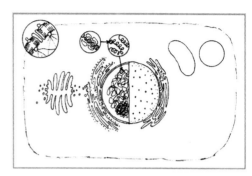

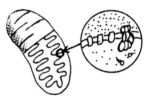

**14)** The last organelle for this drawing session is the lysosome. Draw an oval below the mitochondrion. Make it a little smaller than the mitochondrion. Making a dividing line to separate the outer view from the inside view. You can shade the outside to make it look round. For the inside view, draw some small dots of various sizes and shapes to represent the enzymes found inside the lysosome. Make them tiny! At this scale, they still might be too small to see, but we are going to make them visible.

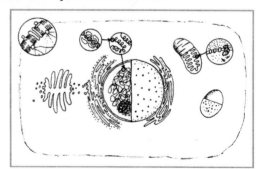

You can go over the organelles and insets with final lines, either pen or darker pencil.

NOTE: DON'T DRAW FINAL LINES FOR THE PLASMA MEMBRANE YET. We still need to add some details to it. Strange as it may seem, the plasma membrane will be one of the last things we will fill in with final lines.

# CHAPTER 7

## 1) ART PROJECT:  SECOND SESSION OF CELL "MINI-MURAL"

In this session, the students will finish the drawing they started in chapter 6.  Because this is a continuation of the project, not a new project, we won't start over with numbering the steps.  Rather, we will pick up where we left off and continue with number 15.

**15)** Draw another small oval below the lysosome.  This will be the peroxisome.   Make a line dividing it in half and show the outside as a smooth, round shape.  On the inside, make little dots along with some lines, representing the crystalline core that is full of enzymes.  Of course, in a real cell there would be hundreds, or even thousands of peroxisomes, and also lots of mitochondria and lysosomes. But for clarity, we are putting only one of each in our cell.

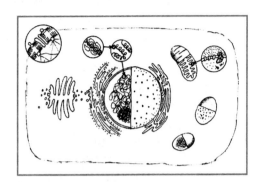

**16)** Ribosomes are very small.  You already put some ribosomes along the rough ER.  We will draw a close-up of one ribosome making a protein chain.  Draw a circle somewhere in the empty space below the Golgi body.  Make this circle about the same size as the circles you drew for the DNA and the electron transport chain close-ups.  Inside the circle show a ribosome with its two parts.  Draw a piece of mRNA going in one side and coming out the other.  Also show a finished protein chain coming out the other side.  Then draw some tiny tRNAs, each bringing an amino acid to add to the protein chain.

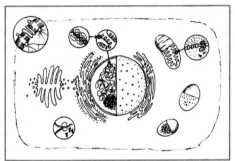

**17)** The last organelle is the centrosome.  Draw a wiggly circle right below the nucleus and then put two barrel-shapes in side of it. (Remember, the two barrels are called the centrioles.)   Ideally, they should be perpendicular. An easy way to do this is to draw the front barrel first, then put the other barrel behind it.  Start each barrel by making the circle end first.

**18)** For this step, you will need to find four places in your drawing that have large enough blank spots so that you can add four more small insets.  It doesn't matter where they go. Just find four places and draw four inset circles.  They can be a little smaller than your other insets if your drawing is filling up.  In these four circles, we will put close-up views of the "raw materials" that are floating around in the cytoplasm.  In one circle, draw a few little hexagons.  These will represent glucose molecules.  In the second circle, draw a few circles with line going out from them.  These will represent fatty acid molecules.  In the third circle, draw a few ovals.  These will represent amino acids.  (If your ovals are large enough, you could even write the first three letters of some amino acids, such as "PRO" or "VAL" or "LYS.")  In the fourth circle, draw a nucleotide.  You'll remember that a nucleotide is made of a phosphate, a sugar, and a base.  It's a piece of DNA ladder consisting of one rung and the side piece it is attached to. It looks a bit like a "T" lying on its side.  If drawing a phosphate, sugar and base is too complicated, just draw some T's.

glucose

fatty acid

amino

nucleo-tide

or

enzyme

**19)** If you have one last spot available, draw one last circle.  Inside this circle draw one or more enzymes.  An enzyme can be drawn as an oval with a weird shape either going into it or coming out of it.   Remember, enzymes are not nutrients.  They are keys that put things together or tear them apart.

**20)** Add some more ribosomes floating around in the cytoplasm.  Just make little dots here and there in the "background" space you have available.  You could also make a ribosome right near your ribosome inset circle and make an arrow pointing from the circle to the little ribosome dot.

**21)** Now it's time to draw the final line for the plasma membrane. But first you need to sketch in some little details. Make a few places where pinocytosis or phagocytosis is going on. These would look like little indents in the membrane, some shallow and some deep enough that they are about ready to pinch off and become vesicles inside the cell. Draw some little dots to show the things that are being brought inside the cell. Then sketch in some areas where exocytosis is occurring. These would look like little bumps sticking out from the membrane. Once again, they would have little dots inside them to show the contents that are being exported out of the cell. Once you have these areas sketched in, you can then begin to trace around the membrane with your pen or dark pencil. Remember, you don't have to follow your sketchy lines exactly. If your sketchy lines don't look the way you want them to, you can erase them and move them.

**22)** Once you have your plasma membrane completed, draw in the cytoskeleton. The cytoskeleton lines should be fairly light so they won't obscure the other objects in the drawing. Think of the cytoskeleton as decorative background. That is not to say that the cytoskeleton is unimportant, it's just that dark lines going all over the place will make the drawing look very confusing. So keep the cytoskeleton line on the light side. If you are doing your final lines in pen, you might want to consider keeping the cytoskeleton lines in pencil and not tracing over them in pen.

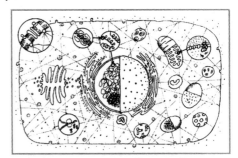

Lay the ruler across the drawing (anywhere, at any angle) and draw a light line with your pencil. As you are drawing your line, if you run into any organelles, lift your pencil and don't draw over the organelle. Then move the ruler to another place and do this again. Don't draw on top of any organelles. Make it look like the lines are going behind them. Of course, in a real cell, the microtubules would be running in front of them as well as behind them, but for clarity in our drawing we will leave them behind the organelles. Keep moving your ruler to different angles and adding more lines. Eventually it should look like a network of very light lines running all over the place behind your organelles. The exact number of lines in not important. You could put in as few as a dozen, or as many as several dozen.

**23)** After the cytoskeleton is in place, add some final details such as little vesicles floating here and there inside the cell (or outside the cell). Empty vesicles can be vacuoles. You could also add random dots that you can imagine to be any type of molecule you might find in or near the cell.

**24)** If you have space outside your cell, add some desmosomes. Of course, you will only be able to see the parts of the desmosomes that are connected to this cell. (Although, if you have space at the edges of your paper, you could draw in the edges of some other cells.) Remember, a desmosome is anchored to a cell by little "plates" that are attached to the cytoskeleton just inside the membrane.

**25)** Now you can do any labeling you want to do. You'll have to make the words very small, but this can be done without too much difficulty if you use a pen with a very fine point or a pencil that is very sharp.

If you want to add anything else you've learned in this curriculum, feel free to do so!

*Remember, there is a color sample of this project in the downloadable file at www.ellenjmchenry.com, FREE DOWNLOADS, HUMAN BODY, "Color supplement for Cells curriculum" link.*

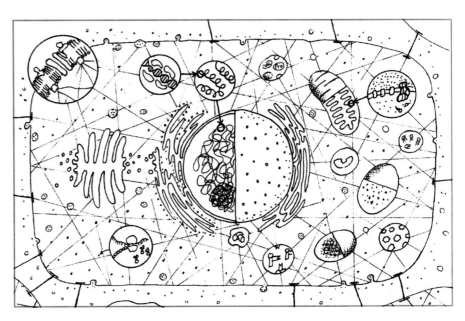

## 2) GAME: CELL BINGO

The boards for this game will look a bit like the cell "mini-murals" the students drew. In fact, one option would be to play this game before finishing the mural.

**Each player will need:**
- A copy of the page with the cell squares (page 127)
- A copy of the page with the blank squares (page 126)
- About 24 tokens ("markers") to place on each square as clues are read
- A pair of scissors
- A glue stick (or other glue, if sticks are not available)

**Set up:**

Cut apart the cell squares so you have 25 individual square pieces. Glue these squares onto the page with the blank squares. (Don't cut apart the blank squares.) The cell corner pieces must go in a corner, the edge pieces must stay on an edge and the nucleus pieces must still form a circle, but other than that the players are free to put the pieces wherever they want to. Each player should create their own unique pattern.

**How to play:**

This is a bingo-type game. The only difference is that to win, you must fill both a vertical row AND a horizontal row. (A diagonal row would also be acceptable.) So winning patterns might look something like these:

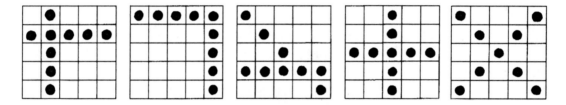

**Giving clues:**

There are three pages of clues. This gives you several options.
- You can play the game three times, getting progressively harder each time.
- You can play just once, selecting the level most appropriate for your players.
- You can keep going even after you have a winner and play through the rest of the clues on that level so that all the clues are used (maximizing review). For example, if someone gets a bingo while you are on question 15 on the easy level, you can just pick up with clue 16 for the next game, then bridge over to the medium clues to finish that game. Then pick up with the rest of the medium clues for the next game.
- You can play all (or most of) the clues on the level if you let the rest of the players keep playing even after a bingo has been called.
- You can do the clues in order, or you can skip around and use the clues you feel are the best review questions for your players. (If you don't go in order, just remember to put a pencil mark next to the ones you've done so that you can keep track of them!)

RE-USABLE OPTION: If you want to use these cell pieces multiple times (for example, a permanent classroom set) copy the cell page onto white sticky-back label paper (the full sheet 8.5" x 11" labels). Then stick these to pieces of mat board or heavy cardboard. (You could also print the cell pages onto card stock, then use spray adhesive to adhere them to the mat board.) Use an craft/utility knife to cut apart the squares. Mark the backs of each set with a number or letter so that if the pieces get mixed up they are easily sorted again. Put each set in a small zip-lock plastic bag. When it is time to play, give each student a bag and have them arrange their 25 pieces into a square. The pieces will not be glued together, just set into place like puzzle pieces with straight edges.

CELL BINGO      Easy Clues

1) This organelle generates energy in the form of ATPs.                                    MITOCHONDRIA

2) This is a dense area in the nucleus that contains the information on how to
make ribosomes.                                                                            NUCLEOLUS

3) This organelle contains many digestive enzymes.                                         LYSOSOME

4) This organelle is often called the "post office" of the cell because it packages
and labels things.                                                                         GOLGI BODY

5) This is the name of the watery fluid inside the cell.                                   CYTOSOL

6) These are sugar molecules that the cell breaks down to make ATPs.                       GLUCOSE

7)  This is called "rough" because it has ribosomes stuck to it.                           ROUGH ER

8) This is how the cell takes in little "swallows" of the fluid surrounding it.            PINOCYTOSIS

9) This organelle gets rid of toxic hydrogen peroxide.                                     PEROXISOME

10) This structure is a central point for the organization the cytoskeleton.               CENTROSOME

11) These are like little "cardboard boxes" that the cell uses to transport things.        VESICLES

12)  DNA is made of these.                                                                 NUCLEOTIDES

13) This is like the library of the cell. It contains all the information the cell needs.  NUCLEUS

14)  These act like little connecting rods between cells.                                  DESMOSOMES

15)  These things bring amino acids to ribosomes that are busy manufacturing
proteins.                                                                                  tRNAs

16)  This organelle consists of a complicated network of smooth tubes.
Its membrane is "continuous with" the outer membrane of the nucleus.                       SMOOTH ER

17)  This is what separates the cell from its environment.                                 PLASMA
                                                                                           MEMBRANE

18)  These are the little manufacturing units that take amino acids and string
them together into long protein chains.                                                    RIBOSOMES

19) These are the largest fibers of the cytoskeleton.  Their structure is similar to
drinking straws because they are cylindrical and hollow.                                   MICROTUBULES

20)  These are what proteins are made of.  There are 20 types.                             AMINO ACIDS

21) These are the smallest fibers of the cytoskeleton.                                     MICROFILAMENTS

22)  Your cells can use these to create and repair phospholipid membranes.                 FATTY ACIDS

23)  These proteins are "stuck" in the plasma membrane and serve quite a
variety of functions, including as portals for letting things in and out.                  MEMBRANE-
                                                                                           BOUND PROTEINS

24)  These proteins help join things together or break things apart.                       ENZYMES

25)  This is basically a very large empty vesicle.                                         VACUOLE

CELL BINGO      Medium Clues

1) This is where the centrioles are located.                                      CENTROSOME

2) This has four layers of phospholipids around the outside.                       NUCLEUS

3) This is basically the same thing as phagocytosis, just on a smaller             PINOCYTOSIS
scale.

4) These are formed by the rough ER and used to transport things over to  VESICLES
the Golgi body.

5) Your digestive system breaks down fats into these.                              FATTY ACIDS

6) This organelle has many functions, including storing calcium and                SMOOTH ER
manufacturing steroids.

7) These are attached to proteins that are bound to the inside of the
plasma membrane.  They give the cell its shape and can also be used to             MICROFILAMENTS
form pseudopods.

8) This organelle gets its name from the Latin word for "empty."                   VACUOLE

9) This is where the electron transport chain is located.                          MITOCHONDRIA

10) This organelle deals with several kinds of toxins produced by the cell.  PEROXISOMES

11) Glycolysis is when a cell starts harvesting ATPs from this molecule.      GLUCOSE

12) Seventy percent of this is water.                                              CYTOSOL

13) This organelle is responsible for labeling digestive enzymes so that      GOLGI BODY
they get transported over to the lysosomes.

14) These are made of two pieces—a larger one and a smaller one.              RIBOSOMES

15) This contains lipid rafts.                                                     PLASMA MEMBRANE

16) About 40 different kinds of these are found inside lysosomes.             ENZYMES

17) This is where ribosomes are made.                                              NUCLEOLUS

18) This is the smallest type of RNA.                                              tRNA

19) This organelle pumps protons into itself.                                      LYSOSOME

20) This organelle has docking ports for ribosomes.                               ROUGH ER

21) These are the highways along which motor proteins can travel.            MICROTUBULES

22) Some of these act as "flags" to identify the cell as part of the body.    MEM-BOUND PROTEINS

23) These connect skin cells to each other and give skin its stretchiness.    DESMOSOMES

24) The nucleus contains lots of these, all joined together into a twisted     NUCLEOTIDES
ladder shape.

25) When proteins have been thoroughly digested, they break down into      AMINO ACIDS
these simple molecules.

124

# CELL BINGO      Harder Clues

1)  This is the only organelle that doesn't have any phospholiipids in it. **RIBOSOMES**

2)  Although usually located towards the center of the cell, much of what this organelle does involves sending its products outside the cell, often to cells that are very far away. **SMOOTH ER**

3)  This organelle is full of chaperone proteins.  Somehow they stay in place even though the organelle is in constant flux. **GOLGI BODY**

4)  These bind to something called a substrate. **ENZYMES**

5)  During the last part of mitosis, the movement of these causes the cell to pinch in the middle. **MICROFILAMENTS**

6)  Tay-Sachs Disease is caused by a malfunction of this organelle. **LYSOSOME**

7)  This has an inner region called the matrix.  The walls of the matrix contain ion pumps. **MITOCHONDRIA**

8)  Serine, proline, lysine, arginine, and valine are examples of these. **AMINO ACIDS**

9)  Inside this are little "snipper" proteins that can snip off the ends of protein chains being manufactured by ribosomes that are on its surface. **ROUGH ER**

10)  This is where glycolysis occurs. **CYTOSOL**

11)  This can be filled with waste and sent to merge with the membrane. **VACUOLE**

12)  This has an anti-codon. **tRNA**

13)  One of this organelle's main jobs is to break down long chains of fatty acids.  It also can detoxify alcohol and other wastes. **PEROXISOME**

14)  The result of this process is to form a small vesicle filled with water, minerals, and hopefully some food molecules. **PINOCYTOSIS**

15)  These were discovered by using antibodies stained with a fluorescent dye.  The antibodies attacked and covered these, then the dye made them show up on a screen. **MICROTUBULES**

16)  This is where you would find histones with DNA wound around them. **NUCLEUS**

17)  This contains 6 carbon atoms and its basic shape is a hexagon. **GLUCOSE**

18)  This has thousands of sets of instructions for making just one thing. **NUCLEOLUS**

19)  These are formed by both smooth and rough ER and by the Golgi. **VESICLES**

20)  The structure of this is sometimes described as a fluid mosaic. **PLASMA MEMBRANE**

21)  These are phospates and lipids connected by a glycerol. **FATTY ACIDS**

22)  Some of these act as receptors, receiving chemical messages from other cells. **MEMBRANE-BOUND PROTEINS**

23)  These are attached to the inside of the plasma membrane with a plate-like structure.  The plate is then connected to the cytoskeleton. **DESMOSOMES**

24)  This is made of a base, a sugar, and a phosphate. **NUCLEOTIDES**

25)  This is made of two barrel-shaped things inside a blob of protein. **CENTROSOME**

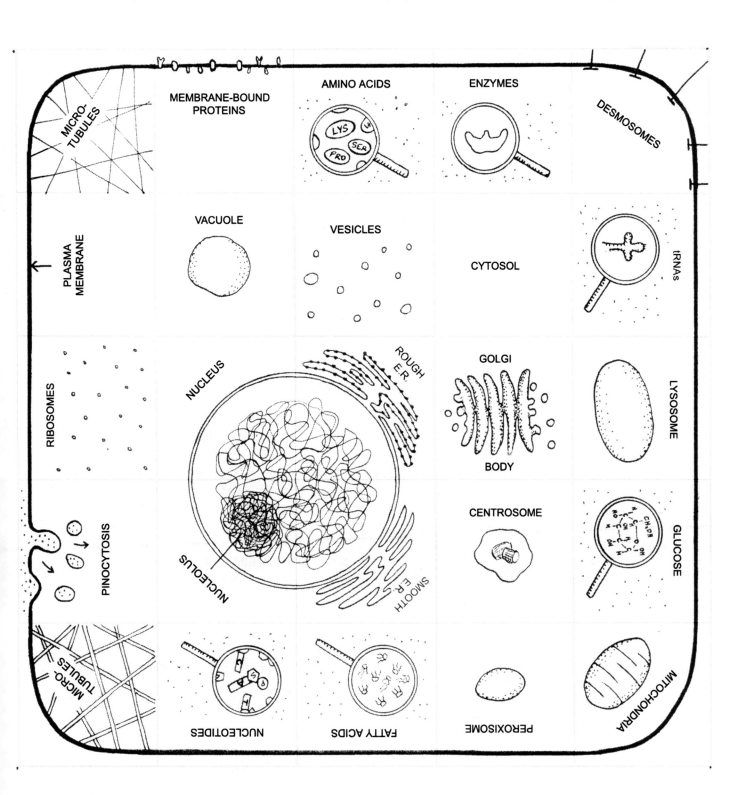

MICRO-TUBULES

MEMBRANE-BOUND PROTEINS

AMINO ACIDS

ENZYMES

DESMOSOMES

PLASMA MEMBRANE

VACUOLE

VESICLES

CYTOSOL

tRNAs

RIBOSOMES

NUCLEUS

ROUGH E.R.

GOLGI BODY

LYSOSOME

PINOCYTOSIS

NUCLEOLUS

SMOOTH E.R.

CENTROSOME

GLUCOSE

MICRO-TUBULES

NUCLEOTIDES

FATTY ACIDS

PEROXISOME

MITOCHONDRIA

LYS
SER
PRO

127

## 3) RELAY RACE: "RESPIRATION RELAY"

Still confused about respiration? It's really complicated! It's difficult to comprehend how all the parts (glycolysis, Krebs cycle, E.T.C.) go together to make one long process. This active game will help the students see the whole picture of how the processes involved in respiration fit together.

**You will need:**
- two pairs of scissors
- two staplers
- a piece of black paper
- several pieces of white paper
- a piece of colored paper (any color, just not black or white)
- some cotton balls
- white glue
- yarn (any color will do)
- some rope or heavy string (or a different color of yarn) to be the membrane of the mitochondrion
- a large piece of cardboard (or box) or 4 pieces of poster board
- a black marker
- your Electron Transport Chain ion pumps and synthase machine (from chapter 3, activity 2)
- the beans or small items you used for the E.T.C. relay
- a stopwatch or clock (if you want the relay to be competitive)

**What to tell the students:**
*This relay race will help you understand how all the parts of respiration fit together. You will act out what happens in a mitochondrion. Some of you will be the scissor-and-stapler enzymes. Others will transport acetyl-CoA through the Krebs cycle factory or run the ion pumps at the electron transport chain. You will see how both glucose and fats can be used by a mitochondrion to make acetyl-CoA fuel for the Krebs factory. And the best part is that you'll remember playing this game long after you've forgotten what you read in the text! If someone asks you what happens after glycolysis, you can just tap into your memories of this game. You'll remember cutting and stapling to make acetyl-CoAs. You'll remember crawling through the Krebs factory on your hands and knees and throwing some ATPs and carbon dioxides out the window. And of course, you never forget putting electrons through those crazy ion pumps!*

**How to prepare:**
There are two stages of preparation needed. The first can either be done ahead of time by an adult, or it can be done by students during class time. You will need to make these parts:
- long fat molecules (4 should be enough, if they are pretty long)
- glucose molecules (about 10-12; more if you have a large group of players)
- oxygen molecules (two for each glucose)
- CoA tags (two for each glucose, plus at least another dozen)
- ATPs (just a few, as you can recycle them)
- carbon dioxide molecules (just a few as the relay race itself will be producing more of them)

To make carbon atoms, cut circles or squares of black paper. For the fat molecules, cut a long piece of yarn (we used red) and glue the black pieces of paper to it, leaving a bit of space between the papers. For a glucose molecule, glue six black papers to a piece of yarn, then tie it into a circle. For oxygen molecules, glue two cotton balls to a short piece of yarn. For CoAs, cut ovals out of white paper and write

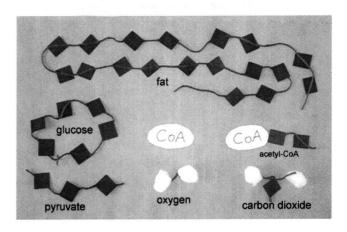

"CoA" on them. Make some carbon dioxides by gluing two cotton balls and a paper carbon square to a piece of yarn. Lastly, make some ATPs by gluing circles of colored paper to short pieces of yarn. (You've made ATPs before, so they are not shown in the picture.)

The second part of the preparation is setting up the mitochondrion. This illustration shows the basic set up. Put a piece of rope or string or yarn on the floor in a large circle. This represents a mitochondrion. Use four objects (anything—pieces of paper, shoes, fabric, books) to make two portals in the membrane. One portal will be where the pyruvate (half a glucose) comes in, along with an oxygen and a CoA. The other portal will be where a fat molecule comes in. Put a scissor and stapler right on the first portal. Put a scissor and stapler inside the mitochondrion somewhere near the second portal.

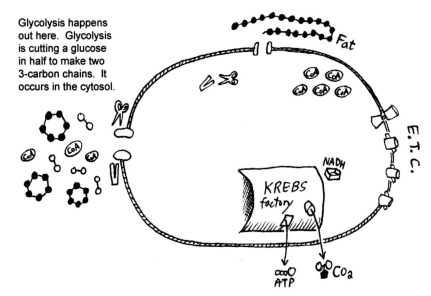

Glycolysis happens out here. Glycolysis is cutting a glucose in half to make two 3-carbon chains. It occurs in the cytosol.

Make a Krebs factory out of either a large box or piece of cardboard, or several sheets of poster board taped together to make a tunnel, similar to the one shown on page 55. Make sure it is large enough so that even your biggest player will be able to crawl (or wriggle) through it. Write "Krebs Factory" on it. Cut a little window on one side. Also cut a circle (for a chimney) near the top. Roll a sheet of paper to make a short chimney and attach it to the chimney hole. Make sure the chimney is not pointing straight up, or the carbon dioxides will fall right back into the factory. Place the parts of the E.T.C. on the edge of the rope and park the NADH "shuttle bus" right outside the Krebs factory. Put a supply of ATPs and some carbon dioxide molecules (just a few) inside the Krebs factory.

**How to play:**

You will have to adapt this relay to your situation. If you have a lot of players, you can distribute just one job per player and makes team of 5 or 6. If you have fewer players, you can have each player do two jobs. You could even have one person run the whole relay by themselves, doing all the jobs. In any case, if you want it to be a competitive race, you'll have to time each run and then compare times.

The goal of the relay is the goal of respiration—to produce ATPs. At the end of the line is the electron transport chain. The students should recognize this set-up from the chapter 3 activities. The final result of this relay will be to make 4 ATPs. When the high energy electrons come out of the Krebs factory, the E.T.C. runs the same way as described in chapter 3, activity 2.

You will need to adapt this relay to the space you have, the number of players you have, and how long you want each "run" to be. You will need to make the decisions about how many jobs each player will have.

Here are the jobs that need to be done: **1)** glycolysis—cutting a glucose in half to make two 3-carbon pyruvate chains, **2)** at the portal enzyme: cutting a carbon off a pyruvate and stapling the 2-carbon chain to a CoA to make acetyl-CoA, and stapling the lone carbon to an $O_2$ molecule to make $CO_2$, **3)** bringing in the fat chain and snipping off some 2-carbon sections, then stapling them to CoAs, **4)** taking an acetyl-CoA to the Krebs factory, **5)** crawling through the Krebs factory, dropping the acetyl-CoA inside, putting an ATP out the window, a $CO_2$ out the chimney and an electron into the NADH shuttle, **6)** taking the shuttle to the E.T.C. then operating the E.T.C. (the instructions for the E.T.C. are on page 95).

NOTE: You may also want to add a box or bowl near the fat portal and require that, as part of the race, the team put in a certain number of extra acetyl-CoAs that will be used for building cell parts.

# CHAPTER 8

## 1) ADDITIONAL INFORMATION
Here are a few more links you may want to use with your students.

- **TELOMERES:**
Here is an easy-to-read illustrated page of information about telomeres. Telomeres are sections of non-essential DNA at the ends of each chromosome. The telomeres are like protective caps on the ends of the chromosomes to keep the essential information from getting damaged. However, each time the cell goes through mitosis, these protective telomeres get a little bit shorter. You start life with about 8000 base pairs in each telomere. By the time you reach 35 years old, you're down to 3000 telomeres. Scientists are studying telomeres in the hopes of finding a way of slowing down this process. Find out more by going to the web address below:
**http://learn.genetics.utah.edu/content/begin/traits/telomeres/**

- **INHERITANCE OF FOUR KINDS OF DNA** (autosomal, X, Y, and mitochondrial)
This is an online audio-visual presentation about inheritance of DNA and how it can be used to trace ancestry.
**http://learn.genetics.utah.edu/content/extras/molgen/index.html**

- **MATCHING UP PAIRS OF CHROMOSOMES**
Here is an online interactive activity where you match up single chromosomes into pairs. (This is called making a "karyotype.") They use micrographs of real human chromosomes.
**http://learn.genetics.utah.edu/content/begin/traits/karyotype/**

- **MEIOSIS MISTAKES**
Here are some brief animations you can click on that show you possible scenarios for genetic mistakes during meiosis—mistakes that will cause the offspring to have genetics syndromes or disorders (such as Downs Syndrome).
**http://learn.genetics.utah.edu/content/begin/traits/predictdisorder/**

## 2) VIRTUAL LABS
Here are some labs you definitely can't do at home. But with the magic of the Internet (and thanks to a lot of talented computer graphic artists!) you can have all the fun of doing these labs without any of the expense or mess or long waits.

- **CLONING**
Cloning is when you skip meiosis and make a new organism out of a regular cell. How can this be done? Find out by cloning a mouse in this virtual online lab.
**http://learn.genetics.utah.edu/content/tech/cloning/**

- **GEL ELECTROPHORESIS OF DNA**
This lab procedure uses electricity and a gel medium to sort DNA into various lengths so that patterns can be seen.
**http://learn.genetics.utah.edu/content/labs/gel/**

- **PCR LAB (Polymerase Chain Reaction)**
This procedure is used to make billions of copies of just one tiny piece of DNA. The tricks is to target one part of the DNA with "primers," then use enzymes and heat to switch various natural processes on and off. (This is a great review of what the students learned in chapter 4.)
**http://learn.genetics.utah.edu/content/labs/pcr/**

## 2) MITOSIS FLIP BOOK

This is a standard cell biology project for middle or high school students. Listed below are two options, both color and black and white. The third option would be to make one from scratch, which would be the best learning experience, but also very time-consuming and probably beyond the patience of most students.

**You will need:**
- Patterns for flip book, printed onto card stock
- Scissors
- White glue (not white "school glue" because it really doesn't stick as well)
- Fine sandpaper (a belt sander is even better!)

### Option 1: Use color pattern pages

If you would like to make a flip book from actual micrograph pictures, check out this address: **http://www.exploratorium.edu/imaging_station/activities/flipbooks/flipbooks_mitosis.php** The pictures are from fruit fly embryo cells. There are many cells on each picture, not just one. The cells were stained with red and green and the background is fairly dark. The pictures are very saturated with color. The text says that fruit fly embryo cells multiply very quickly. The series shown in the flip book took about 10 actual minutes.

### Option 2: Use black and white pattern pages

Patterns are provided on the following pages. Copy them onto card stock. The stiffer paper will make the book more flip-able. Cut out the pages very carefully. The neater you cut, the better the book will work.

Decide whether your flip book will flip from the bottom or top. (Imagine you have a flip book in your hand and flip it. Was picture 1 on the bottom or top? Did you use your right hand or your left?) Stack the pages accordingly. Page 1 can be on the top or the bottom, as you choose.

As you glue the pages together, make sure the ends opposite the numbers are lined up as perfectly along the edges as possible. The natural inclination of the students will probably be to line up the edges where the numbers are. However, the spine of the book (where the numbers are) is not the crucial edge. The edge where your fingers flip the book is the edge you want to focus on. Line up the pages from this end so the book will flip smoothly.

Use only a TINY amount of glue. If any glue at all seeps out from the crack, you are using too much. Just put on a tiny drop and spread it out with your finger. White glue is very strong.

Several blank pages are provided so that you can design a cover for the flip book, or add a few pages at the end to make it flip better. Before you put on a cover, decide whether you will be flipping the book with your left hand or your right hand. If you are going to flip with your left fingers, design the cover so that the spine of the book will be on the right of the cover. And vice versa for right hand.

After you have finished all the gluing, hold the book very firmly in one hand, and hold a piece of sand paper down on the table with the other hand, and pull the book across the sand paper in one direction. Continue sanding in this one direction until the edge is as smooth as possible. The smoother the edge, the better the book will flip. A belt sander is faster and gives a better finish than sanding by hand. (Just make sure to press gently so your whole book doesn't get ground away!) If, when you flip your book, there are pages that get skipped, this means that those pages are a little too short. You can do more sanding until all the pages are exactly the same length.

### Option 3: Make one from scratch

Make several copies of the blank template page (onto card stock). Draw a simple cell on one the pages and mark it as page 1. Then place the second page on top of it and then hold them up to a window or somewhere else where you can see page 1 through page 2. Now make your second picture just slightly different from your first one, but don't stray too far from your first design. Mark this as page 2. Then do the same for pages 2 and 3, and so on. Make the changes very gradually. Don't glue the pages together until you have them all drawn.

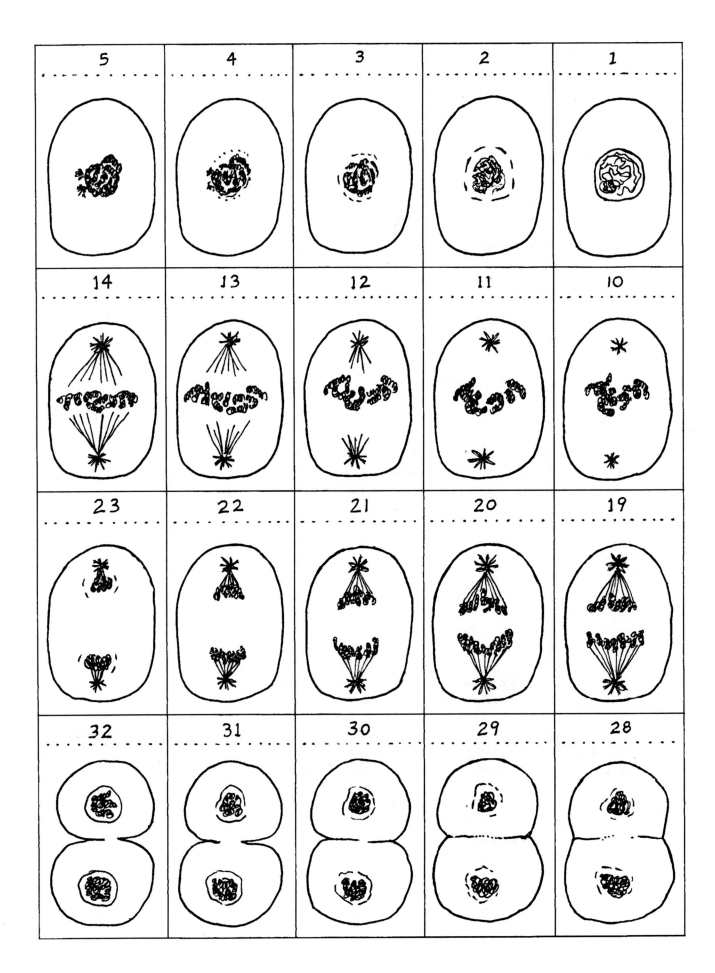

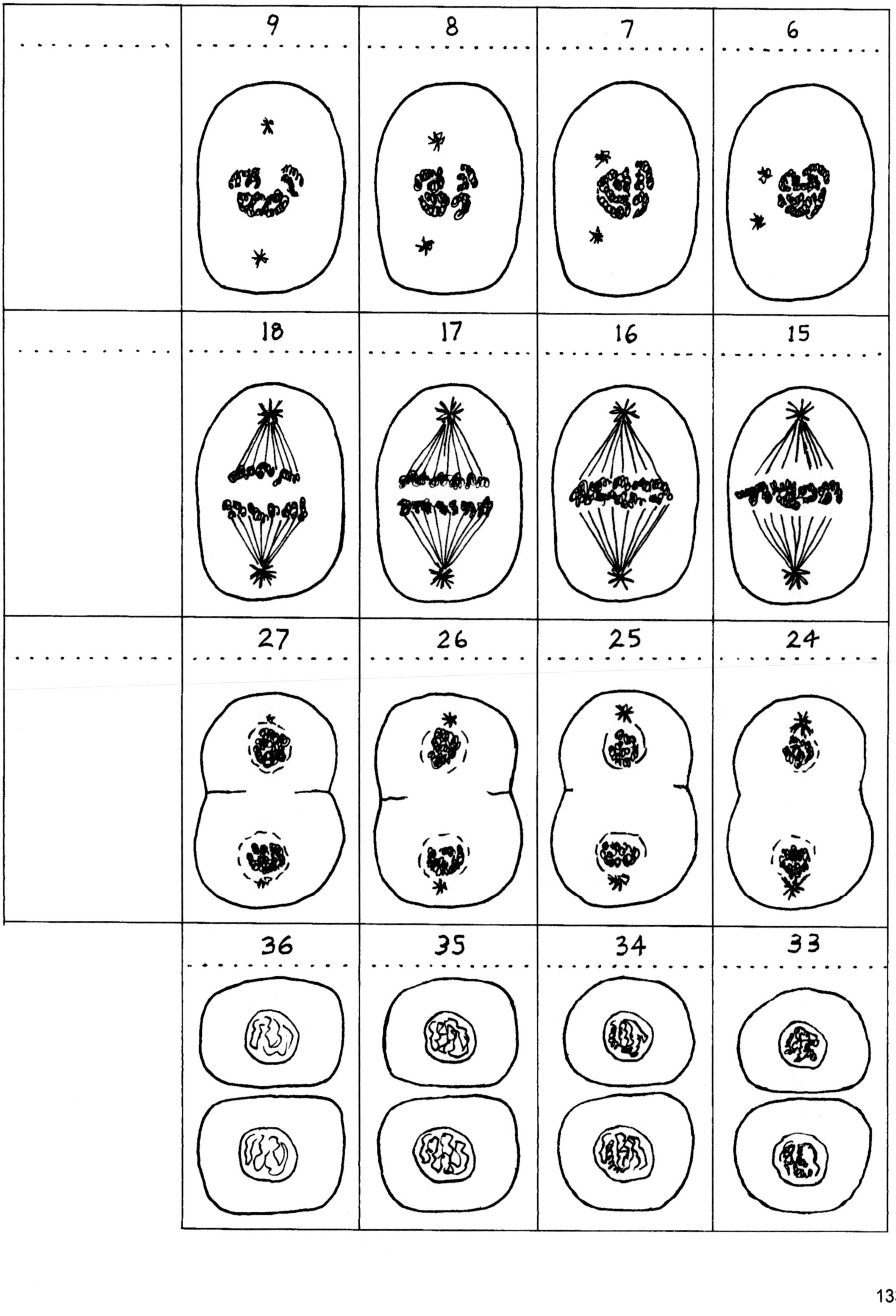
9
8
7
6
18
17
16
15
27
26
25
24
36
35
34
33

# CHAPTER 9

## 1) QUIZ GAME

This is a Jeopardy-style game but the answers don't have to be in question format. Most of the questions are taken out of chapter 9, although there are also review questions about cells in general (disguised as questions about particular cells).

**You will need:**
- A playing board (see note below)
- Some kind of "markers" to put on the squares of the playing board as questions are answered
- The questions on the following pages

**How to prepare:**

If you are playing with a fairly large group you will want to make a version of the playing board that can be put on a wall. This is easily done with a piece of poster board and a marker. Or you can make it even larger, and use a sheet of paper for each square.

You will need some kind of "markers" such as squares of colored paper, or colored sticky notes, for keeping track of which team scores on which squares. You will need a color for each team. If you are playing with a board tacked to the wall you will obviously need your markers to be sticky.

Divide the group into teams. Two teams can work well if you let players take turns answering the questions. Depending on your group, you may want to have the player who is answering the question be able to ask advice of the other group members. This is a particularly good option if you have players that lack self-confidence.

You will note that there are three games available. It does not matter which you choose. They are designed to be approximately equal in difficulty. In other words, game three is not more difficult than game one.

**How to play:**

Choose a team to go first. They may choose any square on the board. They call out a cell type and the number, such as "Nerve Cells for 100" or "Bone Cells for 300." The teacher/adult then reads the question that corresponds to that square. If the correct answer is given, the team gets to put one of their colored markers on that square.

In the television show "Jeopardy" contestants continue to control the board as long as they give correct answers. This format won't work so well in this game and will result in cries of, "It's not fair!" or, "When will it be our turn?!" We recommend having the teams take consecutive turns calling out squares. However, if one team guesses incorrectly, the question can be passed to the next team. If the next team answers the missed question correctly, that doesn't count as their turn. They still get to call out a square.

After the questions have all been answered, add up the scores to determine who won.

NOTE: Have fun watching how players know all the answers when it's not their turn. Then, when they are on the spot, the answers fly right out of their head!

| EPITHELIAL CELLS | SECRETORY CELLS | BONE CELLS | MUSCLE CELLS | NERVE CELLS | BLOOD CELLS |
|---|---|---|---|---|---|
| 100 | 100 | 100 | 100 | 100 | 100 |
| 200 | 200 | 200 | 200 | 200 | 200 |
| 300 | 300 | 300 | 300 | 300 | 300 |
| 400 | 400 | 400 | 400 | 400 | 400 |
| 500 | 500 | 500 | 500 | 500 | 500 |

# GAME ONE:

## EPITHELIAL
100: Epithelial cells divide using this process.    MITOSIS
200: In the word "epithelial" what does "epi" mean?    OUTSIDE or OUTER
300: The epithelial cells in these hair-like structures are responsible for getting nutrients out of your intestines and into your blood.  What are these hair-like structures in your intestines called?    VILLI
400: In the word "epithelial" what does "thelial" mean?    TISSUE
500: Epithelial cells in capillaries use this process to "drink" in nutrients from the bloodstream.  PINOCYTOSIS

## SECRETORY
100: This type of secretory cell makes mucus.  GOBLET CELL
200: The main component of mucus is a protein called _____.    MUCIN
300: The nucleus of a goblet cell is located where? Top, middle or bottom?  BOTTOM
400: Mucin proteins expand after they are released from the cell.  Their volume can expand by how much?  600 TIMES
500: What holds mucin proteins together in a compact shape before they are released? A) negative areas on the protein repelling each other   B) calcium ions sticking to negative areas on the protein molecules   C) Oxygen molecules binding the ends of the protein together        ANSWER: A

## BONE CELLS
100: What does the root word "osteo" mean?  BONE
200: Once an osteoblast is stuck inside the mineral "cage" it has built around itself, it is an ___.  OSTEOCYTE
300: In the word "osteoblast" what does "blast" mean?  IMMATURE CELL
500: When old bone has been dissolved by osteoclasts, what comes in to fill the gaps? NEW OSTEOBLASTS
500: The spiderweb-like network of collagen made by osteoblasts is called the _____.    MATRIX

## MUSCLE CELLS
100: Muscle cells are also called muscle _____.        FIBERS
200: Muscles you can control are called _____ muscles.    VOLUNTARY
300: Name the two proteins that cause muscle fibers to contract.    ACTIN and MYOSIN
400: The bundle of protein fibers inside muscle fibers are called _____.    MYOFIBRILS
500: Muscle fibers have a special membrane around them called the _____.    SARCOLEMMA

## NERVE CELLS
100: The correct name for a nerve cell is a _____.    NEURON
200: The long, thin middle part of a neuron is called the _____.    AXON
300: A neuron receives electrical signals through its _____.    DENDRITES
400: The protective cells around a neuron's axons are called _____.    SCHWANN CELLS
500: When an electrical signal reaches the gap between neurons it must be converted into what?  CHEMICALS or NEUROTRANSMITTERS or A CHEMICAL SIGNAL

## BLOOD CELLS
100: What is the correct name for a red blood cell?  ERYTHROCYTE
200: Where are blood cells "born"?  BONE MARROW
300: Where do B cells mature?  BONE
400: Name the three kinds of granular leucocytes.  BASOPHILS, EOSINOPHILS, NEUTROPHILS
500: Name the three kinds of lymphocytes.  T-CELLS, B-CELLS, NATURAL KILLER CELLS

**GAME TWO:**

EPITHELIAL
100: Apoptosis is when cells do this.     DIE
200: It is in this layer of skin that your nerves, sweat glands and hair follicles are found.     DERMIS
300: This substance is made of long, thin strands of protein which gradually fill up skin cells.   KERATIN
400: Name an organ of the body where you would find epithelial capillary cells that have larger-than-normal cracks between the cells.     LIVER or SPLEEN
500: The epithelial cells of the villi have little holes in them.  The Latin word for this kind of cell means "full of little windows.  What is this scientific Latin name?     FENESTRATED

SECRETORY
100: Name one reason your body makes mucus.
     POSSIBLE ANSWERS:  To keep out foreign substances such as dust or bacteria.   To lubricate places such as the intestines.   To cleanse parts of the respiratory tract such as nose, sinuses or lungs.
     To capture foreign particles such as dust, pollen, bacteria or viruses.  (Or similar answers)
200: Where would you find a lot of goblet cells? A) Circulatory system   B)  Bones   C) Respiratory system
     D)  Nervous system.     ANSWER:  C
300: All types of secretory cells use this organelle to manufacture their proteins.     RIBOSOME
400: What ingredient in mucus causes it to be sticky?   SUGARS
500: What causes mucus to expand after leaving the goblet cell?   A) Negative areas of the protein repelling each other   B) Calcium ions sticking to negative areas of the protein   C) Oxygen molecules binding to the hydrogen atoms in the protein   ANSWER:  A

BONE CELLS
100: Name a mineral that bones cells use to make bones strong.  CALCIUM, PHOSPHORUS, MAGNESIUM
200: What does exercise do to bones?  MAKE THEM STRONGER
300: Where does a bone cell get the information for how to make collagen?  FROM DNA IN ITS NUCLEUS
400: What kind of bone cell breaks down the matrix to release minerals?  OSTEOCLASTS
500: How long can an osteocyte live?  ABOUT 20 YEARS

MUSCLE CELLS
100: Which of these organelles is only found in muscle cells?   A) Smooth endoplasmic reticulum   B) Rough endoplasmic reticulum   C) Sarcoplasmic reticulum   d) Mitochondria     ANSWER:  C
200: When calcium ions bind to myosin proteins, the muscle fiber will do this.   CONTRACT or GET SHORTER
300: Which protein has tiny "oars"—action or myosin?     MYOSIN
400: Why is it an advantage for muscle cells to have more than one nucleus? SO THE mRNA DOES NOT HAVE TO TRAVEL SO FAR TO GET INSTRUCTIONS FROM DNA  (or similar answer)
500: The nerves that carry the signals to the muscle fibers and "shock" them into action are located where?
     A)  On the outside of the cell    B) Attached to the myofibrils    C) In the sarcolemma tunnels  D) Inside the capillaries that feed the cell     ANSWER:  C

NERVE CELLS
100: What is a synapse?  A TINY GAP BETWEEN NEURONS
200: What is the main job of the Schwann cells?  TO PROVIDE ELECTRICAL INSULATION
300: "Dendrite" is Greek for ____.     TREE
400: About how many neurons are in your brain?   100 BILLION
500: Most phospholipid membranes won't let electricity through.  What enables the membrane of a neuron to conduct electricity?  SPECIAL PROTEINS EMBEDDED IN THE MEMBRANE

BLOOD CELLS
100:  What is the correct name for white blood cells?  LEUCOCYTES
200:  Which type of granular cell (ending in "phil") releases histamine and makes a mess?  BASOPHIL
300:  Which type of granular cell (ending in "phil") cleans up the messes made by the basophil? EOSINOPHIL
400:  Why would a detective analyze a neutrophil?  TO DETERMINE GENDER OF CRIMINAL OR VICTIM
500:  Once a monocyte leaves a capillary and goes in among the cells, it is called a _____.  MACROPHAGE

## GAME THREE:

### EPITHELIAL
100: Epithelial cells use this organelle to make ATPs.   MITOCHONDRIA
200: Where would you find very few epithelial cells? A) Skin   B) Bone   C) Intestines   D) Capillaries
ANSWER: B
300: When a cell starts to change its shape as it dies, this is called ___.   BLEBBING
400: Where would you find epithelial cells with no nucleus?   TOP LAYER OF EPIDERMIS or OUTER LAYER OF
SKIN or SURFACE OF YOUR SKIN (or similar answer)
500: What is the 10-step process that epithelial cells use to harvest energy from acetyl-CoA molecules?
(Hint: In your booklet this process looked like a factory.)   THE KREBS CYCLE (or TCA/CITRIC ACID)

### SECRETORY
100: Secretory cells have large numbers of this organelle.   A) Nuclei   B) Peroxisomes   C) Mitochondria
D) Storage vesicles      ANSWER: D
200: Which of these would NOT be produced by a secretory cell?   A) Saliva   B) Hormones   C) Sweat
D) Keratin      ANSWER: D
300: Mucin proteins are processed and labeled for delivery to storage vesicles by this organelle.  GOLGI
400: What causes goblet cells to release mucus?  IRRITATION OF SOME SORT
500: Which kind of secretory gland responds at least somewhat to voluntary control?    A) Sweat glands
B) Tear glands      C) Salivary glands   D) Thyroid glands   ANSWER: B

### BONE CELLS
100: Name one type of food that is especially important for bone health      MILK, ANY KIND OF DAIRY
PRODUCT, VEGETABLES WITH HIGH MINERAL CONTENT (or similar answers)
200: What is the function of the hollow spaces in bones? A) To make the bones light   B) To let bone cells
get oxygen      C) To make the bones flexible      ANSWER: A
300: Osteoblasts weave their fibrous network using this flexible protein.   COLLAGEN
500: Which of these can an osteocyte NOT do?   A) Live a long time   B) Send signals to other osteocytes
C) Do mitosis   D) Control the mineral content of bone      ANSWER: C
500: Osteoclasts come from this type of immature cell.  MONOCYTES

### MUSCLE CELLS
100: Where do you find most of a muscle fiber's organelles—the outside or the inside?  OUTSIDE
200: Which would a muscle have more of—mitochondria or Golgi bodies?  MITOCHONDRIA
300: What does the sarcoplasmic reticulum do?   A) Store calcium ions   B) Manufacture proteins   C) Attach
the muscle cell to a capillary      D) Control diffusion of water molecules into cell      ANSWER: A
400: What three-letter root word means "pertaining to muscles"?   MYO
500: What causes muscle fibers to looked striped?   A) Red and white pigments in the cells
B) The arrangement of the organelles in the cells      C) Areas of actin and myosin
D) The tendency of capillaries to follow the contour of the muscle fiber.   ANSWER: C

### NERVE CELLS
100: What part of a neuron sends out electrical signals? THE TERMINAL ENDS OF THE AXON
200: How long is the shortest neuron in your body? MICROSCOPIC
300: Which of the following does a neuron NOT have? A) ion pumps   B) Golgi bodies  C) nucleus  D) sarcoplasmic reticulum    ANSWER: D
400: Where does glycolysis occur in neurons? A) In the cytoplasm   B)   C) In the Golgi bodies
D) In the mitochondria    D) In the peroxisomes    ANSWER: A
500: Besides insulation, what else does a Schwann cell do for a neuron? NOURISH IT

### BLOOD CELLS
100: What is the molecule in a red blood cells that binds to oxygen? HEMOGLOBIN
200: Red blood cells are red because they contain a lot of this mineral.   IRON
300: How long can a red blood cell live?  ABOUT 3 OR 4 MONTHS
400: Which type of cell makes up about 65% of your total population of white blood cells?  MONOCYTES
500: Which type of lymphcyte makes antibodies?  B-CELLS

## 2) YET ANOTHER EDIBLE CRAFT

If your students having been enjoying the edible crafts, here is another you can do. Watch the "Blood Cell Bakery" videos on YouTube, then make your own blood cell cookies. (There is a color photo in the downloadable file.)

As with the other edible crafts, don't hesitate to adapt this project to your situation. You could use alternative edibles, or you could skip making them edible and use craft dough or colored paper.

**You will need:**

• Cookie dough in various colors (or plain cookie dough and some edible "paints" made from food coloring mixed with a little egg white or water)
• Baking sheets and oven
• Pictures of blood cells (look at some images on the Internet and/or use our pattern pictures in the appendix)

**What to do:**

Use the colored dough and the picture patterns to make your edible blood cell cookies. Perhaps you might want to try a neuron or a goblet cell, too!

# BIBLIOGRAPHY

**Books for young people that I used for reference and comparison:**

Animal Cells; The Smallest Units of Life by Darlene R. Stille.   Published in 2002 by Compass Point Books, Woodbury, NY.  ISBN 978-0-7565-1761-8  (www.cshlppress.com)

Cell Scientists; From Leeuwenhoek to Fuchs by Kimberly Fekany Lee.  Part of the "Mission: Science" series.  Published in 2009 by Sally Ride Science (www.sallyridescience.com). ISBN 978-0-7565-3964-1

Enjoy Your Cells by Fran Balkwill and Mic Rolph.  Published in 2002 by Cold Spring Harbor Laboratory Press, Minneapolis, MN.  ISBN 0-87969-584-6

Cell Communication; Understanding How Information Is Stored and Used in Cells by Michael Friedman and Brett Friedman.  Published by The Rosen Publishing Group, Inc., 2005.  ISBN 1-4042-0319-2

Eukaryotic and Prokaryotic Cell Structures; Understanding Cells With and Without a Nucleus by Lesli J. Favor, PhD.  Published by The Rosen Publishing Group, Inc., New York, NY, 2005.  ISBN 1-4042-0323-0

Cell Regulation; Understanding How Cell Functions, Growth, and Division are Regulated by Lois Sakany. Published by The Rosen Publishing Group, New York, NY, 2005.


**Textbooks used by my consultant to check facts:**

Biology of the Cell by Sylvia S. Mader.  Published by McGraw-Hill, 1993.  ISBN 0-697-15098-4

Biology of Genetics and Inheritance by Sylvia S. Mader. Published by McGraw-Hill,1993.
ISBN 0-697-15099-2

Molecular Biology of the Cell, 5th edition by B. Alberts, A. Johnson, J. Lewis, M. Raff, K. Roberts and P. Walter.  Published by Garland Science, Taylor and Francis Group, LLC., 2002.    978-0-8153-4105-5

Molecular Biology of the Cell, 3rd edition by B. Alberts, D. Bray, J. Lewis, M. Raff, K. Roberts, and J. Watson.  Published by Garland Publishing, Inc., 1994.  ISBN 0-8153-1619-4


**Samples of online referrences I used:**

Detailed info about proteins:
http://www.ncbi.nlm.nih.gov/bookshelf/br.fcgi?book=mboc4&part=A388  (ebook)
http://www.zoology.ubc.ca/~berger/b200sample/unit_8_protein_processing/golgi/lect28.htm

Info about protein sythesis, ER and Golgi bodies
http://users.rcn.com/jkimball.ma.ultranet/BiologyPages/P/ProteinKinesis.html

Translocation of proteins into the rough ER:
http://www.cytochemistry.net/cell-biology/rer2.htm

Animation of how sodium potassium pump works:
http://highered.mcgraw-hill.com/sites/0072495855/student_view0/chapter2/animation__how_the_sodium_potassium_pump_works.html

Cell parts:
http://www.wisc-online.com/Objects/ViewObject.aspx?ID=AP11403

Nuclear pores:
http://www.genetik.biologie.uni-muenchen.de/research/parniske/nucleoporins/index.html

Nulceosomes and histones:
http://scienceblogs.com/transcript/2006/08/nucleosome_binding_sites_1.php

Chromatin:
http://micro.magnet.fsu.edu/cells/nucleus/chromatin.html

DNA binding proteins:
http://www.ncbi.nlm.nih.gov/pmc/articles/PMC2726711/

Protein structure:
http://www.ncbi.nlm.nih.gov/books/NBK26830/

Intermediate filaments and desmosomes:
http://www.cytochemistry.net/cell-biology/intermediate_filament_intro.htm

Capillaries:
http://education.vetmed.vt.edu/Curriculum/VM8054/Labs/Lab12b/Lab12b.htm

Glycolysis and the Krebs cycle:
http://www.sparknotes.com/testprep/books/sat2/biology/chapter6section1.rhtml
http://www.daviddarling.info/encyclopedia/C/citric_acid_cycle.html
http://biology.clc.uc.edu/courses/bio104/cellresp.htm
http://www.elmhurst.edu/~chm/vchembook/612citricsum.html

Digestion of fats:
http://www.annecollins.com/digestive-system/digestion-of-fats.htm

Reproduction of Golgi bodies:
http://books.google.com/books?id=Eb1TaY6P8HwC&pg=PA187&lpg=PA187&dq=how+to+golgi+bodies+replicate&source=bl&ots=vJXxVxslbD&sig=vhY-PxqrvI1PisTH3aOh0c0mOJs&hl=en&ei=sgBXTcTlF4X6lwec-zNWUBw&sa=X&oi=book_result&ct=result&resnum=5&sqi=2&ved=0CD0Q6AEwBA#v=onepage&q&f=-false

NK cell maturation:
http://researchnews.osu.edu/archive/nkstages.htm

Other websites I used are listed in the student booklet at the end of each chapter.

I also confess to consulting Wikipedia articles quite frequently. When checked against other sources, their cell biology articles seem to be very reliable. Their information was consistent with (and sometimes more in-depth than) articles from reliable university (.edu) websites.

CPSIA information can be obtained at www.ICGtesting.com
Printed in the USA
BVOW06s1621280314

349113BV00003B/5/P